HUMAN LIFE IN RUSSIA

by

DR. EWALD AMMENDE

Introduction by
The Rt. Hon. Lord Dickinson, K.B.E., P.C.

Historical Introduction by
Dr. James E. Mace
Harvard University

Cleveland
1984
John T. Zubal, Inc.
Publishers

FIRST REPRINT EDITION

Reprinted 1984 by
John T. Zubal, Inc.
Publishers and Booksellers
2969 West 25th Street
Cleveland, Ohio 44113 U.S.A.

In cooperation with:
The Foundation to Commemorate the
1933 Ukrainian Famine
Montreal, Quebec
Canada

ISBN 0-939738-54-6

Reprinted with the permission of:
George Allen & Unwin Ltd.

HISTORICAL INTRODUCTION
by
JAMES E. MACE
Harvard University

THE GREAT FAMINE of 1932-33 is unique in the annals of human history in that it was wrought neither by some natural calamity nor even by the unintentional devastation created by warring armies. It was an act of policy, carried out for political ends in peacetime. It was deliberately man-made. It was an example of what the Nuremburg Trials would later call "crimes against humanity." Evidence later uncovered shows that it was geographically focused, so that it would devastate only certain regions, inhabited by national and proto-national groups which Stalin wished to neutralize. It was an example of that worst of all crimes against humanity, genocide.

The Great Famine is unique for yet another reason. Like all genocides, its existence was (and still is) denied by those who were responsible. But in this case, attempts of denial were carried out with such success that those who, like Dr. Ewald Ammende, knew the truth and committed themselves to publicizing it, were ultimately unsuccessful. Information about the Famine faded from public consciousness so completely that even scholars have only recently begun to study it.[1] The Famine, therefore, represents that most successful attempt by the perpetrators of an act of genocide to deny their actions. It is as if Hitler had won the war and the world remembered only Theresienstadt, the "model camp" where the Nazis showed foreign observers what purported to be a well-regulated and humanely administered autonomous Jewish community, while the atrocities of Auschwitz and Treblinka remained closely guarded secrets.

When an event of this magnitude fades from the public consciousness, it is important to outline the information we have

[1]A notable exception is the ground-breaking article by Dana Dalrymple, "The Soviet Famine of 1932-34," in *Soviet Studies* (January 1964), pp. 250-284, and (April 1965), pp. 471-474. A number of valuable studies by Ukrainian scholars predate Dalrymple's work, but these were completely ignored in the field of Soviet studies and by the non-Ukrainian public in the West.

about it and, likewise, it is necessary to describe the sources of
our knowledge.

Witnesses to an event that took place over half a century ago
naturally become less numerous with each passing year, but a
substantial number of Famine survivors did manage to escape
to the West in the 1940s and a significant group of them are
still with us in North America. Their recorded recollections
largely corroborate the earlier findings of Dr. Ammende.

Present-day scholarship is particularly indebted to those who
took part in organizations such as the Democratic Organization
of Ukrainians Formerly Repressed by the Soviets (DOBRUS) in
the United States and to the Association of Ukrainian Victims
of Russian Communist Terror (SUZERO) in Canada, which
jointly published in English two volumes of materials on the
Famine and the simultaneous destruction of Ukrainian national
life in the Soviet Union,[2] as well as to those individuals who
published collected or individual testimonies.[3]

The Harvard University Refugee Interview Project also col-
lected oral testimonies from former inhabitants of the Soviet
Union, including the accounts of Famine survivors. However,
due to an evident lack of interest on the part of the Project's
American sponsors it was prevented from collecting as much
Famine-related material as was available.[4]

We are also fortunate to have some accounts by individuals
who were associated in one way or another with the Soviet
government which extracted the means of subsistence from the
countryside, the testimony and published accounts by Victor

[2]*The Black Deeds of the Kremlin: A White Book* (Toronto/Detroit:
1953-1955), 2 vols.

[3]*Cf.* especially Olexa Woropay, *The Ninth Circle* (Cambridge: 1983
reprint); Dmytro Solovey, *The Golgotha of Ukraine* (New York: 1953);
M. Verbytsky, ed., *Naybilshy zlochyn Kremlya* (London: 1951); Yury
Semenko, ed., *Holod 1933 v Ukraini* (Munich: 1963); Pavlo Makohon,
Witness (Toronto: 1983).

[4]A number of interview transcripts indicate that in the later stages of
the project the interviewer would often stop recording when the person
being interviewed came to the Famine in the course of the life-history
interview. The project directors may well have felt that so many
respondents had already told about the Famine that additional information would not advance the Project's primary goal of gathering intelligence.

Kravchenko and Lev Kopelev being the most revealing in this respect.[5] Nikita Khrushchev, who was not in Ukraine at the time of the Famine, recalled how Anastas Mikoyan told him of the protests of a high-ranking Ukrainian Communist official against the policies which created the Famine.[6]

A number of persons who claimed to have unofficial sources of information within the Soviet officialdom indicated that an estimate of ten or eleven million dead from the Famine circulated within the Soviet Union.[7] No one will ever really know, since the prohibitions against unregistered burials, which alone could have enabled the Soviet government to keep an accurate tally of deaths, were widely ignored.[8] The geography of the Famine, the tracing of which has been made possible through examining the age structure of rural women by *oblast* in the 1959 census, indicates massive starvation throughout what was then Soviet Ukraine, the largely Cossack Don and Kuban regions, and to a lesser extent, in the Volga Basin. Along the border with Belorussia and Russia proper, the Famine stopped. This shows that, contrary to Dr. Ammende's belief, the Famine was geographically focused.[9] A comparison of the number of Ukrainians given in the 1926 and 1939 Soviet censuses shows a declines of 3.1 million, and if the natural rate of population

---

[5]Victor Kravchenko, *I Chose Freedom: The Personal and Political Life of a Soviet Official* (New York: 1946); Lev Kopelev, *The Education of a True Believer* (New York: 1980).

[6]"Mikoyan told me that Comrade Demchenko, who was then First Secretary of the Kiev Regional Committee, once came to see him in Moscow. Here's what Demchenko said: 'Anastas Ivanovich, does Comrade Stalin——for that matter, does anyone in the Politburo——know what's happening in the Ukraine? If not, I'll give you some idea. A train recently pulled into Kiev loaded with the corpses of people who had starved to death. It picked up corpses all the way from Poltava to Kiev...'." Nikita Khrushchev, *Khrushchev Remembers* (Boston: 1970), p. 74.

[7]*Cf.*, for example, *The New York American* (August 18, 1935); John Kolasky, *Two Years in Soviet Ukraine: A Canadian's Personal Account of Russian Oppression and Growing Opposition* (Toronto: 1970), p. 111.

[8]A number of eyewitnesses mention this in the files of the Harvard University Refugee Interview Project, currently housed in the Russian Research Center of Harvard University.

[9]Maksudov, "Geografiya goloda 1933 goda," in *SSSR: Vnutreniye protivorechiya*, 1983 (No. 7), pp. 16-17.

growth for the early 1930s is factored in, we arrive at an estimate of over seven million Ukrainians having died in the Famine.[10] This is, admittedly, only a "ballpark estimate," but it is as accurate a figure as we are likely to get.[11] If we include non-Ukrainian victims, the estimate of ten or eleven million Famine dead seems unlikely to be far from the mark.

Today there is little dispute about the immediate cause of the Famine: excessive grain procurements applied in a discretionary fashion against selected territories inhabited by Ukrainians, Cossacks, and the Germans and Tatars of the Volga Basin. These peoples were considered "suspect" by Stalin for a number of reasons which dated to the wars of the Russian Revolution, when they fought against the Bolsheviks with particular vigor and determination.

[10]The natural rate of population growth in the Ukrainian SSR in the years immediately before the Famine are as follows: 2.25% in 1927, 2.15% in 1928, 1.77% in 1929, 1.56% in 1930, 1.45% in 1931. From these rates we may compute that there were 34,165,000 Ukrainians in the Soviet Union on the eve of the Famine. If we subtract 250,000 victims of dekulakization and other repressions, the figure becomes 33,915,000 Ukrainians in 1932, a conservative figure because Ukrainians tended to be concentrated in the countryside where the natural rate of population growth was always somewhat higher than in the republic as a whole. Since there was a blackout on population statistics after 1932, undoubtedly because of the Famine, we can only project back from the average rate of natural population growth observed in the late 1950s, 1.39% annually, to assume 26,211,000 million Ukrainians in 1934, plus 250,000 victims of repressions, making the 1934 figure 26,461,000. Assuming *no births* in 1932-33, we calculate the probable number of Ukrainian Famine victims as:

$$\begin{array}{r} 33,915,000 \\ -26,461,000 \\ \hline 7,454,000 \end{array}$$

[11]This figure might be further lowered by the fact that some persons who were counted as Ukrainians in 1926 were grouped with Russians in 1939. On the other hand, it might be raised because the 1939 census figures were almost certainly inflated, since the officials in charge of the 1937 census (which was never published) were executed when it was alleged that they had engaged in a plot to discredit Soviet policies by deliberately undercounting the population. If census officials were shot for not finding enough people in 1937, it is reasonable to assume that their successors made every attempt to prevent any perception of similar shortcomings in the 1939 census.

There is little doubt that the Famine was most severe in Ukraine, and if we are to understand why it happened, we must understand political developments in Ukraine. The Ukrainians established their own independent socialist state which managed to survive as a territorial entity until 1921 and whose supporters continued to carry on an armed guerrilla struggle for some years thereafter. In 1923 the Soviet authorities announced a policy of Ukrainization designed to endow the Soviet Ukrainian state with an aura of national legitimacy by means of efforts to sponsor Ukrainian cultural activities, recruit Ukrainians into the Communist Party and state apparatus, and to teach the Ukrainian language to Russian communists and state employees. Ukrainization legitimized not only cultural activities but also a measure of national consciousness and self-assertion within the Communist Party (bolshevik) of Ukraine. On the one hand, a large number of former members and associates of the Ukrainian Peoples Republic, including its head of state, Mykhailo Hrushevsky, returned to take advantage of the opportunities, which official sponsorship offered, to conduct scholarly and literary work, thereby providing the Soviet state with the implicit threat of a physically present alternative national leadership. On the other hand, newly prominent Ukrainian Communists began to assert what they saw as Ukrainian national-political rights.[12] In this sense, Soviet Ukraine before the Famine was not unlike what Poland would become after the death of Stalin: it was that part of the larger Russian-centered entity that was most conscious of its national distinctiveness, most assertive of its rights, jealous of its prerogatives, and least willing to follow Moscow's lead in arranging its internal order.

At the end of the 1920s Soviet Ukraine possessed a distinct national communist regime in which the leading figure was the Commissar of Education, Mykola Skrypnyk. The early 1930s brought a protracted campaign to topple him from power, to discredit any manifestation of Ukrainian cultural identity, and to ban the Ukrainian Autocephalous Orthodox Church. Grain quotas were applied to Ukraine and the Cossack areas in a clear-

[12]The problem of national self-assertion in Soviet Ukraine during the years leading up to the Famine has been treated in my *Communism and the Dilemmas of National Liberation: National Communism in Soviet Ukraine, 1918-1933* (Cambridge: 1983).

ly discriminatory fashion, such that they were obliged to deliver to the state amounts of grain far out of proportion to their share of the total Soviet harvest. This, and the fact that this famine stopped precisely at the border with Russia and Belorussia proper, indicate that the Famine was due not, as Ammende believed, to a general collapse of the collective farm system, but that it was deliberately focused against certain areas for political ends.[13] Ammende was one of the few foreign observers to perceive a link between the Famine and the Soviet nationalities policy. But he was wrong in viewing the struggle against the nationalities as a consequence of the Famine. The struggle against the nationalities began before the Famine, and much evidence suggests that it was the Famine which was the concommitant of this struggle.

As one recent study has pointed out, Ewald Ammende worked "almost singlehandedly to draw public attention to the Famine."[14] An ethnic German born in what were at the time the Baltic provinces of the Russian Empire, he grew up with a special sensitivity for the national diversity in the territories between the ethnic homelands of the Russian and German nations.

After briefly working for the independent government of Estonia in 1919, he left the country of his birth to take part in the work to aid victims of the Soviet famine of 1921-22, which followed the wars of the Russian Revolution as the result of rural devastation, inclement weather, and the ruthless procurement policies carried out by Lenin's government. Later he became Secretary-General of the European Congress of Nationalities, a body which had the unenviable task of overseeing the observance — or, more accurately, the lack of observance — of postwar treaty obligations to protect the rights of Europe's numerous national minorities.

In 1933, as word of famine in Ukraine, the North Caucasus, and among the Volga Germans, began to reach the outside world, Ammende was drawn into the work of trying to save lives, despite the denial of the Soviet government that lives

[13]See my "Famine and Nationalism in Soviet Ukraine," in *Problems of Communism* (May-June 1984), pp. 37-50.

[14]Marco Carynnyk, "The Famine the *'Times'* Couldn't Find," in *Commentary* (November 1983), p. 39.

were being lost. In September 1933, as the Famine was coming to an end, Cardinal Innitzer of Vienna formed an interfaith relief committee and named Ammende its General Secretary.

Strong Soviet denials of the Famine's existence impeded the transmission of factual reports to the West. These delays meant that news of mass starvation continued to be received long after the starvation itself had ended. Additionally, there was the fact that the new order of collectivization had produced more or less permanent impoverishment of the countryside throughout the USSR.

Although the situation was less horrifying after 1933, the need for humanitarian relief measures remained a pressing reality through out the 1930s. Various groups with relatives outside the areas truly devastated by famine also received news of their co-nationals' grinding poverty, and made every effort to demonstrate that their peoples were no less deserving of aid than others. All this affected Ammende's treatment of the problems described in his book.

It might be said that Ammende called for aid to the hungry only *after* the Famine came to an end and in areas where the situation was less severe than it had been in Ukraine and the Cossack lands in 1933. The fact is that, while there were no mass graves for the starved in places like Belorussia and Russia, or even in Ukraine by 1934, there was still hunger. And if blurring the distinction between what happened in 1933 and what followed it, what happened in Ukraine and outside of it, could have fed one hungry child, focusing on the fact that children still needed to be fed was the only humanitarian and humane thing to do.

Ewald Ammende wrote for the needy of his day, not for the historians of ours. His work is a testimony not only to the tragedy that he was powerless to stop, but of the energy, the dedication, and the determination of one man to speak the truth and to try to arouse the world to a crime that will forever remain a blot on the historical record of humanity.

CAMBRIDGE, MASSACHUSETTS
JULY, 1984

HUMAN LIFE IN RUSSIA

A struggle for existence

Surrender

HUMAN LIFE IN RUSSIA

by

DR. EWALD AMMENDE

Introduction by
THE RT. HON. LORD DICKINSON, K.B.E., P.C.

LONDON
GEORGE ALLEN & UNWIN LTD
MUSEUM STREET

FIRST PUBLISHED IN 1936

INTRODUCTION

BY

The RIGHT HONOURABLE LORD DICKINSON, K.B.E., P.C.

I ESTEEM it an honour to be invited to write an introduction to this book. Before the Great War I did not know Dr. Ewald Ammende; but soon after its close we found ourselves working together on behalf of the racial and religious minorities, and I then learned to know and respect the singleness of purpose and wide sympathy which have enabled him to become an unknown friend of millions of people.

The war had claimed its dead and wounded; but that was not all. It had left an aftermath of destitute folk deprived of their homes, driven into foreign lands, or placed under new rulers. And multitudes were actually starved to death in the years that followed that terrific cataclysm.

Dr. Ammende, hailing from the Baltic Provinces of Russia and knowing well the conditions in Eastern Europe, threw himself into the task of rescuing these helpless people. With great skill he brought representatives of the "Minorities" into conferences whence it became possible to issue to the Governments and the League of Nations appeals for justice and tolerance. He thus became an effective advocate of the cause of minorities all over Europe.

Later on he extended his sympathy to the toiling masses of Soviet Russia, where poor harvests and incompetent administrators had brought famine into thousands of homes. Mainly by his efforts funds were raised and relief was organized on broad international lines. It is right that the Russian people should learn to whom they are indebted.

Dr. Ammende has died, a victim to his own unceasing activity. He has lived and died for others, and the world is the richer by the example of his life and of his death.

PREFACE

For the last fifteen years the author has championed this view —that the rendering of assistance to those inhabitants of Russia who are in danger of death from hunger or malnutrition is a problem which concerns the whole of civilized mankind and does not depend on political factors. Nor ought it to be affected by the views held with regard to the Communist experiment within the Soviet State, or by the achievements which characterize one department or another of Russian life.

As early as November 1920 I published a description of the situation in the former capital, St. Petersburg, where the population was suffering from famine, coupled with an appeal for help. In the spring of 1921, on returning from a long stay in Russia, I was one of the first to raise my voice and to point out, on the strength of personal observation, that millions of people in the Volga basin were in danger of famine.

Later, when the extermination of the so-called *kulaks* began in Russia, I wrote to the press, and for the last two years, as Honorary Secretary of the "Interconfessional and International Vienna Relief Committee for the Russian Famine Areas," I have been trying to solve the problem of how to bring to the attention of the world the position of millions of innocent people who have been dying in vast numbers since the collectivization of agriculture began. The aim of this book is to make the truth known despite all obstacles, in order that adequate relief may be rendered.

How does it come about that I have been dealing with this question for so long a time? This question must be answered in detail, since anyone attacking the question of the famine and the mortality it has caused during the last few years runs the risk of aspersion and denunciation, or at any rate is felt to be a disturber of the peace by many who are pursuing political and economic aims.

I must therefore ask leave, before entering on my theme proper, to give a brief account of myself and my activities in this question.

By good fortune I was able, in my student days, to visit almost every part of the vast Russian Empire, of which I was a national until the republic of Estonia was founded. In 1913 a journey of investigation took me into certain parts of the basins of the Volga and the Kama, where I had, in connection with a scientific thesis on which I was working, to study the position of the peasants as producers in the Russian grain trade. During this journey I had to cover hundreds of miles by sleigh in winter and by river in summer—for even to-day there are hardly any railways east of the Volga. This journey was a veritable revelation.

The impression which I formed at that time in the villages of East Russia, in the provincial towns and in the great centres along the Volga, through immediate contact with the peasants, the boatmen, and the merchants, who owned dozens of vessels and an extensive system of branches on the various rivers, may be summed up thus. At that time two different worlds stood face to face: a socially and economically privileged class, and a mass of peasants living in economic distress and in primitive conditions. Even at that time the Russian export of grain was in many districts not so much the result of abundance as of the distress of the producers, who were compelled to sell their crops—in part even in so far as they needed them for their own requirements—to cover taxes, debts, and purchases of vodka. Frequently enough—a fact worth stressing as typical of the disastrous effects of the State vodka monopoly of that time—the only sign of the State's activity in the remote Russian villages consisted in the State drinking shops with the eagle over the entrance and the drunken peasants round it. Despite the appearance of order, the entire country was in the midst of a severe crisis, which not even Stolypin's reforms could overcome. The revenues of the State consisted almost wholly of the contributions drawn from the peasants' meagre harvests. To that extent there is a resemblance between past and present. But the importance to the State of the vodka monopoly and of the indirect taxes is nothing like that of the exactions of grain to-day. At that time the mass of the population could despite everything hold its own without being actually threatened by death from starvation, and if occasional droughts led to a failure of the harvest the deficiency could be made good by bringing grain from elsewhere.

Then came the war, followed by the revolution. The vast empire collapsed. In 1918 Bolshevism came into power, and with it a new and fascinating idea. Equality and freedom were to triumph. There was to be an end to the rigours of the old regime, to the vodka monopoly and to the gulf between the upper class and the peasants.

Once again circumstance sent me on my travels—before the war was at an end—as plenipotentiary of my own native province of Livonia, and later of Estonia. I visited extensive areas of Russia, especially in the south, to negotiate for my country supplies of important foodstuffs from the east and the south. After the formation of an independent Ukrainian republic under the Hetman Skoropadsky, it was my task to negotiate with the Ukrainian Government at Kiev on behalf of Estonia and Latvia for the supply of grain and sugar from the Ukraine in exchange for Baltic produce. After 1917 I was also in a position to watch the growth of the Ukrainian nationalist movement during the time of the Rada, of Skoropadsky and at the beginning of Petlura's rule.

The winter of 1920 was a terrible time of suffering for many regions and cities of the former realm of the Tsars, especially for the former capital, Petrograd, now called Leningrad. At that time the economic convulsions and the breakdown of communications rendered the famine most acute. When I returned home (where, as part proprietor of the *Rigasche Rundschau*, the leading German paper in the Baltic provinces,

I was also active as a journalist), I found a stream of people fleeing from Russia. In a state of mental and physical collapse, with hollow cheeks and wearing the indescribable dull look which even to-day is peculiar to refugees from Russia who are fleeing from the famine, they were returning to their old home. Their accounts of events in the "starving city" of Petrograd were terrible, and it was certain that in the absence of rapid help the lives of thousands would be imperilled.

Silence here was out of the question, especially for those who felt themselves linked to the population of the former capital. On November 13, 1920, the *Rigasche Rundschau* published an account of the situation of the inhabitants of Petrograd, written by myself, in which I appealed for help. In Riga and abroad this account attracted a good deal of attention (it was printed in the press of many countries). I published soon after in the *Rigasche Rundschau* another article headed "Relief for Petrograd," containing concrete suggestions for giving rapid assistance to the population with the co-operation of the Soviet Government. The readiness of the people of Riga to help now manifested itself: the Red Cross and the Churches became active. Within a few days an interconfessional committee was formed, consisting of members of the various nationalities and denominations.

But it soon appeared that local endeavours would, despite all efforts, be inadequate to the task. This was a few weeks before the first League of Nations Assembly at Geneva, and it was natural that all concerned should turn their eyes to that city. Surely it might be hoped that the new organization, which was meant for the first time to unite the different states for purposes of common action in accordance with higher principles, might offer support or even solve the problem. A few shiploads would have sufficed to bring relief to the people starving in Petrograd.

Thus it came about that I went to Geneva about Christmas 1920 as representative of the Riga Relief Committee, confidently hoping that Geneva would enable the good work to become a reality. This hope was not so much the result of an overestimate of the task and achievements of the new Geneva organization as of a belief that I might be able to interest a man of unique qualities, who was attending the session, in the work of relief. This man, whose beneficent activities had been known to the entire world for decades, was Fritjof Nansen. It was he whom I wished to interest. A few days before Christmas I had an opportunity of talking to Nansen at the Hôtel Métropole, where he was staying at the time. He immediately approved of the idea of relief for Petrograd; but he did not conceal the difficulties. What distressed him most was that the public conscience had become dulled in the post-war period and did not favour fresh relief action. He considered success possible only if the International Red Cross Committee and an influential official of it, competent to deal with the question, were to support my endeavours.

I went to the Committee without delay. But the conversation with the official, whom Nansen recommended to me, was one of the greatest disappointments of my life. He argued that the public interest ought not be distracted by new relief activities from those which had already been taken in hand. I must confess that the argument that the setting up of any relief organization would represent a kind of competition with relief action already being undertaken made the most profound impression on me. The Red Cross official raised other objections, and allowed me to understand that despite Nansen's interest the International Committee could not participate in the work. This sealed the fate of our endeavours. The Petrograd catastrophe took its course unhindered.

A year passed. The Baltic States had concluded peace treaties with Russia and the time had come to implement them—among other things by securing the return of any nationals interned in Russian prisons. In March 1921 I went to Moscow as the representative of the Estonian Red Cross, my object being to find out to what extent Estonians in Russian prisons could be assisted from Estonia. My journey was greatly facilitated by the personal intervention of the head of the Estonian State, Constantine Päts, my sincere thanks to whom I wish to express here. I was acting on behalf of the Latvian Red Cross as well as that of Estonia.

I reached Moscow before the beginning of N E P (Lenin's New Economic Policy), where I found many thousands of innocent persons in prison as "politicals." They frequently had recourse to hunger strikes. Their mental sufferings were worse than their physical troubles. Peshkova, Maxim Gorki's first wife, was an ever-ready helper. As president of the "Political Red Cross" she did all that was in her power to assist the Russians, Estonians, Latvians, Poles, etc., who were under arrest. Even the omnipotent head of the Tcheka, Felix Djerjinski, bowed to the astonishing authority of this lady.

When the first reports reached Moscow of the famine which was impending along the Volga—reports which it was safe only to whisper—I felt that everything must be done to inform the public opinion of the world while there was yet time. (At that time Russia was practically cut off from the rest of the world with the exception of the Baltic States.) Peshkova shared my view, and arranged for an interview with Gorki in her flat. At this interview Gorki drafted a statement about the impending famine for publication in the press, which he handed to me. This document enabled me to raise at Riga the question of rendering immediate assistance to the people threatened by famine in Russia.

On my return from Moscow personal reasons caused me to break my journey in Petrograd. My experiences in that city had such a decisive influence on my further actions that I must describe them here. One of my brothers had gone to the front at the outbreak of war with a Guards regiment, had been invalided home and had been imprisoned in the notorious fortress of St. Peter and St. Paul for the sole reason that an old military coat was found in his rooms. He left the fortress to appear before his judges a dying man, and he actually died soon after. His body, as I learned later, was buried in a common grave. In Petrograd I had to visit the German cemeteries one after the other and look through the burial certificates in order to discover the place of his interment. On looking through these certificates I discovered that dozens of the people in question had died of starvation, or, as the technical expression was, "of exhaustion." The certificates I held in my hands bore the names of famous men of science, members of ancient and noble families, and all of them had died of starvation. . . . It was just a sample of the great tragedy which had been enacted in Petrograd during the previous year. For the first time I saw exactly what the failure of our endeavours at Geneva had meant.

I must here record another grievous experience in Petrograd. On the day before Palm Sunday of 1921 I went to look for certain relatives whose house was in the Galernaya. It was a glorious day. On reaching the house I was told that my relatives had gone to Estonia and that I should obtain further information from another tenant living in the house. I called on the lady, the widow of an official, and found her in the middle of the room, while on the sofa in the corner lay a boy of about six, worn to a skeleton. The woman told me, weeping, that he was her last child, and that two other boys had died of malnutrition (i.e. famine) during the previous winter. The piteous sight of the starving boy on that glorious early spring day always comes before my eyes when I think of the position of suffering people in Russia.

I called on some other acquaintances during this visit, and everywhere I found the same picture of half-starved people in a state not only of physical, but also of mental collapse. Once proud men and women were now broken to such a degree that they would have been ready to debase themselves before anyone in exchange for a piece of meat or any other food. I also began to understand how it was possible for foreigners living in Moscow or Petrograd to exist in a kind of oasis, having enough, indeed plenty, to eat every day and never becoming aware of the distress of a less privileged class of humanity. The members of this class are in such a state of mental distress—they are so keenly aware of their *déclassement*, their membership of a different world—that they would not venture to appeal to their relatives or to members of the more fortunate classes even if the Ogpu allowed it. Hunger, continual undernourishment, tyranny and unending fear make these people easily governed slaves—especially when malnutrition has become chronic.

The psychological state of these permanently hungry and harried people would certainly demand a chapter to itself. No appeals come from them, no cries for help, no shrieks of despair; which explains why there is here no potential source of revolt. But equally these humiliated wretches know no laughter and no joy, and their look—no other comparison is possible—is that of a beaten dog. In those days in Petrograd I realized for the first time the duty and the responsibility which rests on all those who succeed in escaping into another world, and who know from their own experience the dreadful sufferings to which all those are exposed who live in the Russian famine areas.

In those sunny, spring days of 1921 the contrast between the mass of distressed people and the life of the privileged classes—by which I mean especially the members of the first foreign delegations in the Soviet State—was particularly striking. The result of the extraordinary conditions prevailing was that many of the foreigners attached to various delegations in Moscow participated in the buying-up of Russia. In exchange for spirits, food or foreign exchange, carpets, paintings and jewels could be obtained and enormous profits made in the shortest time. Thus many of the first foreigners who came to Russia in 1919 as members of economic commissions, technical delegations, etc., became the abettors of the regime in the sale of Russian objects of art and of cultural value, and privy to the moral collapse of the country. I have described conditions as I found them at the time in Moscow and Petrograd in my pamphlet *Europe and Soviet Russia*, which was published at Riga (R. Ruetz & Co., 1921) after my return.

It is true that the Governments of the bourgeois states soon put an end to these activities of their nationals; but it is also true that it was on a business footing that foreigners coming to Russia met the representatives of the Soviet State—whether the business was of a political or an economic nature. This in itself was a fact calculated to dull the sympathy of visitors from the bourgeois states for the fate of the famine victims. This was the case, for example, when, at the time of the N E P, a former German Chancellor took over the control of a Russo-German trading company. Things have not changed since; the only difference is that private interests have been replaced by the economic interests of the states.

On my return to Riga I published in the *Rigasche Rundschau* an article called "At the eleventh hour"[1] in which I described the imminent Russian catastrophe and made suggestions for combating it on a purely humanitarian basis.[2] Shortly after I had the satisfaction of finding the foreign organ of the Russian Government, the *Novy Puty* (New Ways), expressing the agreement of Soviet circles with my suggestions. A conference called soon after by the Red Cross also adopted resolutions in this sense. These resolutions provided the foundation for Nansen's Russian relief work, which, together with the great American relief organizations, saved the lives of innumerable persons. If this help from America and Europe had not been forthcoming, the victims of the Russian catastrophe would

[1] Cf. *Europa und Sovietrussland*, Ruetz & Co., Riga, 1921.
[2] I would also mention in this connection that I was enabled to establish contact with Fritjof Nansen, Prince Carl of Sweden, Professor Lujo Brentano and other eminent men in the matter of Russian relief. In the summer of 1922 I was also permitted to publish articles on the Russian famine from the purely humanitarian standpoint in a special Russian issue of the *Manchester Guardian*, edited by Mr. J. M. Keynes.

B

undoubtedly have numbered ten millions or more instead of "only" four millions.

Several years passed. Lenin's new economic policy brought with it an improvement in the economic position of the country, and the danger of famine seemed to be removed for a long time, if not for ever. In 1929, however, there was a drastic change of course. Agricultural collectivization began. Those who were acquainted with the food position in Russia understood at once that the consequences of this revolution, carried through all over the country, must involve, at least temporarily, the gravest rationing difficulties, if not an actual catastrophe.

On Sunday, December 29, 1929, the *Neue Zürcher Zeitung* published a letter from myself written to attract public attention to the danger of a new and acute famine arising in Russia. In this letter I wrote:

"In view of the poor harvest and the results of Stalin's experiment a severe food crisis can be foretold with certainty, in which case the coming spring may bring another catastrophe. . . . It is the duty of the European public to take the initiative in order that timely preparations may be made on behalf of the victims in Russia. If the government should eventually overcome the difficulties, it would still be better that preparations should have been made unnecessarily than that responsibility for the loss of many human lives should be incurred. A first step, therefore, should be for the various national relief organizations to co-operate on the proved foundation of the International Red Cross in order to reach an agreed plan for relief, and to obtain information on the actual food position in Russia."

In view, however, of the flattering estimate of the experiments and the general situation in the Soviet Union published at that time (in the same manner as to-day) in the press of the non-Communist states, this suggestion was disregarded. Indeed, it proved impossible to get the letter printed in German papers outside Switzerland, although it referred specifically to the plight of the Germans in the Volga basin and to the need for help there. To-day, when Stalin's collectivization has caused the death of millions of innocent persons, I have a right to ask whether these terrible losses of human lives in the very midst of Europe might not have been avoided if inquiry had been made into the actual food position in Russia, as suggested by me, and joint action by the various relief organizations on the basis of the International Red Cross had followed.

The catastrophe arrived soon after, not as the result of an act of God, but simply in consequence of the agricultural experiment. On June 26, 1933, the Vienna *Reichspost* published a letter from me containing a full account of the position, together with suggestions for putting an end to the ravages of the famine. For years I had been Secretary General of the European Nationalities Congress, and as such enjoyed the confidence of the minorities of the national groups living in the various states. Many of the nationalities affiliated to the Congress have kinsmen living within the Soviet Union, and I thus obtained authoritative information about conditions in the Russian agricultural districts, which formed the basis of a memorandum published in the *Reichspost* and elsewhere. However, the statements contained in the memorandum were denied by the Soviet Minister in Vienna within a few hours of their appearance, as well as by others of Moscow's spokesmen and friends at a later stage. Thus suggestions for putting an end to the famine were before the public as early as the summer of 1933, when innumerable persons might have been saved by the help of surplus grain rotting in the granaries of European and other exporting countries—a fact which it would be impossible to deny to-day.

On the initiative of Cardinal Archbishop Theodore Innitzer, the "Interconfessional and International Relief Committee for the Russian Famine Areas" was formed soon afterwards in Vienna. Under the leadership of His Eminence it proved possible to gather all denominations for united, brotherly relief work on behalf of the people dying of starvation in Russia.

The Committee made it its main task to enlighten world public opinion on the real position in the Russian famine areas and the necessity of joint action. In anticipation of joint relief action the Committee gives what assistance it can by forwarding private food parcels, an aim which has been vigorously pursued since August 1934. I was made Honorary Secretary of the Committee immediately after its formation.

It was my task to tell the facts about the Russian famine and its consequences in full detail. While writing the book, however, I found that the magnitude of the famine was such that separate treatment of its various phases was essential, the most important task being to show how the sudden catastrophe of the first period turned gradually into a kind of "normal" state of affairs. I further realized in the course of writing that this description by itself would not suffice to make the events intelligible, and that I should have to provide a special explanation of the causes other than natural which led to the famine. Further, I had to deal with its chief consequences, and with the reasons which made it possible to keep world public opinion in the dark as to the facts and which influenced the attitude of the non-Communist states in this purely humanitarian question.

Thus the original description of the catastrophe has turned into a book dealing with the whole group of questions connected with the deaths from famine in the Soviet Union and with the problem of relief. My first chapter on the causes of the famine deals with Moscow's economic policy, which led to these events. The second chapter deals with the catastrophe and describes this scourge in all its phases. The chapter on the national struggle completes this aspect and covers the position of the nationalities, with special reference to the Ukrainians and to the systematic campaign now being carried out against this group with the help of the famine.

Chapter IV deals with Moscow's methods; its object is

to show how the events which led to the famine and its exploitation by Moscow harmonize with the general ideology of Moscow and the procedure of the Kremlin. I here show how, granted the aims pursued by Moscow, the procedure adopted followed of necessity. The fifth chapter, "Propaganda Methods," as well as the sixth, "The Testimony of Monsieur Herriot," are an attempt to explain systematically the methods by which Moscow succeeds in keeping a veil over the real position in Russia and especially over the fate of the non-privileged categories. The chapter on the attitude of the outer world asks why the bourgeois states carry their respect for Moscow so far as to refrain from action even in the matter of a purely charitable intervention on behalf of the victims of the Russian famine. I then deal with the problem of assistance, and describe the struggle with the object of rendering assistance which has now been going on for years.

I have thought it well to sketch for the reader's benefit the contents of this book, in order that it may be easy to follow the general outline from the beginning, and to understand why a discussion of the causes was as necessary as a description of the catastrophe itself.

A word should be said on the sources of this book. The description of Russian events is mainly based on authoritative statements in the Russian press, a press which, of course, is entirely controlled by the State and party authorities at Moscow. Nothing appearing in the press, therefore, can be treated as a baseless invention.

How is it then that the Russian press, and notably the big provincial papers, mingle praises of the achievements of the regime with reports on the real position within the country which are frequently amazingly frank and even pessimistic? One of the most experienced Moscow correspondents, Dr. Just, answers the question by saying that "the damage can be repaired only by means of organized public pressure." This is in fact the correct explanation. The method of exerting pressure through these unvarnished accounts is frequently the one and only means of dealing with the appalling deficiencies in various spheres and of keeping the local officials working properly. Reports on Soviet conditions from Soviet sources are the main foundation of this book. As far as possible they are quoted textually.

In addition there were a number of other sources. There were reports from reliable eyewitnesses, from foreign experts who had been at work in Russia for years, and from refugees of various nationalities who managed to escape abroad across the Dniester and other frontiers. There were also letters from victims of the famine living in various parts of Russia.

I have further made use of reports from certain foreign journalists of different nationalities living in the Soviet Union. Here, however, caution and selective methods became necessary, since most of the foreign journalists in Russia are in a delicate position.

Other books, with a few exceptions, like Mr. Chamberlin's *Russia's Iron Age*, did not provide a useful source. Travellers in Russia show little interest in the fate of the people living there and confine their attention to the external results of the Communist experiment, such as the activity of the giant concerns and the possible profits from trade with Moscow; again, the present book covers the events of the last few years, which have barely been touched on by writers.

Official evidence and statistical figures provided by the government had to be used with the utmost caution for reasons explained elsewhere. Relative rather than absolute figures are the safest to use.

A few words should be said about the photographs which illustrate the book. They are among the most important sources for the actual facts of the Russian position. The majority of them were taken by an Austrian specialist who worked in Russian industry until 1934, and was able to take the pictures unobserved during his stay at Kharkov, at the time when deaths were most numerous during the summer of 1933. The authenticity of the photographs, which form a permanent record of the terrible events in the Ukraine after the agricultural collapse, is undoubted; for an examination made by experts shows that they were taken with a Leica camera of a type which did not exist at the time of the famine of 1921–2, and that the pictures were actually taken in the streets and squares of Kharkov in the summer of 1933, as is also apparent from various details clearly visible in the pictures.

In addition to these photographs taken in Kharkov, the English edition of the book contains also others, which were supplied to the author by Dr. F. Dittloff, for many years Director of the German Government Agricultural Concession —Drusag—in the North Caucasus. This institution was most flourishing in the time of the Stresemann regime and of the German Rapallo Policy, but was liquidated in 1933. The photographs were taken by Dr. Dittloff himself in the summer of 1933, and they demonstrate the conditions then prevailing on the plains of the agricultural areas of the Hunger Zone. A few of them have been published before elsewhere without his permission. Dr. Dittloff accepts full responsibility for the guarantee of their authenticity.

My treatment of the various problems was facilitated by a number of facts which it might be worth while to enumerate. I had a grasp of the economic position because I was acquainted with the economic geography of Russia, more especially with regard to foodstuffs, and because I had studied the agricultural districts in question for a number of years. In dealing with the campaign of Moscow against the nationalities I had the advantage of having been for the last ten years Secretary-General of the European Nationalities Congress, and thus having had to deal with the problem of the nationalities in various parts of Europe. The same applies to the personal observations made during the last fifteen years at almost all the important political conferences dealing with the international co-operation of the states and peoples of non-Communist Europe.

My book differs from most of those written about Russia in that it was written with a purely humanitarian object. Its kernel is simply the fate of the inhabitants of the Soviet State, and all other questions, such as the success or the failure of the five-year plans, collectivization, the construction of the industrial monster works and the rest are of subsidiary importance. The only question is, "Is it desirable and is it possible to render help to the people who are starving in Russia?"

EWALD AMMENDE

GENEVA
November 1935

CONTENTS

LIST OF ILLUSTRATIONS

HUMAN LIFE IN RUSSIA

CHAPTER I

THE CAUSES OF FAMINE IN RUSSIA

ALL serious observers of conditions in Soviet Russia are of one opinion as to the causes of the Russian famine. In their view the real cause is to be found not in any natural events, but in the fiasco of the collective system which was introduced with such excessive haste. Even official Soviet reports referred to the 1932 harvest as of medium quality: poor results or failure were never mentioned, and in January 1933 Stalin proudly declared that 61 per cent of all the peasants' farms had been socialized— 220,000 as collective farms and 5,000 as State grain and cattle farms. But although his plan of campaign seemed to have succeeded, the facts were the reverse: the foundation of all these thousands of collective farms had collapsed. The experiment, which consisted in forcibly detaching the peasantry from their soil, and converting them into proletarian workers in a large-scale State concern, had failed.

A leading expert on Soviet Russian agriculture, Dr. Otto Schiller, who was attached to the German Embassy at Moscow in that capacity, has produced an extremely carefully written scientific work[1] on the subject of collectivization—that unique measure which was carried through, without any preliminary investigation, in a territory with nearly 160,000,000 inhabitants. This is his verdict: "In the work of collectivization one factor of production failed completely: the human factor."

In the author's opinion Dr. Schiller's statement provides the key to an understanding of the present position in the Soviet Union; and it also explains why, as a recent eyewitness

[1] Cf. *Die Krise der sozialistischen Landwirtschaft in der Sowjetunion,* Reports on Agriculture, No. 7, 1933.

expressed it, the Russian machinery and tractor cemeteries "surpass the wildest imagination." In fact, Soviet agriculture, based as it was on mechanization, was wrecked by the backwardness of the Russian peasant.

The publication of Dr. Schiller's above-mentioned work led to a controversy with the Soviet Government. The Soviet claimed that Schiller could not have published his report without the sanction of the German Government, and that his criticism of Russian agricultural policy constituted an unfriendly act on the part of Germany. Nevertheless, Dr. Schiller remains the agricultural expert at the German Embassy at Moscow. Professor Auhagen, a predecessor of Dr. Schiller's in this post, had a similar experience. The Bolshevik Government made difficulties over his reports, and he had to leave Russia.

These incidents show why the experts, or rather their superiors, are unable to publish anything, however scientific or objective, about the real position in Russia. Friendly Governments having diplomatic representatives accredited to Moscow have an interest in preventing such reports from reaching the public, for otherwise their economic relations with the Soviet Union would be jeopardized. There is no doubt that the Foreign Offices of various European states possess reports from their experts containing the full facts about Russian conditions.[1]

Deprived of every economic inducement, the Russian peasant has resisted the demands made upon him. Dr. Schiller well remarks that the Soviet Government, in its dealings with the peasantry, is in the position of a general who has concentrated all his forces to consolidate a new position and improve his technical equipment, but whose troops are suddenly demoralized at the very moment when the external conditions of success appear to be present. "Without abandoning the strategic plan," Dr. Schiller writes, "an attempt is now being made to restore discipline by changes in tactics, material

[1] See chapter entitled "The Outer World and the Soviets."

promises and finally by draconic measures—to a certain extent by the introduction of martial law."

What has happened in Russia is this. Owing to the failure of the collectivized peasant, and the other reasons mentioned above, the 1932 harvest did not amount even to a moderate part of the yield anticipated. Further, a large part of the harvested corn could not be garnered because of the destruction of live-stock. Before the peasants were absorbed in the collective farms, draught oxen were slaughtered in masses: according to Schiller the number of beasts fell from 70·5 millions in 1928 to 29·2 millions in 1932.

The late Mr. Gareth Jones,[1] who visited the Russian famine area in the winter of 1933, writes that the peasants had to give up their cows, which were handed over to the collective farms. The result was a systematic slaughtering of the oxen by the peasants, for no one wanted to hand over his beasts for nothing. He goes on to describe how the collective farms were absolutely unprepared to receive such numbers of cattle and how part of the cattle perished from disease. Stalin himself, in his speech at the Seventeenth Congress of the Communist Party in Moscow, had to admit the disastrous position of Russian stock-farming at the present time. So did Mirsoian, the representative of Kazakstan, whose speech showed that the reduction in the number of cattle had continued until quite recently. Another speaker praised Stalin's frankness in admitting the magnitude of the collapse in the cattle-raising industry.

But the undoubted collapse of Russian agriculture does not suffice to explain the death by starvation of millions in the Ukraine, the Northern Caucasus, on the Volga and in the other agricultural districts which were once the most fertile in Russia. It should be remembered that these parts of Russia used to export to foreign countries vast quantities of wheat

---

[1] It will be remembered that Mr. Gareth Jones was carried off by bandits while on a visit to China in the spring of 1935, and eventually met his death at their hands.

and other grains. Accordingly, despite the decline of agriculture, the remnants of the harvest ought to have sufficed at least to keep the peasants alive. Here we come to the immediate cause of the tragedy which is being enacted in the Russian agricultural districts.

Apart from the process described above, leading to the ruin of agriculture, the diminution of the cultivated areas, the declining yield, the disastrous loss of cattle, and the constant difficulties in garnering the harvest, it must be pointed out that the peasants of the agricultural districts are deprived of almost the whole yield of the harvest through the system of compulsory surrender. This means the total exhaustion of the producers, with the consequence that not even the minimum of grain and other food required to sustain life is left them. The State demands the surrender of impossible amounts of grain: and the peasant resists this pressure from the State by the only possible means—sabotage. Gareth Jones's explanation of the psychological causes of the peasants' passive resistance seems very apt. He writes that anyone who has the blood of a Welsh farmer in his veins would understand what it means for a peasant to be deprived of his land. The Russian farmers wanted to own their land, and if it were taken away they refused to work.

What are the reasons that induce the Soviet Government to pursue a policy which can only be described as the systematic starvation of the agricultural population? Two reasons must be borne in mind to appreciate in its full scope the agricultural policy of the State, which in normal circumstances would be entirely unintelligible. First, the absolute necessity of providing the populations of the districts to which grain has to be transported, especially the capitals and industrial centres, with the necessities of life; secondly, the necessity of keeping alive the industrial system, the real foundation of the Communist State, by exporting—in order, with the help of foreign currency, to obtain the foreign fuel and raw material essential for industry.

Foodshop in Kharkov besieged by the population

Queue at a milk-distribution centre in Kharkov

Starving, homeless children—the *bezprizornie*

Bezprizornie

The first reason is to some degree ordained by Nature. Half the territory of the vast Russian State (the entire north and almost all the industrial regions) have always lived on the imported surpluses of the agricultural south and east. Every year, in spring and autumn, hundreds of trains and barges transport grain from the agrarian into the consuming regions. The whole existence and the future of the Communist State depend on assuring these regions, and especially the industrial centres, the necessary minimum of food supplies. Hence the axiom that the feeding of the industrial districts is the primary task of Soviet Russian economic policy. In practice this means that whether the harvest is good or bad, the minimum of grain needed by the consuming centres must be extracted from the "surplus areas," however great the dearth may be in the latter.

It is otherwise with regard to the second reason. It is no natural catastrophe, but the inadequate fulfilment of the five-year plans, which has led to the requirements of foreign goods and hence of foreign currency far exceeding the estimates. Other causes, too, contributed to burden agriculture. To grasp this fully we must here deal with the Government's policy of industrialization and the effects of its collapse.

The aim of the five-year plans was perhaps most effectively summarized by Ordjonikidze in his speech at the 1934 Communist Congress in Moscow: "He [Stalin] wanted us not only to produce the material for our clothes; he wanted us to produce the machinery necessary to turn out the material. His object was to make us industrially independent of foreign countries. We were to manufacture, in the shortest possible time, not this or that article, but everything we required. In another place and in another connection Stalin put in the foreground Lenin's motto: 'To catch up and pass'; and it was on this that he built up his concrete plan of action." This, Ordjonikidze continued, was based on the idea "the devil take the hindmost," and on the assumption that any "slowing down of the tempo" was out of the question. He summarized the fundamental idea of this plan

c

in these words: "We must see that the efforts of our political economists are directed towards transforming our country from one which imports its machinery into one which manufactures it."

Ordjonikidze illustrated this idea by quotations from Stalin's speech at the fourteenth Congress of the Communist Party: "The authors of the Dawes Plan," he said, "would like to restrict us to the manufacture, say, of boots. No, we want to produce the machinery to make the boots." Addressing himself to Sokolnikov, the Opposition spokesman, he declared: "Here is the difference between the two 'principles of economic policy' [i.e. between that of Stalin and that of the Opposition]. A departure from our principle would be equivalent to a surrender of the goal aimed at by Socialist reconstruction and would mean"—here Ordjonikidze coined a new word—"the 'Dawesification' of our country."

This characterization of Stalin's aim is not exaggerated. It was Stalin's fixed idea that the Soviet Union was to be made independent of foreign countries, not merely in respect of primary necessities, but in every sphere. All this was to be done in a Russia whose population until recently consisted largely of illiterates, for the sake of an idea.

The erection of the "giants" now began, those technical monster concerns which to-day evoke the astonishment of foreign guests of honour. For the construction of these government works, on which leading technical specialists from many different countries were employed, it did not seem necessary to make any calculations as to whether the concerns would pay. When a party of foreign journalists recently visited the new industrial buildings at Kharkov, one of them asked how the new undertaking had been budgeted for and what was the estimated yield. He was told that "that sort of thing was not done." A particularly instructive example is the power station on the Dnieper rapids which has become universally known by the name Dnieprostroi. This gigantic work, which was constructed at enormous financial sacrifice, was built on so much too large a scale that even to-day, many years after its completion, there is no economic possibility of employing a great part of its capacity.

Even the first five-year plan, with its "giants" stamped out of the earth, could not be realized. It was shown that monster concerns, whose output had been estimated on a titanic scale, had in many cases not yet reached the productive stage or had actually not been completed. Thus the Novo-Sibirsk correspondent of *Pravda* reported on March 11, 1934, that the monster mill at Barnaul, whose output of manufactured goods had been calculated at 1,300,000 metres for the current year, was not even approaching completion. "If a classical example of *funkzionalka*"—i.e. general irresponsibility in the economic field—"with all its disastrous phenomena and consequences had been needed, there could be no better example than the erection of the Barnaul works. Every part, every building, every hole and every scaffolding was handed over for completion to a special organization. But there is no unity of control. There is no supervisor to give an independent decision. The leading 'functionaries' who direct the construction of the various parts of the works are solely occupied in quarrelling about their privileges." The correspondent goes on to describe how the highest authorities in charge of the building sit in Moscow and thence send telegrams, wired decrees and instructions to the builders at Barnaul, thousands of miles away. As a result the Barnaul works are far from completion: yet the Moscow economic plan shows it even for the current year as actually turning out the vast quantities of material which it is to produce according to programme. Vast capital sums were invested in this and other giant concerns, of which only a part has actually reached the stage of economic exploitation. Even where the undertaking was completed punctually according to the plan, only a part can be put to real economic use.

To show that occurrences of this kind in the erection of

large-scale concerns are not exceptional, but common phenomena of Soviet construction policy, let me quote another
example. On May 21, 1934, *Za Industrializatsiu* reported on
the results of the construction of the Ural Wagon Works.
The description ends by stating that four dates for starting
work had already been fixed, and that it had still not begun.

Rudzutak, a leading Soviet Russian economic official, who is
at the head of, among other things, the building department,
enumerated (at the Moscow Congress in 1934) quite a number
of works which had had to be reorganized ten times during
the last three years. According to him the worst instance is
that of the Tagil (Urals) engineering works, whose organization plan had to be altered nine times in twenty-six months,
involving a loss of approximately 4 million roubles. In 1932, at
these works, 220 million roubles had been invested in machinery
which was in an unserviceable condition. According to Rudzutak the costs of industry are continually growing. During
the first five-year plan $1\frac{1}{2}$ milliards of roubles were invested in
the metallurgical industry, of which half is at present "frozen"
owing to the prevailing chaos. In other words, the giant
concerns are there, but their actual economic value is often
negligible.

And yet another fact must be remembered. Even where there
is regular production, the entire energies of the managers are
concentrated upon turning out the prescribed amount of
goods at whatever cost—not least because their own existence
depends upon the fulfilment of the prescribed plan. (Once this
has been done they can telegraph that the plan has been
fulfilled.) After all, the quality of the articles produced cannot
be immediately checked. Often enough it beggars description,
because, as was mentioned above, the managers' interest is
limited to the formal fulfilment of the plan. The result has
been that the production of shoddy goods, known in Russia as
brak, has become a conspicuous characteristic of Soviet Russian
industry.

In the speech quoted above, Rudzutak referred to the production of defective goods as the greatest evil of Russian economic life, and quoted as an example the fact that 50 per cent of the manufactures produced by the Stankolit works in Moscow were entirely useless, while a zinc wire netting factory at Kiev was said to be turning out 100 per cent of rubbish.

The systematic and mass production of *brak* has been publicly admitted by the President of the Central Committee of the Communist Party, Kalinin, as well as other leading Soviet officials. On February 10, 1934, the Central Committee and the Council of Peoples' Commissaries thought it necessary to make paragraph 128*a* of the Penal Code run as follows: "The production of incomplete or poor quality goods by industrial undertakings, owing to a criminal and careless attitude towards their work by the heads of trusts, directors of works, and members of the administrative and technical personnel, is punished by deprivation of liberty for not less than five years."

A further passage throws a good deal of light on present conditions in the industrial system: "The systematic mass production of poor quality goods by the trading institutions is punished by deprivation of liberty up to five years."[1] Here is an open confession that the industrial plan has resulted in the production of goods large quantities of which are unfit for use—for which the heads of the industrial undertakings and of the trading institutions whose work it is to distribute the *brak* are henceforth made to bear the responsibility.

The most disastrous effect of this production of defective goods has undoubtedly been seen in a sphere particularly important for Russian agriculture—the production of tractors and agricultural machinery generally. Agriculture has been motorized to such an extent, and the number of draught

---

[1] The decree was published at the Kremlin on February 10th and was published in *Izvestia* on February 17, 1934.

animals so heavily reduced, that the faultless working of the tractors in particular has become a matter of the utmost importance. Even a layman can readily understand what it means if there are no draught animals available at sowing time or harvest time, or even if their number is inadequate. It may easily result in the loss of a very considerable part of the harvest. Indeed, this is one of the chief causes of the famine. Clearly the wastage of the complicated machines on account of the inadequate training of the personnel must be very great. The many vivid accounts of the gigantic machine cemeteries are not really necessary as corroborative evidence. This makes the problem of spare parts and repairs all the more important.

The tractor troubles are very freely reported in the Soviet press. It is often sufficient to look at the headlines of the big Moscow papers, e.g. one in *Pravda* which runs: "Bureaucrats and thieves at work in the tractors factory." *Izvestia* (February 23, 1934) reports from Leningrad that the local works have not completed half the tractors intended. On February 24 the same paper had a report from its Tashkent correspondent to the effect that defective tractor parts were being despatched to that region by the thousand. "Part of the fault," he writes, "is due to the tractor centres, which pass large parcels of defective reserve parts without noticing it. The result is chaos, and the entire repairs time-table is upset." On February 19 *Pravda* summed up its views on the collapse (*proval*) of the tractor-repair plan by quoting an extract from the Leningrad paper *Put Linina* (Lenin's Way). "The chief reason for the collapse of the repair plan," the paper said, "is the scandalous organization of the work. But a number of monstrous occurrences have also contributed to the breakdown of the repair campaign, the non-fulfilment of the plan, and these have been permitted by idiots in charge of the motor and tractor stations."

Recent developments with regard to agricultural machinery are apparent from a decree issued by the Central Committee of the Communist Party on April 19, 1935, dealing with the work of the Kombajny (combined reaping machines). The decree (published in *Pravda* of April 20, 1935) says: "Hitherto the Kombajny have been working intolerably badly both on the Soviet grain farms and at the machine tractor stations. The People's Commissariat for Agriculture of the S.S.S.R. and that for the administration of the Soviet farms omitted to organize the practical application and utilization of the Kombajny. They keep the Kombajny in a poor state and take little trouble about the training and maintenance of efficient Kombajny mechanics." The false system of accountancy used in the State grain farms —directly counter to Government instructions—led to Kombajny mechanics, who fell far short of the daily standard of work, only too often being better paid than those who exceeded this standard by doing more work in a shorter time.

In order to increase the yield of the Kombajny, Moscow has been compelled to revert to capitalist principles and to cause Kombajny mechanics to have the highest possible material interest in increasing the yield of their machines. On this point the *Pravda* leader says: "Kombajny mechanics must be given the greatest possible interest in the efficient working of their machines, and in their not being run at a loss."

The same reasons account for the crisis in another important branch upon whose smooth working the success of industries and agriculture in Russia largely depends. Here again the Russian press continues to publish the most incredible reports. They have to admit almost daily that the chief blame rests with *funkzionalka*, and here again the competent delegates at the Moscow Communist Congress have provided ample confirmation. It is particularly the case with the river traffic, especially on the greatest Russian river system of waterways, the Volga and its tributaries. A special correspondent despatched by *Pravda* to the Volga early in 1934 sent from Gorky (formerly Nizhni-Novgorod) a report which calls for no comment. He begins by describing the astonishing red-tape methods employed and the flood of papers which issues from the head office of the Volga shipping administration. "In 1933," the report goes on, "the number of accidents on the Volga had actually risen. On an average every other vessel has been in for repairs on account of accidents. These accidents constitute a disaster for the Volga transport and are one of the main reasons for the collapse of the shipping plan." It must be borne in mind that the Volga is a river on which there are no accidents due to stress of weather. A greater fiasco could not be imagined. Picture, for the sake of comparison, that every other vessel on the Rhine or the Danube had been damaged and under repair during the past year. It must further be remembered that the waterways, and especially the Volga-Kama system, are of the highest importance to Russian economic life. The correspondent declares in conclusion that at Astrakhan, where 70 per cent of the Volga vessels are laid up for the winter and are repaired, "the plan of repairs was very far from being completed" only just before the opening of navigation. "Astrakhan," he writes, "is a menace to the Volga shipping traffic." And he ends with a positively angry reference to the "liberalizing indulgence which the public prosecutor of the Astrakhan river district shows towards the producers of defective material" (meaning the persons in charge of the repair shops, where "hundreds of instances of careless work in the execution of repairs have been recorded") instead of taking proceedings against them.

It is the same with the railways. On this subject, too, a number of reports are available which were submitted at the 1934 Communist Congress, the most important being one by Andreiev, then People's Commissary for Transport. An article by Andreiev in *Pravda* bears the significant title: "How the railways transport air!" Latterly the collapse of the transport system has induced the highest Soviet authorities to take extraordinary measures and to issue remarkable decrees. By a coincidence—or was it perhaps intentional?—a decree concerning the railways, signed by Stalin in person as Secretary of the Central Committee, and by Molotov as President of the Council of People's Commissaries, appeared on March 10, 1934, the same day on which the above-mentioned decree about the production of defective material was published. Although the decree refers only to conditions on the Donetz railways, it is obviously an exposure of the whole traffic system of the Soviet Union.

It is stated in the decree that "all this refers both to the Permanent Way Commissariat and its instances and also to the management of most of the railways in the Soviet Union." It points out that the managers and their district subordinates have no idea of "the actual condition of stations, the permanent way and the depots." It is further stated that the Donetz railways fulfilled no more than a small part of the transport plan. Finally, the public prosecutor of the Union is instructed "to prosecute all railway and party officials who abuse their position to ruin the transport plan, who accept or give bribes, and who contribute to the dissipation of State property." Significantly, the decree ends with the words: "Station-masters are made personally responsible for the fulfilment of the transport plans." Here again is the cry for personal responsibility as the only means of combating the gigantic *funkzionalka* of the irresponsible Soviet bureaucracy.

On March 23, 1934, a decree was issued by the Council of People's Commissaries and the Central Committee of the Communist Party, signed by Stalin and Molotov (see *Pravda*, March 24th) which throws much light on the critical position of the railways and on the war which Moscow now has to wage against the *funkzionalka* of railway officials who are also members of the Communist Party. In this decree Stalin puts all personal considerations aside and pillories his own party comrades. He declares that an improvement in the position of the railwaymen is impossible without "an end being put to the unbusinesslike ways, the irresponsibility and the frivolity which infect the transport system like a fever."[1]

Nor does the Soviet press hesitate to point out what this failure of transport means for agriculture. An article in *Izvestia* (February 24, 1934), dealing with the impending sowing season, says: "Owing to the transport breakdown the collective farms and the Soviet farms have been deprived of thousands of tons of most valuable seed—the direct result of bureaucratic mismanagement. Are many words needed to show the disastrous effect of the breakdown of water and railway transport, as also the failure in production and repairs, in respect of tractors and other branches of industry upon the Soviet Union —a country where industrial and agricultural mechanization is one of the main foundations of the entire economic system?"

It is not the aim of this work to inquire to what extent the five-year plans were capable of realization. Yet the question of industrialization and of the degree to which it was successful could not be passed over altogether, for it has reacted profoundly upon agriculture and hence upon the food supply, quite apart from the immediate effect upon agriculture of the conditions in the tractor factories and the transport system. The excessive haste with which industrialization was undertaken and, in particular, the impossibility of properly harmonizing the rate of production of the various branches of industry, as well as the faulty investment of capital on an enormous scale, led to a greater and more urgent need for foreign products and hence for foreign exchange. Despite the endeavour to reach autarchy in the shortest possible time, it became apparent that industrialization could not be carried through without the

---

[1] That the transport system has further deteriorated since 1934 is shown by the first decree issued by the newly appointed dictator, Kaganovitch, to the employees of his department. He says: "When we consider that in 1934 19,000 trucks were delivered to the railways and that 64,000 were destroyed or damaged, it is clear that railway accidents and casualties are the root evil and a plague of the entire railway system. . . . People have become accustomed to railway accidents, regard them as ordinary occurrences, and consider the campaign against them a matter of secondary importance."

help of vast quantities of foreign machinery, spare parts and other goods.[1] Indeed, the Soviet Government has for years left no stone unturned to obtain foreign currency at any price. For this purpose it was equally ready to use humanitarian methods like the Torgsin operations (which will be dealt with in greater detail in a later chapter), to suppress the import of articles not required for the process of industrialization but otherwise absolutely essential, or to export food at a moment when millions of persons were being swept off by hunger in the country itself.

This urgent need of foreign exchange also explains the Soviet anxiety to obtain foreign credits. Yet this latter method of financing imports proved of little profit. After concessions ceased to be granted to foreign capitalists, the Soviet Government could obtain only medium or short term credits, and almost exclusively credits for the import of goods, which had to be promptly repaid in order to safeguard the discountability of Soviet paper. Hence for a considerable time only the two first methods have remained advantageous for the financing of the imports necessary for industrialization—the cutting off of all imports not required for industrial reconstruction or for armaments, and the forcing up of exports to a degree almost unimaginable in view of the economic position of the country.

Even a hasty survey of Russian foreign trade statistics suffices to show the extent to which imports of all goods not essential for industrialization have been throttled. At this moment I will confine myself to two striking examples. Tea has been from olden times one of the very few luxuries which even the poorest Russian peasant used to allow himself at all seasons. In a few months the imports of tea were so drastically cut down by Moscow that they fell from 98,000 tons in the first

---

[1] It should be stressed in this connection that the demands, enormous in themselves, made on the population by the hurried process of industrialization, have been very greatly intensified by the fact that a large part of the newly created industry does not serve the needs of the population, but solely the requirements of armaments—a more unproductive aim from the economic standpoint.

six months of the financial year 1931–2 to 10,300 tons in the corresponding period of 1932–3. It is true that this extra-ordinary strangulation of tea imports was followed by some increase in 1934; in the first eight months of that year 40,604 tons entered the country. But even of this quantity, extremely small for Russia, only a part remained in the country; an article in the *Deutsche Allgemeine Zeitung* of October 6, 1934, shows that a considerable amount was re-exported to Germany. The figures for other foodstuffs and consumption goods show clearly how pitilessly the overwhelming majority of the country population is being compelled to do without everything remotely suggesting luxury.

Similar methods are employed with regard to other "indispensable" imported goods, in so far as they are not absolutely required for the consumption of the privileged classes and the needs of the industrial system. This even applies to the most vital drugs and medicines, the import of which is prohibited except for the benefit of the privileged categories (G.P.U. officials, the Red Army and certain industrial workers). All eyewitnesses of conditions in Soviet Russia agree that this lack of the most indispensable foreign medicines leads to the death of an immense number of persons.

A particularly competent foreign expert, who for years held an administrative position in Southern Russia, expressed himself as follows: "There were no drugs for the treatment and cure of various diseases, especially of malaria, which occurred on an enormous scale. Despite the vast burdens placed upon the industrial concerns by the *sozstrakh* [social insurance], amounting to 16 per cent of the money wages of all workers, the equipment of the hospitals and travelling dispensaries was more than lamentable. Everything was lacking. Hundreds of thousands had to perish because the scanty supply of doctors had no medicines at its disposal, especially out in the country. The same was true, of course, with regard to drugs for the treatment of animal diseases. If laboratories for their manu-

facture actually existed in a few places, their practical importance was negligible because the serums delivered were insufficient to meet the demand. The best proof is the disastrous
reduction of the live stock, which without doubt is partly due
to the unchecked spread of epidemics." The stores of drugs
for combating malaria kept at the German *Drusag* concession
saved the lives of numerous persons in the Northern Caucasus;
but as there were not enough of these, thousands perished who
otherwise might also have been saved.

The stimulation of exports is, of course, even more important than the restriction of "unnecessary" imports. This is
not based, as in other countries, on the absorbing capacity of
foreign markets and the surplus at home which can be utilized
without harming the internal economic structure: the sole
consideration is to acquire at all costs the largest possible
amount of foreign currency. Timber is one of the most important articles of export; indeed, as will be understood, Russia's
export trade is entirely in raw materials. The panic will still
be remembered which was caused in the world timber market
when the Soviet Union tried to force all other producers out of
the market by supplying timber at prices which did not even
cover the transport on the Russian railways. An industry entirely directed by the State is, of course, much better able than
other sellers to throw goods on to the market at uneconomic
prices. But the prices asked by the Soviet Government were
possible only because there was an unlimited supply of unpaid
labour. I shall describe elsewhere how numbers of so-called
kulaks[1] were deported to the forests of the far north, where

---

[1] The word *kulak*, literally translated, means "fist." It was used in
pre-revolutionary Russia to denote a rich peasant, often a money-lender,
who exploited his poorer fellow peasants. The Bolsheviks use it in quite
another sense, and apply it to a totally different type of person. According
to the Soviet terminology a *kulak* is almost any villager who owns any
property whatever, even if it be only a cow or a goat. And under the pretext
of fighting the *kulaks*, they have raged a ruthless war against a large
section of the rural population who refused to give up their small private
property and to enter the collective farms.

a large number of them perished miserably of over-work and privation.

The export of petrol and petrol products has been forcibly stimulated in a similar way. The exports of the latter amounted to 3·3 million tons, worth 56·1 millions of roubles, during the first eight months of 1933, and to 2·8 million tons, valued at 40·1 millions of roubles, in the corresponding period of 1934. The result was an extreme dearth of these essential products in the Soviet Union. Incidentally, the abundance of petrol available in Russia, and the high stage of development reached by the oil industry of the Caucasus regions even before the war, should have ensured a production amply sufficient for export as well as for the home market, but for the fact that the same disorganization prevailed in the oil industry as in every other sphere.

But while all other measures to obtain foreign exchange may appear more or less comprehensible, one is not—and that is the exportation of foodstuffs at a time when, in the country itself, famine had reached unimaginable proportions. Here again a few figures may suffice to illustrate the position. 1933 was a particularly critical year for the food supply of the Soviet Union. Nevertheless, 1·8 million tons of grain and other foodstuffs were exported. During the first eight months of the year 466,905 tons of grain, worth 13·2 million roubles[1], were exported, together with fodder and other foodstuffs worth 29·9 million roubles. In the first eight months of 1934, during which period the acute lack of foodstuffs continued, the export was even more considerable; 591,835 tons of grain, worth 13·6 million roubles, were exported, as well as foodstuffs and fodder to the value of 34·5 million roubles. These goods were mostly sent via the Black Sea ports, in the immediate vicinity of which millions were at that time dying of starvation pure and simple. It is obvious that a great number of them could easily have

[1] Here and below the roubles referred to are gold roubles, worth at par 9·46 roubles to the £.

been saved if the export of foodstuffs had been abandoned. But the continuance of the industrialization process was evidently considered more important than the lives of whole regions.

The export figures for 1932 show a considerable decline compared with the previous years. In 1930 exports of grain were worth 207·1 million roubles, and in 1931, 157·8 million roubles. The quantities of grain exported amounted to 4·8 million tons and 5·2 million tons respectively; so that it must be admitted that the Soviet Government did send much less grain out of the country during the famine years than previously. At the same time the fact remains that at the height of the famine foodstuffs were sold abroad which would have sufficed to save the lives of some millions of persons. It is impossible to avoid the conclusion that a more cautious export policy in the preceding years would have allowed the formation of reserves amply sufficient to keep the famine at bay for a long time. It would not have required any very great foresight to build up such reserves. In the hot and dry regions of the south periods of drought, accompanied by bad harvests, recur at almost regular intervals. Nor should it have been hard to foresee that the collectivization of agriculture, which began first during the years of record exports, would necessarily bring about at least a passing reduction in the yields of the harvest.[1]

To sum up, the delays in the process of reconstruction due to the building of giant works, etc., and the production of defective goods (brak) had the result that, to maintain the industrial system, imports of foreign goods had to be continued on a much larger scale than had been anticipated. The demand for foreign currency grew correspondingly and in a manner

[1] In the last two months of 1934 the export of grain and foodstuffs continued, and during this period 780,400 tons of grain were exported. If the export of this "famine grain," as a journalist of long residence in Moscow called it, has latterly shown a tendency to decline, it is still regularly maintained.

quite unforeseen; and this could be for the most part acquired only against exports of raw materials. This is the immediate reason why millions of innocent persons had to starve in what were formerly the richest agricultural regions in the world: they were sacrificed to the export of foodstuffs.

Yet the chief cause of the human tragedy now being enacted in these regions was the ruin of agriculture, in consequence of collectivization carried out with excessive haste. It was this alone which, as previously mentioned, brought about a state of affairs in the south that makes the export of grain possible only at the cost of the lives of millions of local producers. This collapse of Russian agriculture—or, more correctly, of the peasantry who are its mainstay—is perhaps best described in the words of an eminent agricultural specialist who for years was at the head of an important agricultural settlement holding a State concession in the Northern Caucasus: "The decline of agriculture was caused primarily by the great lack of experts. The natural leaders of the village communities, the *kulaks*, and with them all middle-sized holders, were destined to become the victims of the terror and of the campaign against class enemies." Only the economically weakest elements in the village survived, which were willing to act as informers against everyone possessing anything, and, consequently, everyone of any ability. The management of the collective farms was generally handed over to party functionaries, and it is a significant fact that, in 1931, the Moscow Centre of Communist Trade Unions placed 30,000 young trade-unionist factory workers at the disposal of the Commissariat for Agriculture as farm managers. The economic mischief done by these officials in the collective farms can be properly appreciated only by an agricultural expert. But it is proved by the lamentable shrinkage in cultivation, and hence of the harvest, and also by the destruction of approximately half the Russian livestock.

The lack of farm managers, combined with all the results of Stalin's agricultural policy, is one of the chief reasons of the famines of 1933 and 1934. The same applies to the Soviet farms. The Schachty trial of 1928 had put an end to the authority of all the managers on the farms who had received a scientific training in time of peace.

To replace these experts as managers of big farms there came Communist directors, most of whom knew only the agricultural slogans of party politics, and possessed the scantiest information about cultivation, stock rearing and farm management. It was, too, the ambition of the Moscow officials to introduce "100 per cent mechanization" into Soviet agriculture, a measure which could only accelerate its ruin. The new managers were seized with a mania for Americanization; machines were introduced into agriculture without due preparation, while horses and oxen were described as "obsolete factors" which should give place entirely to tractors and lorries.

The fundamental miscalculation of these attempts at Americanization was undoubtedly this. American workers are mostly very intelligent, but few in numbers, and therefore command high wages; or, to put it better, the American farmer who, with his children and a few good employees, works large areas with the most up-to-date machinery and exploits them pretty thoroughly, is in a quite different position from Russian agriculturists, who dispose of unlimited quantities of unintelligent but correspondingly cheap labour. These people could be used for cultivation with horses and oxen, but not with modern machinery like tractors and mechanical reapers. The collapse of the Soviet agricultural organization was inevitable.

It seems to have been realized at the eleventh hour that the root evil of the Communist economic apparatus has hitherto been the removal, indeed the extirpation, of personal responsibility, initiative and interest. It has now been realized that the collapse of the industrial plan is primarily due to the failure of the entire system of organization, to the misdeeds of officials,

D

or, as the latest expression is, to *funkzionalka* and bureaucracy. On this point the entire Russian press is at one, though only in admitting details.[1]

The struggle carried out by the Government and the press and its entire staff of correspondents for a renewal of the economic apparatus and against the bureaucratic system, the general mismanagement and the omnipotence of quite irresponsible departments and functionaries, is nowadays of an almost heroic character. Naturally the main struggle is in the most important sphere—that of agriculture. The open criticism of the agricultural institutions which began with Stalin's remarks at the party congress, and the call for a complete reorganization, grows louder and stronger from day to day. A leading article in *Izvestia* quotes Stalin's words that nine-tenths of the agricultural breakdowns were due to

[1] The expressions, some of them newly coined, used by the Moscow rulers and the press in their criticism of existing conditions, are very instructive for anyone acquainted with Russian. I quote some of the commonest. *Funkzionalka* is used to describe the inefficiency of irresponsible and uninterested officials of all departments, both at Moscow and in the provinces. *Boltologia* is the word coined to chastise the talking and phrase-making instead of acting vigorously, so common among Soviet officials. It is derived from *boltatj* (gossip). *Kantselyastchina* is a very common expression used to signify bureaucratic officialdom. *Otschkoftirateli*, or people who supply others with coloured spectacles, are the officials who throw dust in the eyes of their superiors and the public as regards their own performances in the fulfilment of the economic plans. The word *lyshentsy* covers what may rightly be called the most unfortunate category —the disfranchised members of the former privileged classes. They belong, in so far as they survive, to those elements of the population who were recently deprived of their passports and who belong to the lowest group of the various rationing categories. To these hypermodern expressions a few old terms may be added which have been given an up-to-date meaning. Thus *nakhlebniki* means people who have newly entered the collective farms who constitute a burden in the distribution of the available bread (*khleb*). The *prikhlebateli* (parasites) are a similar category. The new use of this old Russian word in Soviet terminology throws light upon the real issue in the struggle for bread. *Prikhlebateli* are not, as formerly, idlers who are a burden on others because of their idleness, but whole categories of hard-working men, such as country doctors, veterinaries and country-dwellers following the most varied professions, who do not form part of the labour corps of the collective farms and are consequently regarded by Moscow as a burden, or even as "superfluous mouths" to be eliminated as far as possible.

the lack of all control over the actual carrying out of decrees and orders.

The article further describes the desperate attempts made in 1933 to render the whole apparatus efficient: "With the assistance of the political sections, we ejected tens of thousands of people from the agricultural bodies, the tractor and motor stations and the accountancy department, etc." Yet the paper is forced to admit that "all this does not suffice: new and better officials must be found." This is in fact the cardinal task now facing Moscow; to fulfil it (as explained elsewhere) the authorities have reserved for themselves, in conflict with the most important principles of the whole Soviet system, the right to confirm the new officials in their posts, or rather to appoint them.

Daily the cry grows louder for an entire renewal of the Soviet system by the introduction of a new and responsible or, as the press puts it, a "concrete" staff. It has been recognized that the irresponsibility and lack of interest of the Soviet officials are a cancer in the body politic. The call, therefore, is now for the abolition of the colleges, committees, etc., whose functions are to be taken over by responsible individuals. In this respect the decree issued on March 16, 1934, relating to steps for the organization of the Soviet economic system, is highly characteristic. The People's Commissaries and the heads of various important organizations are requested to liquidate the colleges within a fortnight. A variety of other decrees—e.g. that relating to the reorganization of water transport—echo this demand. In short, great efforts are being made to put men with a sense of responsibility—the type exterminated in previous years—in the place of the colleges, commissions, etc. In a time of acute crisis and demoralization a complete change in the system of collective institutions, hitherto described as the ideal, is demanded; at a day's notice men of initiative and interest in their work, and above all with a sense of responsibility, are to take the place of the *funkzionalka.* It must be emphasized, however, that even after the renovation things cannot improve. Moscow rulers and the Soviet papers are obliged to admit that the root evil of the system—lack of interest and responsibility—still remains. *Izvestia* concluded an article on the work of the agricultural organizations by admitting that the agricultural apparatus must be reconstructed. "Conditions must be created"—note the following words—"in which, both in the provinces and at the centre, concrete persons shall be responsible for every task." The unusual term "concrete" was first used by *Izvestia* and was meant to give striking expression to the real need of the moment—concrete men, i.e. living men of flesh and blood.

Stalin himself has declared that 90 per cent of the agricultural collapse is due to the breakdown of the organization and economic system as it has existed hitherto, in other words to communization. This remarkable utterance of Stalin's disposes of the false statements as to the cause of the collapse of agriculture—the bad harvest, intrigues of the *kulaks*, saboteurs and enemies of the Government.

The whole fault lies in the illusion that, in a country with a largely illiterate population, a grandiose State Socialist apparatus could be swiftly improvised and a system created which would render the country independent of all foreign imports.

It is not my task here to answer the question whether Stalin will ultimately succeed in renovating the entire Russian economic apparatus by introducing new men at Moscow. But the statements of the Government and the press at least justify the assumption that some time must necessarily pass before this work of renovation is completed—given that it does succeed. But until this is done there can be no decisive change in the conditions I have described. If this inference is correct, famine and malnutrition will—at least for a long time to come—be a permanent and not a transitory phenomenon. It was possible for people to die in multitudes in 1933, although the 1932 harvest, as expressly stated by the Soviet Government, was a medium harvest, and certainly not a failure. The statement is confirmed by all the agricultural experts present in Russia at that time. It follows that the agricultural distress in Russia has little to do with the nature of the harvest in any given year: the state of things as it is to-day cannot be changed by a better or a worse harvest in one year or another. At the same time, if a future harvest were severely injured by climatic or other natural causes—as was the case in 1933—the catastrophe would once more reach vast dimensions.

Thus there are two questions. The first is whether the communist experiment will succeed and State Socialism will become a fact; all the world is interested in the answer. Another question, and a most pregnant one, is what will become of the people in the Soviet Union. It is all too clear that many consider this a question of only secondary importance.

CHAPTER II

THE CATASTROPHE

In undertaking a description of the catastrophe with all its attendant phenomena—a description based on the accounts of reliable eyewitnesses, of journalists of standing, of Soviet newspaper reports and of the victims themselves—we should distinguish between three different phases: the year 1933, down to the new harvest in the autumn; from then onward to the harvest of 1934; and the period beginning in the autumn of 1934, which had not drawn to a close when this book was written.

THE FIRST PHASE. UNTIL THE AUTUMN OF 1933

The first phase of the famine, which embraces more particularly the first seven months of 1933, was undoubtedly a human tragedy of far greater magnitude even than the famine of the years 1921-2. I propose to begin by explaining in detail the course of events during this first phase in the Ukraine, in the Northern Caucasus, etc.

There was a shortage of food among the peasants of these regions as early as the beginning of the winter of 1932-3, and then a famine which grew more acute daily. Appeals for help were beginning to make themselves heard from various parts of the Soviet Union even at this early period. The relief organization at Geneva, the German relief organization, the Jewish Aid for Russia organization, etc., were then fully informed of the growing danger. It should be mentioned that in almost all the letters containing appeals for help to Russians living abroad the terrible situation of the writers is described with the utmost frankness. The explanation is given by the American journalist, Harry Lang,[1] who agrees with many other

[1] Of the New York Jewish paper *Forward*.

eyewitnesses in stating that the reason consists in the writers' complete indifference to a life which had ceased to have any value. Fear of persecution or death had no longer any effect on them, since they were in a position where none of them had anything to lose. Lang found this attitude particularly common among the Jews in the smaller towns of the Ukraine.

It is another question why the Soviet authorities permitted these appeals for help to reach the outer world. The explanation is that the receipt of Torgsin parcels from abroad was a valuable source of foreign exchange for the Government. The regime, therefore, had a direct interest in these appeals, paradoxical though it may seem. Not till quite lately did this attitude change. Now, owing to the rigorous measures taken by Moscow, no more "famine letters" pass the frontiers. The intention now is to prevent the truth about the continuation of the famine from being known abroad.

It will remain a lasting merit of the *Manchester Guardian*, that great English newspaper well known for its benevolent attitude towards the Soviet Union, that it sent a member of its staff, Malcolm Muggeridge, to Russia, and published a series of articles written by him. These reports, based on personal observation, have been confirmed by the statements of other eyewitnesses of various nationalities. They may be regarded as valuable historical documents on the first phase of the famine of 1933. It should be mentioned that Mr. Muggeridge was not one of those foreign journalists who are permanently resident in Russia, so that he could tell what he saw without being influenced by the desire to be allowed to continue his journalistic work from Moscow. This is perhaps the explanation of his success.

When the famine broke out at the beginning of the winter, Mr. Muggeridge left Moscow in order to travel through the famine areas, part of his journey being actually made on foot. He put down in writing what he saw and heard in direct intercourse with the population. He described the utterly neglected fields, the complete absence of cattle. It would be less than the truth, he wrote in March, to say that there was a famine in the most fertile areas of Russia. There was, he said, not only hunger, but also—and this was true also of the north— a state of war and of military occupation. The grain collections in the Ukraine and the Northern Caucasus had been carried out with such ruthlessness and brutality that the peasants were left completely without bread. Thousands were expelled, and in some instances the entire population of a village was sent to do forced labour in the forests of the north.

Elsewhere he describes the "everyday sight" of whole parties of men and women, so-called *kulaks*, being dragged along in the custody of armed guards. Only the military and the G.P.U. officials—i.e. those engaged in the forcible collection of grain—had enough to eat. All the rest had to go hungry.

In December 1932 the position of the peasants had further deteriorated. Almost simultaneously with the beginning of the struggle with the Ukrainians, the White Russians and other nationalities, the Government resolved on much severer measures than hitherto for the exploitation of the peasantry. Under such slogans as the pursuit of "saboteurs," "counter-revolutionaries," "enemies of the State" and so on, stronger pressure was exercised to extract from the peasants the grain they still possessed. Moscow exerted itself to the uttermost to seize the peasant's last reserves for the requirements of a privileged category and for the fulfilment of the five-year plan; in other words, for the maintenance of exports. From now on even those peasants who hitherto had been best off began to suffer from the famine. Mr. Muggeridge describes the exodus of the peasants from the villages to seek help in the towns. But they gained nothing from this; on the contrary, a decree about the issue of passports drove thousands, whose presence in the cities was considered undesirable, out into the country—to death.

Mr. Muggeridge then tells us, in a gripping passage, how, on his return to Moscow, he heard an address by Stalin at a meeting of representatives of all the collective farms. This speech revealed to him more clearly than anything could have done the contrast which dominates everything in Soviet life— the contrast between the reality, the suffering and misery of the peasant masses, on one side, and the catchwords of the Soviet officials living in Moscow on the other. Stalin declared in the course of his speech: "I am of the opinion that not less than 20,000,000 people who belong to the peasant population have already been saved from poverty, ruin and the slavery of the *kulaks*, and this thanks to collectivization, for it is that which assures the people's prosperity. . . . Comrades, this is a great advance, unique in the whole world and paralleled in no other State." Here Mr. Muggeridge touches on the struggle between the machinery of State and the starving peasant— though at that time the struggle, which was to rise to such a pitch in the months that followed, was only beginning.

Mr. Muggeridge describes the position in the winter of 1932–3, i.e. before the real catastrophe began. The disaster did not reach its climax until the months before the new harvest. The new sowing campaign had to be begun. The peasants were enfeebled by hunger, and the campaign could not be properly conducted. Force had to be employed, for if the quantities of grain required for the industrial population and for the indispensable exports could not be collected, not only the lives of a large part of the peasant population, but the very existence of the Soviet system and the maintenance of the five-year plan would be endangered. This was Moscow's chief anxiety.

Stalin decided to intervene with ruthless energy, especially in the Ukraine. There was to be an end of the leniency which, in the view of Moscow, was displayed by the local Communists when collecting grain from their starving fellow-countrymen.

While Mr. Muggeridge's reports give the best account of the position in the winter and spring, the situation in the summer of 1933 is most aptly described in a message to the

Temps. Berland, the Moscow correspondent of that paper, describes the struggle being waged "between a Government of fanatical ideologues and a peasant mass hostile to collectivization." In particular he describes how, from spring onwards, Moscow "mobilizes the most reliable Communist forces to carry on a regular campaign in the villages against the counter-revolutionary stronghold." In March the notorious "political sections," bodies of men carefully selected to take over the management of collectivized agriculture, and all devoted adherents of the Communist party, were despatched into the country. The same method had been followed by Moscow in the winter of 1928-9, when the famous "twenty-five thousand" were despatched. These consisted of a body of fanatical Communists who, while they ensured the success of collectivization, provoked the hatred of the peasantry by their terroristic methods and deepened the gulf between the villages and the towns. The real offensive now began.

About this time Moscow realized that the whole system must collapse unless sufficient grain supplies were ensured for the needs of industry, the towns and export; and, by virtue of a decree issued in February of the previous year, martial law was now declared everywhere. It was administered by an emissary from Moscow, the head of the tractor and motor station, and a third Soviet official, such as the head of the nearest Soviet farm. The court had the right to condemn to death any person committing a punishable act and to carry out the sentence in a few hours. Like the G.P.U. in the towns, the "Political Sections" are all-powerful in the provinces. To be denounced as a saboteur, or enemy of the State, is a prospect which terrifies everyone, for such an accusation is a matter of life or death. In Berland's words the aim was "to force the peasants to work 'honestly' for the State"—i.e. the privileged classes—in other words, to carry out the sowing plan and afterwards the collection of grain, so that the regime might be saved from collapse. This was the task which the Kremlin set the political sections, and with this in view it gave them powers over the rural population.

Thenceforward the local Soviet officials, the Communist party representatives, the secretaries of district committees, the presidents of executive committees, etc.—all these bodies were enumerated in the decree—were made personally responsible for seeing that the instructions given and the standards set up by the Central Committee were in no single instance modified by local concessions. "Contrary to the practice in previous years, no dereliction of the duty of delivering grain immediately will be tolerated." "Contrary to the practice of previous years," the decree goes on, "grain deliveries will take place solely in accordance with fixed standards [i.e. those laid down by the Government beforehand]. In no circumstances and in no case will the introduction of 'contrary plans' by local modifications be tolerated." In other words, the local authorities were to be prevented from taking pity on the peasants' distress and correspondingly reducing the amounts requisitioned. "Contrary to the practice of past years," so begins the third paragraph, too, "the grain must be delivered immediately without delay, since the decisive months are always the same." Another passage lays down that the trade in grain hitherto permitted to the *Zakupkhleb*, the official purchasing organization, is prohibited, and all the State and party officials— the categories being once again enumerated—are made personally responsible for such "crimes" in the case of any infraction.

The purpose of this decree (based on the law of January 10, 1933), becomes apparent from a speech delivered from the Ukraine Dictator, Postyschev, at a plenary meeting of the Central Committee of the Communist party in the Ukraine. It is hard to believe that, in a time of the most acute distress, when the whole world was already beginning to be aware of the calamity, the emissary of Moscow in the Ukraine capital could make a declaration amounting to a strict order to his subordinates to set aside all human emotions in collecting the grain. But it was Postyschev's mission to save the foundations of the Soviet regime by assuring the supply of all the consuming districts and industrial centres. For him and for Moscow, therefore, there was only one way: to collect all the grain that could be got hold of and hand it over to the State.

As Postyschev's remarks give a better idea than all the detailed reports in the world of the struggle which, to this very day, Moscow is waging with the local population in all the agricultural districts of the Union, I propose to give certain extracts here. He begins by openly admitting that the previous grain campaign had been a complete failure, and describes it as "last year's disgrace." Now, he went on, not a day, not a minute must be lost, and all eyes must remain fixed on the one great duty of collecting the grain with all possible energy and determination, since on this depended the position of the Soviet regime and— note these words—"the maintenance of its influence abroad." "The task can only be fulfilled," he went on, "if we reflect upon last year's mistakes."

What were the mistakes which, in Postyschev's view, led to the fiasco of the previous year's grain collection? This was not due to the "objective causes" (diminution of the harvest, famine, etc.), but to the "leniency" (*serdobolie*) with which the local authorities discharged their duty of taking the grain from the producers. To illustrate this harmful "leniency" he quoted a number of examples, e.g. a regulation issued by the Odessa district committee that the first hectare threshed "was to be kept available for local or public consumption." Postyschev commented on this as follows: "Need I waste words in pointing out how wrong such an instruction is, which assigns a secondary position to the delivery of grain to the State, while the feeding of the community is placed first? Is it not the best possible proof that some of our district committees were influenced by consumers' interests, thus promoting the class interests of our enemies to the detriment of the proletarian State? Can

such leniency strengthen our system of collectivization? No;
the Bolshevik struggle has no room for such leniency."

Surely these words reveal the whole tragedy of the situation
more clearly than any reports.

Since Postyschev made this speech, the nature of the famine
now prevailing in the Ukraine and the other grain districts
of the Union has been admitted even by Bolsheviks. It can
no longer be concealed that the Kremlin is allowing the population of the agricultural regions to starve in order to save the
Soviet regime.

How were things now—in the summer—at Kiev, at Kharkov,
in all the towns where the food position was supposed to be so
much better than in the countryside? Here, too, hundreds of
thousands of people, all who did not belong to the privileged
categories, were condemned to starve, if they had not actually
died of starvation. A month's earnings—especially for those
who had no work permit—barely sufficed to buy a few daily
rations of bread, meat, fish or milk at the fantastic prices ruling
in the open market, and consequently people died in multitudes
in these big towns just as in the country. As time went on the
number of starving persons lying in the streets and squares of
Kharkov, Kiev, Rostov and other cities increased. Most of
them were peasants who had summoned up the little strength
left to them in order to reach the town. In the streets and the
courtyards scenes were often witnessed which are hardly
credible by European standards. While at first passers-by
would take some notice of these appalling pictures of misery,
this soon changed, and it was particularly shocking to see people
carelessly passing the corpses of those who had died of starvation. The number of corpses was so great that they could
only be removed once a day. Often no distinction was made
between the corpses and those not yet quite dead; all were
loaded on to lorries, to be flung indiscriminately into a common
grave.

This burial work was done by convicts from the local prison.

From morning until evening they were busy digging the graves. Fifteen bodies were usually buried in one grave, and the number of graves is so great that these famine cemeteries often recall a stretch of sandhills.

The local authorities were as powerless as though confronted by a natural phenomenon. There were occasions when some high Soviet official on a visit from Moscow, shocked at the scenes of misery, tried to take "special measures." For example, the People's Commissary, Mikoian, during his stay in Kiev during April, was enabled, in Berland's words, "to realize the tragic nature of the situation." He ordered that the reserves destined for the Red Army should be diverted to the aid of the population. Some hundreds of "commercial depots" were opened for this purpose; at the same time, sales outside a radius of twenty kilometres were prohibited.

But such measures of Soviet officials impressed by the tragedy they witnessed could at best bring about but a temporary alleviation. The supplies in the shops barely sufficed for the needs of the privileged categories. This was indicated by the shops for the privileged classes, which were either closed or had nothing on show but empty bottles or even pictures of the Moscow rulers. Such desolation was an everyday sight in the big towns. Frequently enough even ticket-holders found the shops shut. If food was being distributed anywhere, the queues were of such a length as to suggest a regular riot.

In the countryside, where the misery was still greater and often passed the bounds of imagination, thousands of starving men, women and children thronged into the towns in defiance of the authorities, like migrating peoples. They left their homes to their fate; their one aim was to seek refuge in the city. Once arrived, the majority collapsed from sheer weakness.

The *Neue Zürcher Zeitung* published a report from an eyewitness, a foreign engineer employed in the Donetz industry, who had to go regularly to Kharkov. His train arrived at about 7 a.m., and as he drove from the station into the town he was always faced by the same spectacle; in the streets of the former capital of the Ukraine lay the corpses of peasants who had died of hunger. They had arrived by still earlier trains to beg for food in the town, but were so weak that they fell down dead. In the industrial towns of the Donetz basin also the houses of better situated technicians and engineers were besieged by starving peasants from morning till night. A similar description is given by a German agricultural expert, who travelled all over the Soviet Union in 1933. He writes: "Conditions in the provincial centres of the south are infinitely worse than in the capitals. When the train arrives one enters the station building. It is clean, and no one is to be seen but the railway officials and Ogpu agents. But then one goes into the open air, on to the station square. The whole square is covered with dead bodies. Dreadful skeletons lie in the dust on the stones. Some are still moving, the rest are motionless. If one approaches the latter, one sees that they are corpses. All victims of the famine. They fled from their villages to escape the famine, but fell victims to it in the town."

The same eyewitness then describes in particular the terrible fate of the children in the famine areas. In one of these accounts he says: "It was beyond my comprehension. I would not at first believe my own eyes. Some of the children dragged themselves to their feet for the last time and gathered their remaining forces to look for something eatable in the street. But they were so weak that they fell down and remained lying where they fell. The poor children were the strongest impression of any journey. At Kharkov I saw a boy wasted to a skeleton lying in the middle of the street. A second boy was sitting near a heap of garbage picking egg-shells out of it. They were looking for eatable remnants of food or fruit. They perished like wild beasts. . . . When the famine began to haunt the villages parents used to take their children into the towns, where they left them in the hope that someone would have pity on them. . . . Their lot was better in the towns than in the country villages, because child murder in the towns is obviously more difficult than in the country."

The conditions in the streets on the outskirts of Kiev are thus described by Mr. and Mrs. Stebalo, Americans of Ukrainian origin.[1] "When we arrived at Kiev, we did not at first find much change in the town, till we went into the suburbs. There the people's appearance horrified us. Most were lying down and not moving. Their legs were swollen. They seemed to be ill. Others were walking in pairs, bent double. Their eyes were unnaturally distended and stared straight ahead. No one uttered a word."

Harry Lang was talking to an old woman at Kiev when she pointed to the crowd which surrounded them and muttered in a hoarse voice: "Those are not people, they are corpses."

Such are conditions in the towns of the south. But all eye-witnesses declare that things there are far better than in the country, though even in the towns only the members of the so-called "privileged categories" are at all well provided for. The "non-privileged" masses have to starve and die. In the countryside of the Ukraine and Northern Caucasus the population of certain districts is better off. If you look at these districts from the train windows on the journey to the health resorts in the Crimea and the Caucasus nothing particular will be noticed. Everything looks more or less orderly. It could not be otherwise. Thousands of people pass along this line daily, not only from Russia but also from Western Europe. But it is enough to go five or ten miles away from the stations, into the hinterland, and conditions are quite different. There are corpses lying on the roads, with flocks of ravens wheeling around them; the villages are desolate, dead, abandoned; the fields are overgrown with weeds. It was in the winter and summer of 1933 that most of the population perished.

Of all the accounts by foreign witnesses who visited Russia, and especially the Ukraine, during the summer of 1933,

[1] The report of Mr. and Mrs. Stebalo was published on August 29, 1933, in the *New York Times*, and on August 30 and 31 in the *Matin* of Paris.

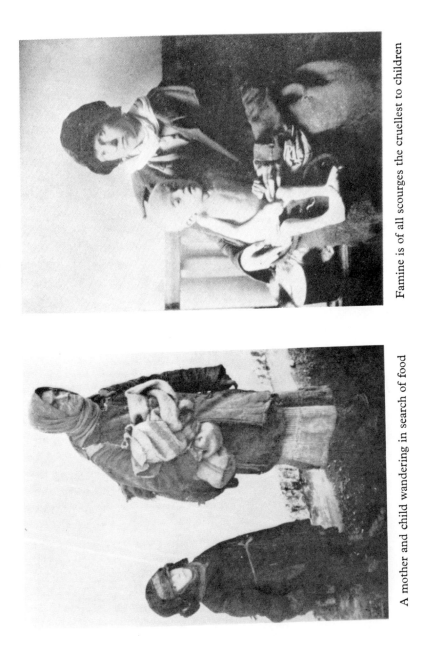

Famine is of all scourges the cruellest to children

A mother and child wandering in search of food

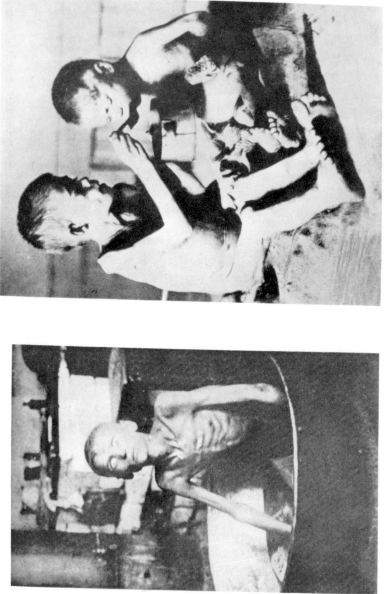

Brothers in distress

Another child victim of the famine

perhaps the most valuable is that given by Mr. and Mrs. Stebalo, mentioned above, who, after many years in America, came to visit their relatives in Kiev and Podolia, travelling via Leningrad; and that of Harry Lang, who, on the conclusion of the Zionist Congress at Prague, visited the various Jewish settlements in Russia as an ordinary "Intourist" traveller, journeying by car with his wife. These records may some day be appreciated as the most important contemporary documents for a region which witnessed one of the greatest tragedies of all time.

The Stebalos left Kiev for the surrounding villages, where they had relatives. "How astonished we were," they write, "when instead of the happy, cheerful villages we had left years ago, we found ruins. Not a flower, broken fences, no leaves on the trees. A hideous graveyard silence. An atmosphere of death. When, with heavy hearts, we reached our native village, we got out of the train and saw people coming towards us. Their bodies seemed gigantic, but when they approached us we found that their size was due to their swollen limbs. They were covered with sores, too, which gave out a putrid smell. Instead of clothes they were dressed in rags."

When the news spread that the "Americans" had arrived, the pair were surrounded by inhabitants and conducted to Stebalo's mother. Like the others, she was swollen with hunger, and her body was covered with sores. But when she finally grasped that her children had arrived, she wept without uttering a word. For two years she had received none of the money that was sent to her. When the Stebalos had distributed bread among the inhabitants, the latter became talkative, though terribly afraid of being denounced. They told how hunger compelled them to eat the leaves of the trees and the most loathsome refuse just to have something inside them, and said that the whole population of the village would probably die, and that they could not touch the harvest in the fields, for these were guarded by armed detachments.

E

The Stebalos then continued their journey into Podolia, to the village of Pisarevka. Here they found the same terrible conditions. The village where their relatives lived was half-deserted, and they were told that all their kinsmen had died of hunger—and during the last month. The few survivors said, "We shall all die." In this village of 800 inhabitants, 150 persons had died of starvation since the spring, while during the Great War only seven inhabitants had been killed in the field. The Stebalos proceed to describe terrible scenes—the savage greed with which the people flung themselves on any food given them, and the dreadful screams of the children who could not sleep at night; cases of mania and cannibalism.

The Stebalos reported what they had seen in the Ukraine on their homeward journey, in Paris and in America. It is no exaggeration, no description of a particularly fearful exceptional case. It depicts what is happening in thousands of villages in the Ukraine, Northern Caucasus, the lower Volga, all over the wide spaces of the Russian famine regions.

Harry Lang confirms the Stebalos' story as regards the Jewish settlements in the Ukraine. "The people are afraid of each other," he writes, "they are afraid of every superfluous word, and above all of any stranger. They are even afraid of relatives and acquaintances, and fear to tell them anything of their troubles."

Lang describes how at first nobody would be open with him. "We visited some Jews in a little place in the west, for whom we had brought letters from relatives in America. We found them in a great state of agitation because our conversations with them might arouse the suspicions of the local authorities." Not till Lang and his wife were taking their departure did one of the Jews whisper to him: "To-morrow at three o'clock at the Jewish cemetery." When they arrived at the cemetery next day they found a number of the people who hitherto had refused to talk to them. "They were standing by their family graves and praying aloud. We listened. Their words were words of prayer addressed to the Lord, but words of confession were mingled with the prayer. One person had been arrested and died of weakness, another had perished of hunger, and so on. Nothing but family tragedies which these people had experienced. These were not the forbidden revelations to foreign correspondents, but a personal and therefore as yet unforbidden conversation with God."

Lang describes how he went from grave to grave, listened to everything and wrote down what he heard in his note-book. He addresses to those of his faith the following appeal: "The Jews of the whole world must not forget their brethren in Soviet Russia and must render them assistance in every way. . . . The distress of the Jewish community in Russia, even in that part which is concerned in the process of production, passes all imagination. Hunger oedema and death from starvation are everyday occurrences."[1]

Lang concludes by stating that Jews and non-Jews alike have become the victims of the distress in Russia, but that the Jews come off worse because they have always been in a worse position socially. "There are degrees of suffering," he continues, "which alienate people from one another. These conditions prevail in Russia. Every man is every man's foe. People behave in the nastiest manner to their relatives just to gain some petty advantage. If someone gets a bit of help, a few dollars from abroad, and wants to keep part of the sum for even harder times, he must conceal this intention from even his nearest relatives, or he runs the risk of being denounced to the Ogpu."

Here, in the last sentences of this description, Lang shows that the Russian famine is characterized not only by material distress, but also and inevitably by a moral decline, internecine strife, denunciation, envy and hate.

These accounts by Ukrainian and Jewish eyewitnesses of conditions in the Russian famine areas are fully confirmed

---

[1] In compliance with Lang's request the French Chief Rabbi and a number of leading Jews in various countries published an appeal.

from a third quarter, the German colonists in the south of the Soviet Union. The famine gripped their villages and settlements like the rest. Hundreds of letters from these German settlements have been collected by the "Brethren in Distress" Committee; heart-rending documents, some of which have been published in the pamphlet *Hungerpredigt* (Eckardt, Berlin). Some of these German settlements affected by the famine are on the Black Sea, close to the frontier of Bessarabia (now part of Roumania). The frontier is formed by the Dniester —a river reddened with blood. During the past few years it has been the scene of tragedy after tragedy—the killing of refugees from the Soviet Union, shot down before they could reach the farther bank. But many succeeded in reaching the Roumanian bank. The state of things across the Dniester is, therefore, thoroughly appreciated in Bessarabia. A letter from a German colonist on the Russian side to his relatives living in Bessarabia was published at the end of 1933.[1] He wrote: "All those dreadful swollen figures. . . . They die at the street corners and often lie there a long time. At night cartloads of naked bodies are taken from the hospitals and thrown into common graves; a few days later the same grave is filled up. Our friends went into the hospital the other day. Their friend, a schoolmaster, had received a letter from the hospital on the 24th to say that his mother had died on the 21st. He had not been allowed to visit her while alive, but now he was sent to the mortuary with his friends and told to pick out his mother. They entered two rooms with locked doors; on the stone floor there were many dirty and naked corpses. Like skeletons, nothing but skin and bones, flung down in different positions, just as they had died. Our woman friend had a hysterical attack. The schoolmaster's mother was not to be found, so she was in the common grave already. Another schoolmaster succeeded in getting his dead sister out of the common grave.

[1] In the *Deutsche Zeitung für Bessarabien,* the organ of the local German minority at Tarutino.

Other friends of ours were visited one afternoon by a naked skeleton of a man, who said he had nearly died of starvation, had awakened under a heap of corpses and made off. They gave the man food, but he soon died. Outside some Russian villages black flags are hoisted to show that everyone in the place is dead. . . ."

Thus under the eyes of the Germans in Bessarabia—the houses and people on the Russian bank can easily be seen across the Dniester—their friends and brethren starve to death in Soviet territory. The Germans had a surplus of grain, fruit and other food. In the summer of 1933 they raised twenty truckloads of grain, to place them at the disposal of a relief organization for their countrymen across the frontier. In vain; their help was declined. They had to go on watching their kinsmen perish across the Dniester.

A visitor to Bessarabia named Walter Eidlitz has given a horrifying account[1] of his conversations and inquiries made in this Roumanian frontier district, where everybody has, or rather had, relatives on the other side. He describes an old peasant woman in the Swiss-German colony at Saba rising with difficulty and, leaning on the table, telling which of her friends and relatives had died in Russia. She described how the last survivors crept through the streets of the great city of Odessa until they collapsed somewhere and died of hunger oedema with distended bodies. At the end the toilworn peasant woman rose to her full height and put the question: "What does Europe think of it?"

All the papers printed for German groups settled in the States bordering on the Soviet Union have again and again published letters from Russia or accounts from refugees. Now it is a seaman who has returned from Russia to Estonia,[2] now a Saxon from Transylvania who had been a prisoner of war for eighteen years and had settled in Russia, but was driven by hunger to leave everything and make his way

[1] In the *Neue Zürcher Zeitung.*   [2] *Revalsche Zeitung.*

home.[1] Russians, Ukrainians, Jews and Germans all agree. Relatives of persons of other nationalities settled in the famine districts—Bulgarians, Finns, Estonians—also confirm that many millions of innocent persons have died of famine in Russia.

Valuable evidence on the Russian famine and all its victims is contained in reports emanating not only from eyewitnesses who have visited the famine area, but also from the German employees of the great German agricultural concession, the *Drusag*, which was founded in Stresemann's time in the Northern Caucasus and led in some respects an independent existence in Russia for nearly ten years. Managed by Dr. Fritz Dittloff on modern economic principles, it was, all foreign visitors agree, a positive oasis in the desert of the Northern Caucasus famine area. Year after year the *Drusag* was able to record large surpluses of grain and other foodstuffs, even in 1933, when the terrible famine broke out all round. (This is probably the best proof that the theory of the cause of the famine being dependent on good and bad harvests is untenable.) Later the hundreds of *Drusag* employees had to see their neighbours—apart from a small number living around the concession, whom the *Drusag* was able to help from its stored surplus —starving in numbers under their eyes. The people perished at their very doors, and among them—a particularly tragic element in the situation—were a large number of Germans, those admirable settlers who quite recently had been pioneers of agricultural progress. Leading officials of the *Drusag* tell how starving German settlers used to come to them and ask: "Are you really going to let us die?"[2]

[1] *Kronstädter Zeitung.*
The *Rigasche Rundschau*, the *Deutsches Volksblatt in Neusatz* and the *Nordschleswigsche Zeitung* also contain accounts from different sources which agree in confirming the extinction of the German settlements in Russia.

[2] Nevertheless, Dr. Dittloff and his staff were able with the stores at their disposal to save the lives of many thousands who sought refuge on the concession, and grateful acknowledgments should here be made to them for their great humanitarian effort.

THE SECOND PHASE: AUTUMN 1933 TO AUTUMN 1934

What has happened since the autumn of 1933? Have suffering and misery, famine and death from starvation now come to an end, as Soviet propagandists claim? Far from it. As was shown in the first chapter, there was a temporary improvement after the new harvest; but the loudest proclamation of the record yield could not alter the fact that the Russian statistics of the size of this bountiful harvest were not in agreement with the real state of affairs.

The Soviet authorities and all the journalists who are friendly to them telegraphed all over the world that "last year's magnificent harvest" had yielded 89,000,000 tons, and this assertion served for months to mislead public opinion on the Russian situation. Now it is generally admitted to be wrong. It appears that the statistical authorities in Moscow calculated the yield, not on the actual figures, but from hypothetical assumptions, a method differing from their own former practice and from that of the rest of the world. The record figure, therefore, was only a theoretical calculation, which did not tally at all with the actual yield.

After the world had been misled for months by the record figure of 89,000,000 tons, even the Soviets had to admit that the figure was a simple estimate, made by non-experts. According to the English press,[1] Ossinsky, the head of the Moscow Statistical Office, himself admitted that the real yield of the harvest was 30 to 40 per cent less than "could be gauged by the statistical estimates"; and he incurred the displeasure of high places on account of his achievements, which had for months been the basis of all news supplied to foreign countries. In the Moscow papers, too, such as *Pravda* and *Za Industrializatsiu*, Ossinsky was quite openly attacked for the "lack of reality" of his figures. This, however, did not take place until May: until then any criticisms of the Moscow figures had been rejected

[1] *The Times,* May 29 and June 2, 1934.

as hostile slander due to enemies of the Soviet regime. Indeed, both the political and the trade propaganda abroad had continued to enlarge on the economic advance the country had made thanks to the abundant harvest of the previous year. Now those are proved right—among them were almost all the foreign agricultural specialists who had worked in the Soviet Union in the last few years—who declared as early as the autumn of 1933 that the yield of the harvest was about equal to that of the previous year—i.e. only 55,000,000 to 60,000,000 tons.

Moscow had meanwhile succeeded admirably in spreading the story of the record harvest. Its journalistic friends reported an amazing superfluity from various regions. They claimed, indeed, on the basis of the improvement which actually took place after the harvest, that the danger of famine in the future was now removed. Their thesis was that things had been bad (a retrospective admission), but that now all was for the best. But this was not how things turned out. Hunger and distress reappeared—in many places almost as severe as before—in the Ukraine, the Northern Caucasus, on the Volga, and this time above all in the west, too—in White Russia and Volhynia.

This had been predicted as long before as the spring and summer of 1933 by a number of foreign observers who had travelled through Soviet Russia. They reported unanimously on the neglected fields, the astonishing masses of weeds, etc.— things which were bound to have an adverse effect on the harvest over wide areas—quite irrespective of good or bad weather and the natural condition of the 1933 crops.

I will quote some of these observations. An Austrian agricultural expert, who had lived for many years in Russia and in the summer of 1933 travelled through various Russian districts, including the Ukraine, found that even at that period a large part of the fields was in an extremely bad condition owing to inadequate sowing. He added that in certain districts, e.g. along the Volga, this fact was partly due to the complete failure of a new experiment, the so-called mud sowing. Pierre Berland, the *Temps* correspondent, wrote in his report on the summer of 1933 that on a short journey in the Black Sea region he had been impressed by "the astonishing prevalence of weeds in the fields."

In the spring of the same year Malcolm Muggeridge came to the conclusion that there was no hope of things getting better. In fact, he anticipated their growing worse, because the winter sowing had been neglected and general conditions in the country, especially transport conditions—despite every endeavour on the Government's part to bring about an improvement—would prevent the spring sowing from being a success.

An engineer named Bassèches, in a report published in July 1933 in the *Neue Freie Presse*, said: "The plan [i.e. the cultivation area for 1933] falls short of last year's by no more than eight million hectares. What counts is the quality of the cultivation." But even where the work was tackled with energy, it was impossible that year to clear the fields of the mass of weeds that had sprung up in the previous years. "It is a task that will require several years of concentrated effort. One's general impression is that the quality of the work varies extraordinarily in any given district." These prophets were to be proved right.

In the autumn of 1933, when the harvest had just been brought in, a special correspondent of the *Kurjer Warszawski*, particularly well informed on Russian affairs, was staying in the Soviet Union. He summed up the position as follows: "Even now, before winter has set in, it can be said that the official optimism about the new harvest was premature. It appears that the collectivization of agriculture, and the famine prevalent in Southern Russia during spring and summer, will have much worse effects than even the enemies of the regime could have foretold. The collapse of agriculture in the Ukraine and the Northern Caucasus is so devastating in its effects that even the best harvest would not have sufficed to make it good. Greater caution and reserve should have been observed in judging the position. All the reports reaching Moscow from the Soviet Ukraine reveal the fear of a new catastrophe. It is enough to mention that on October 1 five million hectares had been cultivated in the Soviet Ukraine, i.e. only half the area planned. It is impossible to increase this area; and if Soviet statistics are read with the necessary caution, the conclusion is unavoidable that even these five million hectares are an overestimate. The Ukraine, where less than fifty per cent of the planned area was cultivated, is the best proof of the harmful effects of collectivization."

At the same time, i.e. in the autumn of 1933, various reports, not least those published in the Soviet press, put it beyond all doubt that the excellent harvest, despite its good condition, had had its yield most adversely affected by a number of factors.

So much for the harvest. But the decisive factor this year, too, was the ruthless collection of grain from the peasants. On June 15, 1933, a decree was issued in Moscow organizing agricultural "cells" on the lines of the industrial "cells," and placing them under the control of the party. Berland's comment was: "The effect of this is very great; but the local fighters who have thus been exposed are full of indignation, and their hatred may some day become dangerous." The judicial autonomy of the federated states was suspended with respect to the protection of the harvest and the grain transports. On June 21 *Pravda* announced the appointment of Comrade Akulov as All-Russian Commissioner and public prosecutor for this special task. The decree of the central committee of the Soviet republic appointing him, dated June 10, was the basis for the entire struggle between Moscow and the grain producers, which in severity and determination exceeded all previous measures against the peasantry. These orders cancelled all the regulations of earlier years.

Postyschev's principle—"away with compassion"—was followed to the letter. No pity, no consideration for the suffering population were allowed to interfere with the collection of grain in the Ukraine or elsewhere. The political sections and the courts martial saw to that. Those who resisted were treated as separatists, saboteurs; in short, as enemies of the State. To this extent the position had grown worse in comparison with the autumn and winter of 1932, when the brutal seizure of grain had reached its zenith. In another respect, too, there was a change in the position. After the experiences of the previous year, when news of the famine and the vast number of deaths had quickly reached the non-Communist world through letters and eyewitnesses' accounts, the Kremlin now resolved to take timely steps to render the events "invisible," to systematize the process and, as far as possible, to erect an invisible Chinese Wall separating the starving populations from the rest of the world. The fact was that in 1932, as Pierre Berland rightly stated, the authorities had been surprised by the magnitude of the catastrophe. A repetition was to be avoided. Now there was time to take all necessary measures. The most important step in this direction was undoubtedly the great cleaning-up process, by which the hungry populations were removed from the visible into the "invisible" zone.

The energy and speed with which the Government set about this task was without doubt a remarkable achievement. In the future it would be impossible to see people dying and dead of starvation in the streets. The towns were to be freed from those categories of people who could not or must not be helped. This was done mainly with an eye to those taking part in the trips organized by the Soviet Russian tourist bureau and to foreign guests of honour, visiting the capitals and provincial centres according to a prearranged plan. Radical measures were therefore adopted to ensure that death should overtake some of these starving people not in the towns, but outside the urban zone—sixty miles away. As described elsewhere, many thousands of starving people were expelled; the authorities refused these unfortunates permission to stay on the ground of a new passport law. Muggeridge, Berland and other eye-witnesses have described the intense distress caused by this system and the attendant expulsion of the victims, above all to the so-called *lyshentsy*, the "anti-State" elements, in fact the unemployed.

Another measure for getting rid of the famine victims was their banishment to the north, to Siberia and to other remote regions. The system of banishment now reached its climax. Thousands of people had to vanish at the shortest notice into distant regions, where nobody could see them or trace their fate. Most of them never returned. Only by accident does news come now and again that they have disappeared or died. This method, which was employed more than any other towards the Ukrainians, the Volga Germans and others, is dealt with elsewhere.[1]

To the same category belong all those measures taken by the Kremlin with the object of hermetically shutting off the Russian provinces from the outer world—such as the pro-hibition of all travel to the provinces by journalists and other foreigners, except under the complete control of the "Intourist" organization and other Soviet authorities. As for Russian nationals, they were prevented from getting out of the country and reporting the true position by the most rigorous methods, including the death penalty and the persecution of the *émigrés*' relatives.[2] These measures taken by the Government did, in fact, succeed in rendering the famine almost invisible as compared with 1933.

Nevertheless, we have irrefutable evidence regarding the famine and the deaths caused by it during this second phase of the catastrophe. First of all, statements in the Soviet press, from the autumn of 1933 onwards, contained unmistakable hints (certainly not intended for foreign countries) of the continuance and intensification of the famine. As early as

---

[1] See Chapter IV, "Moscow's Attitude."   [2] Ibid.

February 1934, in the issue in which it reported the opening of the Moscow party meeting, *Pravda* contained a report showing clearly that the stocks of grain in the south were insufficient to feed the peasants on the collective farms. Seeking a credible explanation of this "strange phenomenon," it fell back on the "faulty distribution" of the stocks of grain collected. It quoted in full various official decrees to prove that it was the fault of the population, and not the Government. The hungry peasants of the collective farms were reminded that they had the right to increase their stocks of corn by setting up certain reserves, so that it was their own fault if the Communist organizations of the cities and the industrial centres succeeded in obtaining more than their fair share by "inflating" their own reserves. The fact, however, was that, as in the previous year, all the available grain was simply taken away from the peasants and the local organizations.

The cruel mockery of the starving peasant population implied in such statements is best seen from certain instances quoted by *Pravda* to show that the peasants of the collective farms were themselves to blame for their distress. "Some examples of the system followed by the collective farms in the Kiev district will show how the working days were calculated there." These are the surprising facts discovered: "In the Shevtschenko collective farm in the Petrovsk district, the village doctor was put down for fifty-four working days, for no ascertainable reason." A number of similar examples are then quoted. So the starving peasants are told that they have been wasting their grain by unjustified distributions to such *prikhlebateli* as the village doctor, etc. (It is notorious, by the way, that if anyone is in a difficult position it is village doctors and other brain workers.)

Another argument put forward by *Pravda* to prove that the inhabitants are to blame for the existing state of things is extraordinarily significant. The paper claims that "in dozens of districts in the Ukraine, the Azov-Black Sea district, the

Northern Caucasus, etc., the grain from thousands of hectares and hundreds of barns has not yet been threshed and that no special measures to carry out the threshing are apparently being undertaken." Here again, according to the *Pravda*, the local population is to blame. This last statement, incidentally, confirms the allegation made long ago from the other side that a large part of the last harvest could not be threshed and in all probability could not even be garnered owing to the destruction of draught cattle, the reduced amount of labour available, and the disastrous position of transport. About the same time *Pravda* published a very significant decree which ran as follows: "It is decreed that the grain to be surrendered by the people on the collective farms and by individual peasants is to be taken only from an area determined for that purpose in accordance with the plan and on the basis of the present decree. It is further decreed that grain grown either by the people on the collective farms or by individual peasants on any area in excess of the plan shall not be collected by the State." Why was this decree issued? Because the danger had been recognized—as can be clearly read between the lines of *Pravda*—that the hungry peasants thus deprived of their crops would not carry out next year's spring sowing properly by way of protest.

A decree of the Council of People's Commissaries and the Central Committee of the party, published in *Izvestia* on February 25, 1934, shows clearly that in the winter of 1933-4 the members of many of the collective farms, so specially favoured and privileged by the Government, were already going hungry. The decree shows that in 1934 as well as in 1933 the peasants of the collective farms had been granted advances in kind, not only for sowing purposes, but also for food. The decree fixes the dates at which, after the next harvest, these advances of grain were to be reclaimed. There can thus no longer be any doubt that even the privileged peasants of the collective farms were, in the winter of 1933-4, in a position which made Government help necessary—and in the shape of advances of grain.

But an article published by *Pravda* on March 10, 1934, is particularly significant. It deals with the necessity of an immediate reorganization of the agricultural apparatus. Dealing with the position in the Northern Caucasus, the article said: "Last year was only the beginning of the recovery. The good harvest was not gathered in its entirety. The region failed to observe the dates fixed for the prescribed agricultural work. The necessary working discipline is lacking on the collective farms. There was no control of operations."

As is always the case with these forced admissions, they were followed by a demand for the final destruction of the "class enemies," who were charged with "pilfering and destruction of crops, barbarous treatment of horses, non-observance of the daily standard of work, and deliberate reduction of the amount of bread delivered—attempts to disorganize the 'collective farm brigade.'" Here is an open admission of the loss of part of the 1933 harvest and of the disorganization of agriculture.

A speech by Kalinin delivered on February 16, 1934, and reported in *Pravda* of February 27, is an equally frank confession. After mentioning the "model collective farms," Kalinin said: "If these collective farms [meaning those which had a good harvest] were the majority, the problem of prosperity would by now have been solved. But the number of these collective farms is unhappily very small." Kalinin went on to declare that the good harvest of the previous year proved that there were good crops "only in those collective farms where the work was well done." It is thus admitted in open words that even the good harvest of 1933 was unable to improve matters where bad work was done, or, more exactly, where the state of agriculture was not what it should have been.

This indirect evidence was reinforced rather later by an important direct admission from Moscow relating to the distress in the Ukraine and the other agricultural districts. On April 11,

1934, the official Swiss telegraph agency published the following Moscow message: "Details published by the Soviet authorities of the food situation in various parts of the Ukraine show that the supply of flour, meal, sugar, fish, butter and fats is insufficient. A scarcity of food is also reported from the timber districts of the north."

The *Neue Zürcher Zeitung* and other papers saw in this report a first confession by the Government that the position in the Ukraine and elsewhere was unsatisfactory. A full confession soon followed, at the end of May, when the Kremlin decreed an increase of 100 per cent in the price of bread. It is surely obvious that this increase was caused by a shortage of bread and not, as the decree says, by the destruction of part of the coming harvest, which would not have been garnered for some months. At the same time Russian grain purchases for the Far East—a region previously supplied from Siberia—on the London, Rotterdam and other exchanges, caused a sensation. Now, in the summer before the new harvest, the distress of the population had, as in the previous year, reached its climax.

To-day, fortunately, we possess eyewitnesses' evidence on the real conditions existing in the "invisible zone" in the summer of 1934. In the first place, that of refugees, who from time to time succeed in evading the cordons and escaping abroad to break the great silence which broods over the famine areas. They tell how, as in the previous year, the peasants left their settlements and houses in order to escape the famine. Thus peasants from Volhynia, including German and Russian Baptists, migrated to the neighbouring regions. The very fact that groups of people are continually trying to cross the frontier, despite pursuit and danger, is eloquent. *Dilo*, the organ of the Ukrainians in Lemberg, describes as follows the escape and appearance of a group of refugees who crossed the Zbrutsch:

"A chain of Russian sentries is posted on the far side of the Zbrutsch, the frontier river. These are picked Bolshevist troops from the interior and from Siberia, who are charged with the control of the Russo-Polish frontier. They stand facing east-wards, ready to fire. They are on the look-out for Russian citizens in hiding near by, who cast longing looks at the river. . . . They are Ukrainian peasants who, driven by hunger, cover hundreds of miles in bands and stream towards the frontier. They seek safety in flight. . . . Their faces are pale as though marked by death. Their bodies are clothed in rags. They are more like mummies than living beings. . . . They wander about at some distance from the river, awaiting a favourable opportunity to get across. No Ukrainians may be placed on sentry duty here, for they might be moved by sympathy and compassion to turn away and give their fellow-countrymen an opportunity of escaping from a dreadful fate in the Soviet Union. The Ukrainians are hungry, barefooted and ragged—as helpless as any living creature could be. They were driven by torturing hunger to leave the places where they once worked happily. They have fled to beg their bread across the frontier. Once other peoples lived on the superfluity of their rich and blessed country."

What is said here of the Ukrainian refugees is equally true of all the other groups of refugees, such as the Germans who fled into Manchuria, or the Jews who escaped to Persia. The fearful sufferings of the Jews have been described by *The Times* correspondent at Teheran. He expressly states that they undertook the terrible hardships of the flight to Persia only because they were driven by misery and hunger.

The fate of the refugees from Russia is undoubtedly a particularly tragic chapter in the history of the famine victims in the Soviet State. Imagine that parties of German settlers escaped, not only into Manchuria, but some even across the Pamir mountains into India. The sufferings of these refugees are often not at an end even when they have crossed the frontier. A group of German settlers who had succeeded in reaching Harbin had to live for a month in the criminal and prostitutes' quarters of that city. The greatest efforts had to be

F

made by the German relief organizations to extricate them from this position and to send them in a specially chartered steamer to Brazil, where they were finally settled.

The evidence furnished by certain foreign observers who succeeded in evading the authorities' precautions and in reaching the famine areas is, perhaps, even more important than the above accounts. In August 1934 a London paper published an account by a young English "Intourist" traveller, who had managed to elude the control of the authorities for a time and to travel for some days through the Ukrainian provinces, the district of Poltava, Belgorod, etc. His observations coincided to a considerable degree with those made in the previous year by Malcolm Muggeridge, Harry Lang and Mr. and Mrs. Stebalo. Most of the famine victims with whom this traveller was able to talk confirmed that they had to starve because they had been deprived of their grain in the autumn of the previous year. They said "they would have had enough bread to live on if members of the Red Army had not taken away their harvest." The author describes a scene witnessed at Belgorod, near Kharkov, where he entered a cottage in a small village. It was, he writes, "a typical hut with dirt floor, thatched roof and containing, as the only piece of furniture, a bench. The occupants were a very thin girl of fourteen and her brother of two and a half years. This younger child crawled about the floor like a frog, its poor little body so deformed from lack of nourishment that it did not resemble a human being. Its mother had died of starvation when it was one year old. This child had never tasted milk or butter and only once in its life had tasted meat. . . ."

This Englishman's evidence refers to the Kiev-Kharkov district. He describes further the terrible effects of hunger in a village twenty miles distant from Kiev, where most of the inhabitants had died of starvation. The author finally succeeded in returning to Moscow without having been stopped or arrested by the local authorities, and placed himself again under official guidance as an ordinary tourist. He lived in the

Hôtel Métropole and enjoyed all the advantages and blessings of this Bolshevik luxury establishment, the chief of them being the possibility of having a hot bath, and was enabled to appreciate the vast difference between the life of the privileged classes at Moscow and the conditions in the famine zone of the south.

Almost simultaneously this account was confirmed from another quarter, by two Polish airmen, the brothers Adamovitch, American citizens, who were the first to fly across the Atlantic to Poland and were received there with enthusiasm in the summer of 1934. Later they were the guests of the Soviet Government at Moscow, and thanks to this were able to get permission to visit their sister in their native village in the Ukraine.[1]

"When we arrived in our car at our native village," they wrote, "we found it completely changed. The trees had been uprooted, the cottages and yards were in a state of ruin. We looked in vain for our parents' cottage, where our sister was living, and could not find it. At last the peasants had to show us what had been our parents' farm. In the cottages we saw a wretched, pitiable figure, whose body was covered with nothing but a ragged old sack. With the help of our neighbours we recognized in this figure our sister. She looked many years older, and the terrible sufferings which she appeared to be undergoing had so distorted her face that even her own brothers could not recognize her. When we asked her about our father and mother, she told us that our mother had died of starvation because she could not adapt herself to the diet of the other inhabitants, who lived chiefly on herbs. . . . Our sister's pitiful appearance, and her strange, macabre story, took our breath away. Two-thirds of the inhabitants have died of hunger in the village, and those who are left are more like corpses than living people. They live without hope, know no pleasure, and do not know how to smile. A few asked us when the war would begin; war—salvation! We said we would like

---

[1] Their account was published by *America*, the organ of the Catholic *émigrés* from the Ukraine, and was reprinted in *Dilo* of October 31, 1934.

to drive to the next village to visit relations there, but we were stopped: the village no longer existed. The inhabitants had died of starvation, and the few recalcitrants who remained had been sent to Siberia."

This account speaks for itself as evidence of the real state of things in the famine areas. Famine and mass deaths continued during this second phase. If the picture, as one of the foreign correspondents in Moscow of many years' standing put it, "was materially better than the year before," this was to be attributed, in his opinion, not only to a better harvest, but also to a "more flexible system of collection and distribution."[1] And in fact it was this "more flexible system of collection and distribution" which constituted the main difference between 1933 and 1934. The collection and distribution of grain had been skilfully adapted to the new position: the famine had become invisible, and could be most thoroughly exploited by the Kremlin for its political ends. The good harvest had afforded no more than a temporary relief; the famine began later than in the previous year and the number of victims was less. But even in the summer there could be no doubt that the famine would continue next year.

THE THIRD PHASE: FROM AUTUMN OF 1934 ONWARDS

The third phase began after the harvest of 1934. The position was then much clearer than it had been a year before. Even in the summer Moscow had been compelled to admit that a large part of the new harvest had been destroyed by the terrible drought and, as mentioned above, had used this admission as a pretext for increasing the price of bread by 100 per cent in May. The striking decrease in the yield of the harvest in wide areas of the country led to the campaign for the extraction of grain from the peasants being prosecuted with greater rigour even than in the previous year.

We quote below the evidence of an eyewitness whose

[1] Cf. Arthur Just's account in the *Memeler Dampfboot*, June 3, 1934.

competence even the Soviet authorities are not likely to question. Harold Denny, Walter Duranty's assistant in the Moscow representation of the *New York Times*, stated on July 26, 1934, that the struggle for the current harvest was of a character and an intensity probably never witnessed in the world's history; indeed, the struggle was being organized and carried through like a military offensive. He described in detail how the plans were worked out during the preceding winter in Moscow, where there was an iron will, and how instructions were then issued to the autonomous republics and by them in turn to the regional authorities, which he compares to army corps. By them the orders were passed on through the further stages of the hierarchy—the tractor stations, the heads of the collective farms, etc., for execution. He described how the workers on the State farms were divided into brigades of one hundred men, and how the whole military apparatus then moved forward as though to battle. During the summer decrees were issued by the Kremlin at certain intervals which gave instructions "like battle orders" for the carrying out of the attack. Not the slightest deviation from these rigid orders was permitted. No excuses for failure were accepted, and deliberate disobedience to an order was punished like a crime.

Against whom was this unparalleled campaign directed? The object of the struggle was the provision of bread, "this absolutely necessary foodstuff," as Mr. Denny naïvely calls it, without which people remain hungry even when there is a superfluity of other foodstuffs (as though there were any such superfluity). The second objective, as appears from Mr. Denny's account, was the forcible carrying out of the collective system and with it the destruction of the remaining individual peasants. Thus on the one side we have a mighty military apparatus, on the other the starving peasants of the agricultural districts, who are to be deprived of the remnants of their harvest by the use of an unparalleled military offensive. Is it possible to characterize in more pregnant terms the tragedy which is still being enacted in the Soviet agricultural districts?

One cannot help asking why it was necessary to use force, if in fact it were only the peasants' surplus grain that was to be collected, as the Soviet authorities always claimed. No, the object of this military offensive is not the collection of a surplus; the peasants are being deprived by force of the minimum necessary for existence. That the peasants should offer a desperate resistance is a matter of course: they are fighting for their existence, for their bare lives. But resistance is in vain, for, as Mr. Denny rightly states, Moscow knows no compromise and no mercy. The result is that Moscow is in a position each year to celebrate the victorious conclusion of the grain campaign, a victory which makes it necessary to deprive the peasants of the agricultural districts of their supplies the same autumn, immediately after the harvest, and thus to leave them at the mercy of hunger and distress.

It sometimes happens that local officials, despite their devotion to the Communist party, cannot bear to see the peasants deprived of the minimum remnant of their crops which they need to keep themselves alive, and thus condemned to death by starvation. What is done with such officials? They expose themselves to the severest persecution. Mr. Denny himself refers to the persecution of local officials, and that in a passage in which he speaks with profound admiration of the strength and energy with which Moscow is wagering the bread war. He quotes the removal from his post of Tsetkov, the representative of the all-state committee for the collection of agricultural products in the Crimea. His crime was that he had protested against the full collection of the grain quotas laid down by the State in the regions afflicted by the drought. Mr. Denny also mentions that similar events are reported in the press.

By the autumn of 1934 the authorities found the success of the grain collecting campaign gravely menaced. A large part had already been destroyed by the drought. In some regions official figures showed that only a small part of the amount which should have been collected by October 1 had been secured. Thus in the extremely important district of Western Siberia only 40 per cent (in some districts 58 per cent) of the requisite amount of grain had been delivered by way of taxation up to October 1. Is it surprising that in these circumstances the Government, true to its principles, took the most vigorous steps against all officials who, from "leniency" or other reasons, refused to participate to the desired extent in the plundering of the population? It goes without saying that the Moscow press, with its eye on the outer world, reported none of these things.

Yet at the moment when *Pravda* and *Izvestia* were completely silent about this development, a local paper at Cheliabinsk, in Western Siberia, published a report of a case heard before the local district court which throws a flash of light on the position. It says that three Soviet officials were condemned to death. Why? The Moscow correspondent of the *Sunday Times*[1] says that one of the officials had been for fifteen years President of the Commune of the First of May and a member of the Communist Party. He was accused of open sabotage in estimating the yield of the harvest and of having said that if the full amount demanded were surrendered to the State, "nothing will be left for us." The leader of a workers' column, Tschernishev, and an inspector of long standing, Gniesdiel, were also condemned to death. The judge said: "Stalin has shown us where the class enemy is to be looked for: it is in the collective farms, and the number of cases which come before the local courts shows that the enemy is resisting desperately."

So the position is that anyone resisting the fulfilment of the grain plan is declared an enemy and executed. It is true that this method has had an unexpectedly favourable result. On October 20, 1934, Moscow was able to declare triumphantly

[1] October 28, 1934.

that in Western Siberia the fulfilment percentage of the delivery plan had increased since October 1, i.e. in less than three weeks, from 40 (or 53) to no less than 83 (or 93). The State had thus won a decisive victory over the starving peasants in their struggle for existence. It is the same result as was obtained in White Russia in December 1932, when the fulfilment of the delivery plan reached 106 per cent, and a large part of the population died of starvation. We have here another proof of the fact that, if Moscow succeeds, as in 1933, in collecting the grain required for its purposes, this is no proof that the food position as a whole is normal, still less that it has improved. On the contrary, the prosecution of the "unprecedented military offensive" against the population of the agricultural districts, and the employment of the most extreme terroristic measures, even the execution of Soviet officials, only proves that the requisite amount could be collected in 1934 only with the greatest difficulties and with the heaviest sacrifices on the part of the agricultural population. It further confirms the statements of eyewitnesses that a large part of this population had been deprived of the minimum supplies of grain necessary to support life even before the end of 1934.

Let us turn now to the position in the Ukraine, the Volga district and other important agricultural regions. I mentioned above the misleading Moscow report, published in the summer of 1934, that the harvest would reach 89,000,000 tons. What are the actual facts? The official Moscow figures do not permit of an answer, because the Government publishes no authentic figures for the harvest.[1] But we know that as late as September the delivery quotas for some of the most important districts, e.g. the Volga district, Western Siberia, the Southern Ukraine, etc., were most unsatisfactory and suddenly shot up only when a "firm hand" was employed for collecting the grain. We know further from Postyschev's and Kossior's evidence, as well as from an official Kiev report on the "preliminary" agricultural

---

[1] The real nature of the Soviet statistics is dealt with in detail elsewhere.

figures for 1934, that—contrary to the Moscow statement that the 1934 harvest would equal that of 1933—the average harvest was "considerably below that of 1933." We also know from other accounts that the harvest in the Soviet Ukraine was so bad that the combined reaping machines could be used only in a few exceptional cases even in the most fertile regions, because, as *Izvestia* and *Pravda* repeatedly declared, the machines could be used only where the corn grew to a normal height, which was not the case in that year. There is no need to stress the significance of the fact that the grain did not reach a sufficient height to be reaped by these machines in a country so fertile as the Ukraine.

Authentic reports, whose reliability can at any time be confirmed through the Vienna relief committee, show that by the end of 1934 the position in the German Volga district was disastrous, and that the German peasants did not possess the minimum quantities of grain even for the near future. We know that some of the big German villages have lost 50 or even 60 per cent of their population in the last few years.

The position was worst, however, in the Southern Ukraine. Messrs. Denny and Duranty, the two Anglo-Saxon journalists who enjoy the highest esteem of the Kremlin, had to admit that the harvest dropped to zero in the places affected by the drought, and that even in the autumn the individual peasants in the Ukraine had such scanty supplies that there could be no doubt that they would be afflicted with famine.

These remaining individual peasants are the chief martyrs of the food shortage. Mr. Denny, whose impressions of the future development of the Russian food situation is admittedly based chiefly on visits paid to collective farms and on information given by the heads of these institutions, resolved in July 1934 to visit some individual peasants also. As a result of his conversations with them he had to admit that they would soon be without reserves—in other words, would be starving. Many of those to whom he talked said that they did not know how they would come through. The taxes they had to pay were heavier than those of the collective peasants. Many declared that the taxes alone would absorb the whole of their wretched harvest. Thus even the statements made to foreign journalists under Ogpu surveillance show that the individual peasants must become victims of the famine unless they can find work in Kiev or elsewhere. The systematic method pursued by Moscow to make the individual peasants victims of the catastrophe is best shown by the decree issued in the late autumn of 1934 on the collection of taxes from these peasants. This decree, whose contents were published all over the world, burdened these unfortunates not only with a money tax, but further ordained that anyone "maliciously" failing to carry out the sowing plans should be taxed double. Finally, it ordained that the local authorities might increase the tax by 50 per cent where there was a particularly good harvest. The aim of these decrees is evident. As Mr. Chamberlin has pointed out in his reports, the Soviet Government exploits the famine in order systematically to destroy certain categories of people.

At the end of October the Moscow correspondents of the *New York Times*, having made a further journey to the Ukraine, were compelled to admit frankly, despite all their former optimistic utterances, that an "interesting migration" of the population, as these gentlemen call it, from the drought-stricken district of Apostolovo had begun. Some thousands of people, they telegraphed, would be leaving this district before winter, many of them because of the failure of the harvest through the drought. The mere fact that thousands were leaving the district, they went on to say, proved that there would be no famine that winter in the Apostolovo district, because there would be all the more bread for those who remained behind. One would almost feel that Mr. Denny regarded the flight of these unfortunates from starvation as a positive cause for satisfaction. The movement (the "interesting migration") was not proceeding in a panic-stricken manner, but quite regularly.

Mr. Denny tells us of one particular party of Apostolovo refugees—a smallish group of emigrants who had come into the Apostolovo district because they were attracted by the previous year's record crop. He mentions that, unlike the permanent dwellers in the region, they had no grain reserves, had nothing to lose, and packed up their scanty belongings in the hope of finding better things in more distant fields. This time they were going to Western Siberia, where the current harvest was good but the harvesters were inefficient. He observes that they might spend their whole lives looking for a good harvest and that they would always be a year too late.

If credence may be attached to reports which reached Warsaw about events in Central Asia during this period, there were regular battles between the peasants and the Government troops during the grain-collecting campaign. The accounts say that hundreds were killed and wounded in the fighting between Red troops and local Mohammedans who opposed the removal of the grain by State officials. After the fighting, representatives of the various villages, including several Mohammedan clerics, were executed by a special detachment of the Ogpu. Only then was it possible to deprive the peasants of the yield of the harvest "according to plan."

The Kremlin was compelled during this period also to sacrifice the vital interests of the agricultural population to those of the workmen and privileged classes. An example is to be found in a wireless debate (pereklitschka), which took place on December 24, 1934. This was one of those conversations between Moscow and individual local officials on the local food supply situation which for a time took place almost every night. One of Stalin's most trusted assistants, Comrade Jakovliev, was talking to Koporovsky, the representative of the Soviet officials at Minsk. The latter said that no more than 30 per cent of bread requirements were covered up to January 1,

so that the Minsk district (White Russia) was unprepared
for the change to be introduced on that date. During the
conversation Jakovliev told the Minsk official that he must
first of all see that the workers in the local paper mill (called
"the Labour Hero") were supplied and not the surrounding
inhabitants. In his care for the industrial workers' welfare,
Jakovliev went to the length of demanding that the bread
should be delivered at their dwellings "so that they should not
have to stand in the queues outside the shops." He said that
this method had already been adopted successfully in Moscow
and Leningrad, and held in prospect a supply of lorries for the
purpose.

If further proof were required that there would be famine
in wide areas of Soviet Russia during the financial year 1934-5,
a declaration of the Soviet Government at the end of December
1934 provides it. This decree refers to an "elemental catastrophe" and not merely to a "partial destruction of the harvest
through drought." The districts affected are enumerated and
it is decreed that over a million tons (69,179,000 poods) of
grain are to be set aside as a relief supply "for sowing, food and
cattle fodder."

This decree was issued on December 26, 1934, and published
in *Pravda* on the following day. Significantly enough, while the
title of the decree speaks only of "assistance to the collective
farms in their sowing campaign," the text also refers expressly
to food or fodder supplies. The decree enumerates one by one
various districts in the famine zone, and gives a complete
picture of the vast territory suffering from "elemental" distress.
It is as follows: the whole of the Ukraine, excepting parts of
the Kiev and Chernigov districts, half of the former Central
Russian black earth zone, the whole of the Northern Caucasus,
the Don region, the lower and middle Volga and, finally, a
large part of Western Siberia—in other words, a territory
inhabited by about one-third of the entire population of the
Union. The Ukraine is allotted more than half of the amount

$(38\frac{1}{2}$ million poods)—a further proof of the condition of this once most fertile region. The Commissary for Agriculture in the Ukraine, Paperny, is quoted as saying, in the autumn of 1934, that by the spring 75 per cent of the smaller collective farms would have to obtain their seed grain from outside.

The fact that Western Siberia is among the districts granted additional grain proves that the "elemental catastrophe" was not confined to the south, and indicates the value of the Soviet press assertions that the deficiency due to drought in the south would be compensated by surpluses elsewhere.

Compared with this admission of the distress in the collective farms, what significance has the alleged success of the harvest campaign, with its "two million tons more" than the "record harvest" of the previous year? It is noteworthy, too, that in the carrying out of the decree care was taken to protect the seed corn delivered to the collective farms from the clutches of the starving. This is shown by a telegram[1] from Odessa stating that the district organizations had the strictest instructions to see that the grain given to the collective farms was protected. They were to keep a close eye on the personnel of the sentries and take care that the stocks were watched day and night.

It is characteristic that officially these grants are made only for a period of a few months; in autumn, directly after the new harvest, the stocks have to be repaid to the Government, plus 10 per cent. Everywhere else in the world goods or money advanced in connection with an act of God is repaid over a series of years. It is also striking that the decree does not contain a word about assistance to individual peasants. This confirms that the physical destruction of the remaining individual peasants is a special plank in the Government's programme.

Although, as stated above, the decree speaks of food relief, this is quite a secondary matter. The chief aim is not to assist

[1] Published in the *Socialisticheskoe Zemledelie*.

the people who have been deprived of their reserves and are at the mercy of famine, but to save the remaining cattle and above all to make sure of the spring sowing. A collapse of the sowing campaign would simply have meant that Moscow would in future be unable to collect the indispensable quantity of grain even at the cost of the lives of the agricultural population. The swiftest action was necessary, and was taken by means of the decree of December 26, 1934. Compared with the great importance of these measures to secure the spring sowing, relief for the famine victims was, from the standpoint of the Soviet regime, absolutely uninteresting. If it had been Moscow's intention to ensure for the peasantry the minimum of food essential to support life, there would have been no need for this unique military offensive to remove the grain.

In order to prove that all the statements made about the distress or famine in the agricultural districts are incorrect, the Government has for some months past been pointing to the abolition of bread cards at the beginning of 1935. I must, therefore, briefly point out what the abandonment of this system really means. The abolition of the system can naturally have no effect on the position of producers, especially in the agricultural districts, since the whole system of bread cards exists only for the distribution of food to consumers, i.e. to the urban population, etc. Whether the bread forcibly extracted from the peasants at dirt prices is distributed to the consumers by the card system or some other, and whether the Government gets an even higher price than before in the State shops, can in no way affect the disastrous position of the peasants—the overwhelming majority of the population.

It would also be a mistake to see in this measure a proof that the yield of the harvest in Russia has at all increased or improved. The amount of grain collected by the Government depends on the result of the collecting campaign, quite irrespective of the yield of the harvest as such.

But even the position of the urban population as a whole has, if anything, deteriorated through the new arrangements and the abolition of the bread cards. The new system greatly increases the price of the bread, which used to be handed out to the holders of bread cards.

A correspondent of the Vienna *Neue Freie Presse* (January 27, 1935) describes the effects of this innovation as follows: "As from January 1 the free sale of bread, flour and other rationed foodstuffs has begun. If part of the population were pleased to be relieved of this bureaucratic fetter, yet the pleasure was very mixed. There can be no doubt that the abolition of the bread cards does material injury to the ill-paid. The price of rationed bread has been increased, and that of bread formerly sold without restriction has been lowered. Thus the cost of living of highly paid officials, who were not content with their card ration and bought the better qualities for sale in the State shops, has somewhat declined. But for workmen, who used to obtain enough from their bread cards alone, it has considerably increased. Wages have been somewhat raised, but the largest increase is 24 roubles a month. A worker's family of four spent last year 54 roubles per month on bread. To-day an equal quantity costs 90 roubles."

A very large profit—and this is probably the real purpose of the change—is made by the State, which notoriously takes their grain from the peasants at a very low price. Admittedly the State has promised employees and workers higher wages as an alleged equivalent for the increase in the price of bread over the bread-card price. But these increases, as a Moscow radio talk put it, would be adapted to individual conditions and above all to the quality of the individual's work: in other words, they would be given arbitrarily, in accordance with the fundamental principle of the Soviet regime.

The result is that the Soviet regime only secured a new means of tyrannizing over individual groups and categories of the population. More than ever is Moscow able to determine the fate of individual groups of the urban population.

To some, by an adequate rise in wages, it will be able really to grant an equivalent for the increased cost of living; others, with the help of the new system, it can expose to privation and misery even more than before. This applies particularly to the *lyshentsy*, who draw no wages at all and therefore naturally suffer most from the new rise in the price of bread.

The population is thus doubly menaced by famine and its consequences. On the one hand are those who do not survive the critical period, i.e. die of starvation, while on the other are those who survive the acute crisis, but are in daily peril from disease and epidemics on account of their undernourished, enfeebled state. Even if circumstances should favour the 1935 harvest, so that it equalled that of 1933, this menace would remain undiminished. After a passing improvement, which would afford Moscow an opportunity for the public display of its "superfluity and prosperity" propaganda, large masses of the population, deprived of the necessary minimum of food, would again be exposed to hunger and distress.

I have attempted to characterize the three periods of the Russian famine—from the autumn of 1932 to the autumn of 1933, from the autumn of 1933 to the autumn of 1934, and finally from 1934 onwards. My description would be incomplete if I did not attempt to deal with certain aspects of the tragedy upon which I have not yet touched.

The first question relates to the number of victims. To arrive at exact figures is, of course, impossible; this can be done only in the future, after careful investigations have been made locally. But it is possible to make an estimate of the losses. In principle it may be said that, from the point of view of the relief work for the benefit of those threatened with starvation in Russia, it does not much matter whether the number of dead is 5, 6, 8 or 10 millions; it is enough to show that the figure runs into millions. If sceptics ask that the representatives of relief organizations shall produce exact figures of the number of dead, the answer is that it is the fault of the Government,

Corpses of famine victims who died in the streets awaken at first
the sympathy of passers-by

This famine victim also still attracts attention and pity

Familiarity breeds indifference

Even several famine victims dead in the street cause no emotion in passers-by

which prohibits local investigation, if the number of the starved cannot to-day be accurately calculated. I emphasize this because, in my opinion, this questioning of the number of victims has as its sole object to throw doubts upon the severity of the famine and thus to relieve the questioners of the duty to help. Yet, even if the number of victims were to be arbitrarily placed at a much reduced figure, the fact of the catastrophe cannot be disputed.

There are, however, data enough which indicate the enormous mortality during the first period. The facts are perhaps best characterized by the statement of a foreign journalist[1] in Moscow well known for his knowledge of Russian conditions— a correspondent who has tried for years to make the tone of his despatches as favourable to Soviet Russia as possible. His comment on the optimistic accounts of the 1933 harvest is, "the collectivizing campaign cost at least as many lives as a great war." What a terrible admission these few words contain! The lives destroyed by weapons of all kinds during years of war succumbed to famine in Russia in a bare eight months! The correspondent of the *Kölnische Zeitung*, to prove that the position was becoming somewhat easier, quoted a Moscow report that the bread in the provinces would in future be distributed "among a few million fewer mouths." Mr. Malcolm Muggeridge, previously referred to, says that by March 1933 as many as 24 per cent of the population had died of famine in certain regions, e.g. Kazakstan. This statement was also indirectly confirmed by the Kazakstan representative, Mirsoian, at the seventeenth Communist Party Congress. According to his statement hundreds of thousands of persons had left their farms up to 1933.

In effect all these accounts say the same thing. The *Neue Zürcher Zeitung* expresses itself more definitely when it gives the loss of life in the Ukraine alone at six million. It adds that even Soviet circles talked of a loss of a million or two of

---

[1] The representative of the *Neue Freie Presse*.

lives in the Ukraine. The inquiry undertaken in the autumn of 1933 by the *Manchester Guardian* correspondent in various places in the south—the Ukraine, the Northern Caucasus, etc. —is extremely instructive. He tried to ascertain the decline in the population of these places in accordance with exact figures supplied by the local Soviet officials. He gives the names of the places and the officials, and comes to the conclusion that in some villages the decline amounted to 10 to 15 per cent. Thus in the village of Kazanskaya only 7,000 people were left out of an original 8,000. The correspondent adds that the winter and even more early spring must have been quite terrible in this region. In order to check the statements of the inhabitants, he went to the president of the local Soviet, Nemov, who confirmed that the population had declined from 8,000 to 7,000, i.e. by 12·5 per cent. Similar effects of the catastrophe were found to exist in other places. These discoveries of the *Manchester Guardian* correspondent in the autumn of 1933 confirm the reports sent by Malcolm Muggeridge to the same paper in March. This is important in view of the controversy about the existence of a famine which was carried on for months in letters to the editor of this paper. Harry Lang[1] estimated that in certain parts of White Russia and the Ukraine up to 40 per cent of the population, including a large number of Jews, had been victims of the famine in 1932–3. Similar figures are quoted for the various German settlements in the Northern Caucasus, etc., by the German relief organizations. They put the total of deaths of Germans in the Soviet Union at about 140,000 in 1933 alone.[2]

Another eyewitness who published his impressions in the English press at the end of August 1933 came to far gloomier conclusions than the *Manchester Guardian* correspondent. Like Malcolm Muggeridge, this writer had stayed for some time in the famine areas. He gives the following details with regard

---

[1] Referred to elsewhere: of the New York Jewish paper *Forward*.
[2] Cf. *Nation und Staat*, No. 40, 1934.

to the mortality in various places in the south. In the settlement of Ust-Labinskaya the population had declined from 24,000 to 10,000 in the course of the winter; at Timishbek from 15,000 to 7,000, and at Dimitrievka from 6,000 to 2,000. Other settlements, such as Irbilnaya, Kammenogradska and Losovskaya, were completely deserted. At Stavropol the loss of life was 50,000 and at Krasnoda 40,000. The terrible mortality in the latter place is confirmed by accounts given by employees of the German *Drusag* concession.

The judgment of Mr. W. H. Chamberlin, the Moscow correspondent of the *Christian Science Monitor*, who spent twelve years in Moscow, and is an undisputed authority on Russian affairs, is particularly valuable. In an article of May 29, 1934, he wrote: "Some idea of the scope of the famine, the very existence of which was stubbornly and not unsuccessfully concealed from the outside world by the Soviet authorities, may be gauged from the fact that in three widely separated regions of Ukrainia and the North Caucasus which I visited— Poltava and Byelaya Tserkov and Kropotkin in the North Caucasus—mortality, according to the estimates of such responsible local authorities as Soviet and collective farm presidents, ranged around 10 per cent. Among individual peasants and in villages far away from the railroad it was often much higher."

In his book, *Russia's Iron Age*, published towards the end of 1934, Mr. Chamberlin, while plainly anxious to make a cautious estimate, puts the number of victims in the famine area at three or four millions.

That millions of people have died of starvation in Russia is a fact which, I am sure, no one can any longer seriously dispute; in fact, no effort to deny it is now made even in Moscow[1].

[1] The Ukrainian People's Commissary, Petrovsky, speaking on October 6, 1933, at Kharkov, stated that the population of the Ukraine in 1933 was 31,687,000. In 1932 the same man estimated the population at 32,122,000 (*Visty*, November 7, 1932) and also stated that the increase in population for 1933 would probably amount to 622,000.

Unfortunately, I am not in a position to print the contents of a document which I have had the opportunity of seeing, dated February 15, 1923.

But it is not the millions of innocent lives which were lost which are especially characteristic of the Russian famine, but the fearful attendant phenomena to which it gave rise. To deal with all of these here would exceed the scope of this book; for it would demand most extensive studies on the spot to explain all the social, moral and physical decay which has been a consequence of the famine. I must therefore confine myself to the most conspicuously significant attendant phenomena of the famine. One cannot help feeling an inner repulsion in treating of a phenomenon which speaks more clearly than any other of the state of utter barbarism to which the famine has reduced the populations of the areas afflicted by it. I refer to cannibalism and the killing of children and of sick persons for cannibalistic purposes. That these practices occurred during the famine of 1921–2 is a fact which can no longer be denied, for we have evidence of this from officials of the American relief organization and from foreign journalists who accompanied it.

During the more recent catastrophe the same causes have had the same effects. Here again there is irrefutable evidence in the shape of the accounts of reliable eyewitnesses and of letters in the possession of the various relief organizations. The evidence available shows clearly that the starving people began by feeding on the most disgusting things—refuse of every kind, mice, rats and the bodies of animals which had died of disease—and went on to eat not only corpses, but the flesh of the human beings who were least capable of resistance—sick

consists of the formal report of a discussion between doctors at a place in the middle of the then famine area on the Volga, and is in the possession of one of the great Anglo-Saxon relief organizations which then conducted the relief work in the Soviet Union. The matter in hand was an objective analysis of "four cannibals and eight corpse-eaters"; the report consists of statements by different doctors on their observations and examinations of these patients. The motives leading to these perversions are carefully stated. In one instance it was a mother who killed her husband, who was ill in consequence of the famine, in order to provide for the "surviving and hungry members of the family" food in the shape of a broth made from the dead man's flesh. The report is drawn up in proper form and signed by all the doctors present.

persons and children. These unfortunates were killed in secret so that their flesh might be eaten or even sold. The Moscow correspondent of the *Neue Freie Presse* has reported on these occurrences on the basis of judgments in the Courts. Professor Auhagen gives a similar account after hearing the statements of Russian refugees in the Schneidemühl camp. "Horrible cases of cannibalism are reported," he says. "There are 150 people in prison at Kiev for cannibalism." Mr. and Mrs. Stebalo, in the story of their Russian travels, say: "Human flesh and the flesh of animals which have died of disease is salted and dried. It is then minced and baked into rissoles. Not only the flesh of people who have died is eaten, but also that of persons who have been killed. A mother killed her sick son almost under the eyes of the other villagers in order to eat him. Nobody can feel sure of not being killed in his turn to-morrow. It is true that cannibalism is punished, but not nearly as severely as, say, the theft of a horse or a cow from the collective farm."

This account of the Stebalos tallies fully with the accounts of other witnesses, above all Harry Lang, and the letters of German settlers. One of these writes[1]: "There is cannibalism in the Russian villages. In one of these villages a son had eaten his father, so they tied his head round his neck and made him walk through the village."

The occurrence of cannibalism is also confirmed by the German specialist, mentioned several times above, who was able to visit every part of the country. He says: "Cases of cannibalism have undoubtedly occurred in the governments of Poltava and Chernigov. I was told the names of villages where they happened, for example Choshevatoy, a village close to Wynitsa, where the flesh of people who had died was eaten quite openly. The same thing happened at Maikop." Elsewhere he writes: "A woman left Moscow to visit her brother in a small town in the Ukraine, probably Kremenchug.

[1] In the *Deutsche Zeitung Bessarabiens*.

Her brother was an official there and had recently married. She stayed with him for several days and had taken food with her, for the ration in the town was only 500 grammes of maize every other day. Immediately on her arrival she was struck by the abnormal appearance of her brother and the absence of his wife. Upon her insistent inquiries after her sister-in-law her brother took her by the hand and led her to a dark closet, where she saw lying on the ground the woman's body, with clear traces of flesh having been torn away."

We have already pointed out that the children, as the weakest and least able to resist, were the principal victims of cannibalism. A few words may be added about the fate of the children in general, the children who have been the greatest sufferers from the course of events in the Soviet State.

Now that Moscow has largely succeeded in destroying the family and family life, the problem of destitute and neglected children, the so-called *bezprizornye*, is one of the chief troubles of the regime. Indeed, it may be claimed that in Russia, more than in any other country in the world, these suffering and neglected children form a problem of paramount importance, a fact which beyond dispute is most closely connected with the destruction of the family and of religious life. In May 1935 the official Moscow Tass agency published a report to the effect that the Council of People's Commissaries and the central committee of the party had adopted a decree "on the removal of the abuse of neglected and unsupervised children." The decree blames for the existing state of affairs "the bad work of the local organs and the lack of interest in the matter of the Soviet public." As happens so frequently in Russia, the removal of an abuse was simply undertaken out of hand through a decree. While the fate of numbers of children, left to their own devices, perishing in distress and neglect, is typical of Soviet life in general, this is particularly true of the famine areas, where there are special as well as general causes. The parents have either died of hunger or have fled in order to escape the famine, with the result that in these regions—especially in the towns—the number of neglected children has grown enormously. There is yet another reason why the lot of the children in the agricultural districts is particularly hard—the peculiar mental conflict to which they are exposed as guardians of the interests and principles of the Soviet State against their parents and other relatives. In collecting the harvest from the peasantry it has been one of Moscow's cardinal rules persistently to work upon the children and make them the guardians and supervisors of the interests and property of the State against their own parents. An incident reported in May 1934[1] will perhaps best serve to make the position clear. "Pronya Kolibin is the latest Communist 'hero,' " the message began. At the age of thirteen, it continued, he won the praise of the Soviet authorities for reporting that his mother was stealing grain from a collective farm in a district near Moscow. Such grain thefts are punishable with death. To reward Pronya for the betrayal of his mother the Soviet Government awarded him a cash gratuity. Pronya commemorated his mother's misdeeds in verses which were published in *Pravda*. Two lines run: "Mother, you do harm to the State; I can no longer live with you." The report ends by saying that it was not known whether the mother had used the stolen grain in order to supplement the rations of her children.

The case here dealt with is typical of what is going on in the various agricultural districts of Russia. It throws a light on the severe spiritual struggles which are taking place to-day between parents and children. Indeed, the catastrophe is remarkable as much for mental struggles and sufferings, a description of which lies outside the scope of this book, as for the physical sufferings and privations of the population.

[1] Reuter's Agency, May 21, 1934.

CHAPTER III

THE STRUGGLE OF THE NATIONALITIES

THE account of developments in the Soviet Union given in the first two chapters would be incomplete without some treatment of an attendant phenomenon of the "fight for bread" there described. Parallel to the fight for bread, a determined fight against the nationalities, their rights and their cultural individuality, has been carried on for some time. This struggle, too, may be regarded as, to a certain extent, a consequence of the famine.

Moscow has to secure the maintenance of the Soviet system and, in particular, the carrying out of the Five-Year Plan. It has, therefore, to collect the requisite quantities of grain to feed all the supporters of the existing order of things, which in the present conditions must necessarily lead to the complete exhaustion of the agrarian districts. As these regions are largely inhabited not by Russians but by other peoples and races, it follows that, apart from the great human tragedy of the famine, all national movements of the local populations are mercilessly attacked.

It is a matter of course that the peasants in the Ukraine, White Russia, Kazakstan, the German Volga region, etc., feel aggrieved at being drained for the benefit of Moscow, and the muttered grumblings in the different regions often break out into open protests, which the terrified and starved population is altogether too weak to emphasize by action. In view of the entire attitude of the Soviet regime it is inevitable that this dissatisfaction should be ascribed to the machinations of alleged "counter-revolutionaries," "saboteurs," or some "elements hostile to the State." The more so that the protests against Moscow's methods are actually accompanied by a stressing of local interests, and emanate from the intellectual class of the local population, such as the teachers, the doctors, the representatives of the newly created cultural institutions, and also the officials of the local Communist organizations. The most drastic steps are now being taken against this class— the so-called "national elements" among the Ukrainians, White Russians, Germans, Armenians, Finns, Bulgars and the rest, even if they have hitherto been the most convinced Communists. Obviously the fight for bread must be greatly exacerbated by the introduction of this national element—must, indeed, assume quite a new character.

The figment that Europe has abandoned development on national lines has long been exploded. All those who dreamed of the birth of a "European nation," one single nationless European mankind, have been sadly disappointed. Nationalism and national peculiarities are emphasized once more, and it is they that form the key-note of developments in Europe. Non-national pacifists have proved wrong, and those who believe that international understanding can be reached, if at all, only by admitting the existence of divergent nationalities, have been proved right, which applies also to those who see in the mutual recognition of national rights (and hence of the rights of minorities) a first condition of such an understanding. And present conditions in the Soviet Union confirm the correctness of this view.

To understand the full scope of the national struggle which has blazed up in the Soviet Union, I must touch briefly on Lenin's policy with regard to nationalism during and after the foundation of the Soviet State. When Lenin arrived at St. Petersburg with his companions in that special train which had carried him across Europe, he not only promised the expectant throng "bread and peace," but also assured the millions who had lived under Tsarism as so-called "aliens" that they should have full freedom to develop on national lines and that local states on ethnographic principles should be formed within the Federated Soviet Republic. Now at that time the old guard of "national Communists" from the Ukraine, White Russia, the Caucasus, etc., stood by his side. These were men who, in view of the centralization and chauvinism of St. Petersburg, had all their lives made their social demands go hand in hand with the nationalist aspirations of their peoples and races. Thus Lenin's "old guard," while revolutionaries, were also to a large extent supporters of the national aspirations of their peoples. Only thus had they been able to gather a large number of adherents, despite the fact that Communism on principle rejects nationalism. Of these old comrades drawn from the "alien" peoples in Russia, the chief was Lenin's old friend, the Ukrainian Skrypnik. He shared in the foundation of the Soviet Union and, until his death, remained Deputy-President of the Council of People's Commissaries. He shares with Lenin the merit of having, in the establishment and construction of the Soviet State, given full weight to the ethnographical element.

The peoples and races of the old Empire which thus obtained a nationhood of their own undoubtedly felt that the structure of the new Soviet State meant a victory over St. Petersburg's centralism. There had always been a contradiction between the realization of pure Communism as envisaged by Lenin, and the fulfilment of those wide national aspirations which St. Petersburg had denied all right to national distinction. It is significant that the representatives of these various nationalities in the first Duma immediately formed a "union of supporters of autonomy." To Lenin, who steadily aimed at the realization of a non-national world communism, this recognition of local nationality—as his successors in Moscow continually insist to-day—was merely a period of transition in order, as Postyschev recently put it, to bring about "socialism of Lenin's stamp" (in other words, Communism) under a national disguise. Two tendencies thus met: that of pure Communism and its exponents, who watched nationalist tendencies in various parts of the Union with the greatest suspicion, and the efforts of those who attempted locally to bring about a compromise between Communism and the national-cultural movements of the peoples and races. It is significant that Moscow saw in the local universities, academies of science, etc., only a means of putting the local languages at the service of Communism. In this respect the experiences of eminent foreign visitors to the Jewish Scientific Institute at Kiev, quoted elsewhere, speak clearly.

Simultaneously, the local Communists of nationalist tendencies at Kiev, Minsk and elsewhere were attempting to do justice to the national individuality of their peoples within the framework of the Communist State. Inevitably, in the autonomous Soviet republics, local and national peculiarities came in practice to be strongly emphasized, and in this respect local Communists even co-operated with former bourgeois elements. Despite all the obstacles interposed by Moscow, local cultural life began to develop. Above all, schools were built. As these steps were taken under the leadership of local Communists and indeed simply expressed their desires, and were certainly not due to intrigues by mysterious counter-revolutionary circles (as has been maintained more recently), no resistance could for the time being be offered by Moscow. There is no doubt that throughout this period Moscow had to simulate a satisfaction which it was far from feeling. It had already recognized that this stressing of the national element stood in contradiction to pure Communism, which is a supernational order. Wherever it was possible the influence of national forces was opposed. Some time ago a German author discovered that the boasted nationalities policy of Moscow aimed at anything but the cherishing of the national-cultural interests of the various peoples and races within the territory of the Soviet Union. The national desires of the local populations were considered up to a certain point only because it was impossible to disregard them.

The famine, with all its attendant phenomena, changed this

position altogether. The local Communists resisted, as far as possible, the drastic measures for the collection of grain in their starving districts. And so, in due course, the "fight for bread" came to be accompanied by the "fight against local nationalist tendencies" as the real foundation of the machinations of all enemies of the State, *kulaks* and grain saboteurs. A reckoning with the local Communists, to whom this development was due, though long avoided, had now become inevitable; and at last the Government proceeded to eliminate every stressing of local and national peculiarity as inimical to the State and the regime. A tardy justice was done to one of the first demands of theoretical Communism. Naturally the fight was fiercest in the Ukraine, which, next to Great Russia, is the biggest of the federative republics of the Soviet State.

At the last Communist Congress at Moscow the representatives of the various districts inhabited by distinct nationalities rose one after another and declared that, in the collection of the harvest and the fight against national movements, things had gone exactly as Postyschev had expounded in his great speech before the Congress about the Ukraine. Gikalo spoke for White Russia, Mirsoian for Kazakstan, and so on. And, indeed, events in the various regions simply were a reflection of the happenings in the Ukraine. Thanks to Postyschev's statement and other reports from Soviet sources, much more is known about developments in the Ukraine than in the case of many other regions. It will, therefore, be expedient to describe the course of events in the Ukraine and, having taken this region as an example, to deal briefly with the course of events among the White Russians, Georgians, Germans, Jews, etc.

It is superfluous here to take sides in the dispute whether the Ukrainians are an independent people or, as many Russians claim, are only one tribe of those that form the Russian nation. It is enough to say that to-day even nationalist Russians mostly hold the view that Ukrainian claims to ethnographical individuality and hence to freedom to develop on local cultural lines must be recognized, even if Russia is to be regarded as a single organism for political and economic purposes. It seems to me important that this should be made clear, for I am of the opinion that the Soviet measures against the national-cultural movement in the Ukraine are by no means, as is sometimes asserted, according to the desires of the non-Communist Russians. Least of all are they in accordance with the views held by leaders of the Russian minorities in such countries as Estonia, Latvia, Lithuania, Poland, Czecho-Slovakia and Roumania (Bessarabia).

Baron Steinheil, the president of the Union of Russian Minorities in Poland, expressed this view in his New Year's manifesto of 1934. "The Ukrainian question must be cleared up," he said. ". . . We must admit that part of the population [meaning that of the Ukrainian districts of Poland] describes itself as the Ukrainian people." Baron Steinheil goes on to say that such a view conflicts with the historical truth that this population actually forms part of the greater Russian stock. Nevertheless, it is the case that the Ukrainians are distinguished by special peculiarities of language and tradition. "In view of all these circumstances," he said, "our policy must be not opposition to Ukrainianism as a distinctive feature, but opposition to Separatism."

Baron Steinheil thus clearly declared that the Russian minorities oppose only Ukrainian separatism, but do not deny that the Ukrainians form a distinct ethnographic group. Finally he has a word to say in criticism of the Great Russian chauvinists. "The Separatist movement is promoted not only by the *Samostiniki* [Separatists], but also sometimes by people who stand on the Great Russian platform, but fail to recognize the many valuable properties of local peculiarity and confuse it with separatism. . . ." The manifesto concludes as follows: "It is, therefore, of the utmost importance to clear up the whole situation and to seek to promote a feeling of respect for all the historic peculiarities of the populations of Volhynia, Galicia and Polessya, but not to foment a chauvinism which can do nothing but harm to the true Russian ideal."

Between 1916 and 1919 a spontaneous national awakening can be traced among the Ukrainians of the former Russian Empire, as well as among various other peoples. This, as is well known, happened much earlier among the Ukrainians of the old Austro-Hungarian monarchy. This awakening took place at the time of the Ukrainian Rada—that is immediately after the collapse of Tsarism—and continued vigorously while General Skoropadsky was hetman and under the domination of Petlura. It was based on the ancient traditions slumbering within the people and on the consciousness of Ukrainian national individuality.

Then Bolshevism came into power in the Ukraine. At the head of the Ukrainian Soviet Republic, a part of the Soviet Union, was a pure-blooded Ukrainian, Lenin's friend Skrypnik. In this period also the national consciousness and cultural development of the Ukrainians made further progress. Not that the Communists under Skrypnik's leadership had any separatist tendencies. But they were all filled with the consciousness of the distinctive nature of their people and the special mission of their nationality within the frame of the composite Soviet State. Consequently they considered themselves justified in vigorously maintaining the linguistic and cultural rights of their people in the Soviet Ukraine.

How the views of these Ukrainians differ from those of such exponents of Moscow's policy as Stalin's friend Postyschev is best seen from the dispute in connection with the law on the utilization of land in the Soviet Union. The first paragraph of this momentous law provides that all land is to be regarded as the property of the U.S.S.R. On this Skrypnik commented as follows: "The new law lays down that the land is not the property of the Republic, i.e. the Ukraine, but of the entire Soviet Union. The acceptance of such a law would mean that the sovereignty of the different Soviet republics consisted in the possession of a separate government, but not of a separate territory. In my view such tendencies should be vigorously opposed." In other words, Skrypnik wished the Soviet Union to be really a federation of independent peoples with territories of their own, and not a structure of states autonomous only in name.

Another utterance of Skrypnik's well illustrates this standpoint of the Ukrainian Communists. "I protest," he declared, "against the foundation of an all-Russian Agricultural College, i.e. an agricultural college for the entire Soviet Union. There is not an atom of sense in creating such a college, for the time has come to depart from a policy which would make this college an all-Soviet institute." (It is significant that, after Skrypnik's death, the agricultural college at Kiev was radically reorganized by Postyschev.)

Postyschev, in his speech in December 1933, characterized the attitude of Skrypnik and his Communist adherents in the Ukraine as follows: "Skrypnik resisted all totalitarian movements literally with the bayonet. In the Union of Soviet Republics he saw a kind of league of nations, where people would meet from time to time and talk, but which was to have no real influence on the life and work of the various constituent republics. Local nationalism does not see what unites and brings together the working masses of the nationalities of the Soviet Union, but what separates them."

Skrypnik and his friends represented what may be called a Ukrainian brand of Communism, combined with a strong insistence on regional and national interests. Whether such an attitude is in the long run compatible with the principles of the Soviet State is another question. It may be assumed that even without the famine a conflict between the Ukrainians and the Russian Communists would have come and that the famine only accelerated it. In any case the way in which the Moscow Communists looked upon Skrypnik and his friends is characteristic.

Stalin's remarks at the seventeenth Party Congress are particularly illuminating. "The essence of local nationalism consists in the tendency for the group to separate itself and shut itself up in its own national shell; in the endeavour to cloak class conflict within the nation; in the endeavour thus to seek protection from Great Russian chauvinism, at the same time moving aside from the general stream of Socialist reconstruction; in the endeavour not to see everything which binds together and unites the working masses of the nationalities within the Soviet State, and to see only what separates and divides them."

If the utterances of the two representatives of Communism, at Moscow and Kiev, are contrasted, the magnitude of the difference in the basic views of the two tendencies within the Communist Party will be realized; the more so since the views of the Ukrainian Communists agree with those of many Communists in White Russia, the Caucasus, Kazakstan, and other districts having a non-Russian population.

Is any compromise possible between these two tendencies? Or is it the case, as Postyschev later stated in one of his big speeches, that the recognition of local cultural rights on a national basis must inevitably lead to a conflict with the principle of the international proletariat as the ultimate factor and basis of the relation between the various peoples and the Soviet State?

In any case it is clear that the views of Skrypnik and his adherents have nothing to do with the machinations of any separatists abroad. But the position taken up by the Skrypnik group had the result that the foundation of the Ukrainian Soviet State was followed by a vigorous increase of national-cultural work in the Ukrainian schools, in the publication of Ukrainian books, etc. The ci-devant bourgeois Ukrainian intelligentsia, some of whom had been recalled from abroad, took part in this work. Certainly there may have been among them people who aimed at the restoration of a non-Communist order and possibly were connected with certain foreign

circles. Yet generally speaking it may be claimed that Skrypnik's fellow-workers, like him, aimed solely at the promotion
of Ukrainian cultural interests and were glad to be able to serve
them in the Ukrainian Soviet State. The indisputable loyalty
to the Soviet of Skrypnik and the other Ukrainian Communists
fully guaranteed this—as did the presence of the Ogpu, which,
in the Ukraine as elsewhere, is, as a matter of course, always
fully informed about the relations between the local elements
and foreign countries.

A definite change in the situation took place only when the
collectivization of agriculture and all its attendant phenomena
began. The consequences were naturally felt with particular
severity in the Ukraine, as a purely agricultural region. The
ruined Ukrainian agriculture and the Ukrainian peasants were
exploited to the last degree for the maintenance of the Communist regime in Great Russia. When the conditions became
more and more terrible and men began to die in multitudes,
the inevitable happened: Skrypnik and the Ukrainian Communists protested openly. They stepped vigorously into the
breach on behalf of their perishing countrymen against the
fearful injury wrought by collectivization; they demanded
that the bread produced by the Ukrainian peasantry should be
used first to safeguard their own lives, and only the surplus
should be handed over to Moscow and the rest of the Soviet
Union. But the Kremlin, determined to continue its "historic
experiment," would not accept the demands of the Ukrainians
and began to see, in the rise of a national resistance movement
in the Ukraine and elsewhere, dangerous separatist tendencies.

On December 14, 1932, the Central Committee of the
Communist Party and the Council of People's Commissaries
in Moscow passed the above-mentioned resolution for the
elimination of "bourgeois nationalist" elements from all party
and Soviet organizations. Further, the Central Committee of
the Ukrainian Communist Party and the Council of Ukrainian
People's Commissaries were officially requested carefully to

examine the personnel of the Communist organizations in the Ukraine and to watch systematically all efforts towards Ukrainianization. According to a later statement by Postyschev this resolution of December 14 was the beginning of the ten months' struggle carried on by Moscow in the Ukraine—not only in order to bring in the harvest, but also to crush local nationalism. Obviously Skrypnik and his adherents could not submit to this decisive blow. The Ukrainian delegates in Moscow opposed the passing of the resolution and, dramatically enough, were arrested in an open session of the Central Committee of the Communist Party. Stalin's inexorable resolution was once again fully manifested.

Things now developed with increasing rapidity. Hitherto the Ukrainian Government (the Council of People's Commissaries of the Ukrainian Soviet Republic) had been autonomous within the frame of the Soviet Union: it was now subordinated to Moscow's proconsul, the Great Russian Postyschev. The latter forthwith proceeded to Kharkov, to start the battle on the spot. It is significant that Moscow could no longer entrust a Ukrainian with this task, and selected for this purpose Postyschev, a Russian Communist particularly devoted to Stalin, who had once saved a part of Soviet territory in the Far East from Japanese invasion. Postyschev, a man whose very features reveal an unflagging energy, seemed to Stalin the right man to bend the Ukrainians once and for all beneath the will of Moscow. His instructions were not only to break all resistance to the gathering of the harvest, but to obliterate everything resembling the stressing of a distinctive Ukrainian nationality. Whether his mission cost the lives of hundreds, or thousands, or even millions, was all the same to him, for on its success the existence of the Soviet Russian economic system depended. His opponents were the starving peasants and the various Ukrainian officials who supported them.

The extent of the struggle, and the fact that it did not confine itself to the persecution of a few important or particularly incriminated persons, but was directed against all nationalist elements, whether Communists or otherwise, is apparent from Postyschev's speech delivered in October 1933 on the conclusion of his campaign. He believed that "counter-revolutionaries" and "agents of foreign countries" had established themselves everywhere, who, together with the leaders of the Ukrainian *émigrés* abroad, were attempting, in Postyschev's words, to bring the workers and the rest of the population of the Ukraine once more under the domination of Polish magnates, German barons and British interventionists. According to Postyschev these endeavours were supported by thousands of misguided Ukrainian Communists in all the party organizations. They had crept into every field of activity, whether in the cultural, the economic or the educational sphere. They had penetrated even into influential circles and the leading positions in the Ukrainian Communist Party. They were in the collective farms, the Soviet farms, the agricultural offices, in the People's Commissariat for Education, and in certain departments of the Treasury, where they did the enemy's work.

Postyschev then specifically attacked the People's Commissariat for Agriculture. There, he said, a band of counter-revolutionaries had been at work for years as members of the college of the People's Commissariat, as presidents of sections and as heads of groups. Their counter-revolutionary activity was reflected in the position of agriculture and the course of collectivization. They had penetrated especially into the agricultural administration to prevent the proper organization of agriculture. "They penetrated into various sections of the agricultural planning department, in order, by their own plans, to hamper the collection of grain and increase the supply difficulties in the country."

Thus even the fact that the Ukrainian Communists protested against the intolerable burdening of the peasants by the excessive demands made in the plans is described by

Postyschev as an "intrigue" in the interests of foreign capital and to the counter-revolutionary activities of *émigrés*.

But most significant of all are Postyschev's remarks on Skrypnik's own department, the Commissariat for Education, and the whole system of education in the Ukraine. "For years," he says, "the representatives of all kinds of Ukrainian counter-revolutionary tendencies held numerous posts in this department." According to him all that they did was "to bring about by propaganda a breach between the Ukrainian peasants and workers and the workers of other nationalities, especially the workers of Russian nationality employed in the collective farms"—a most striking admission of the dimensions attained by the movement of protest and resistance in the Ukraine. It ought, by the way, to be clear that the growing antagonism in the Ukraine to Great Russian Communist workers imported from outside was, with men dying in multitudes, an inevitable and uncontrollable phenomenon. "All these elements," Postyschev continued, "attempted at the same time to promote disaffection against the Soviet power among teachers, students and others."

These words of the dictator reveal the position in the Ukraine in a vivid light. So the widest circles of the Ukrainian intelligentsia had entered the struggle; teachers, students, Soviet officials, all thought it their duty to protest against a further sucking dry of the country. Future historians will have to admit that in its campaign against the Ukrainians, during the spring and summer of 1933, the Soviet regime was faced by a united people, a solid front, including everyone, from the highest Soviet officials down to the poorest peasant. (In view of these facts it is surely grotesque that M. Herriot and others should have adopted the Moscow catch-phrase about the whole of the trouble being due to separatist machinations instigated by foreign influences.

It seems to be the fact that this national movement of protest was headed by the All-Ukrainian Academy of Science, where, according to Postyschev, "a considerable number of nationalists were congregated." But further argument to the effect that, under the cloak of the Academy, "an open chauvinist propaganda for the separation of the Ukraine from the Soviet Union was set on foot" has a more than incredible ring. He says: "It is a fact that in 1930, in the schoolbook *The History of Ukrainian Culture*, the Ukrainians expressed the following view: 'In its relation to Asia the Ukraine has always been culturally a corner of Europe, and it is impossible to appreciate its culture and its art without this connection with European art. Ukrainian art is a part of the general European process of evolution.'" Imagine this truth, to which no one is likely to take exception, being used by Postyschev to claim that the Kiev Academy had demanded that Ukrainian culture should look towards the west and away from "Asiatic Moscow"! (his own quotation marks). What would M. Herriot say—M. Herriot, who declared that the synthesis between Moscow centralism and Ukrainian nationalism had been achieved—if he learned that a remark like the one just quoted was enough to render the Ukrainian Academy suspect of separatism and even of treason?

Postyschev's judgment on Ukrainian art and literature is summary and unburdened by investigation or reflection. "Nationalistic productions of a unique insolence and blatancy which for years filled the libraries and bookshops, in order to instil the poison of chauvinism into various groups of workers and Soviet farm labourers." It would be hard to announce more clearly than Postyschev does here that the campaign directed against Ukrainian Communists of every grade, against teachers, the students and the intellectual classes in their entirety, was not directed against the alleged treason of "the agents of Sir Henri Deterding,[1] the Polish magnates and the German barons," but solely and exclusively against the Ukrainian national-cultural aspirations as such.

The second task in Postyschev's campaign in the Ukraine was "to introduce proved Bolshevik elements in every depart-

---

[1] The well-known oil magnate.

ment" and to build up "a Ukrainian Soviet culture" under Bolshevist guidance. Postyschev had not only a negative aim— to destroy the old nationalist movement, which included the elimination of the Skrypnik group; he had also a positive ambition—to build up a Ukrainian Soviet culture by new methods. He has stated precisely what he means by this, and I shall deal with this matter later.

According to Postyschev the national-cultural ambitions of a people are incompatible with the ideal of the Communist International. He is apparently not aware that this admission removes at one blow all foundation for his charge that the machinations of foreign counter-revolutionaries are the cause of the protest movement in the Ukraine. In discussing Skrypnik's sins, he says: "Skrypnik has shown clearly that any attempt by a Communist to harmonize proletarian internationalism with nationalism must lead him into the camp of nationalist counter-revolutionaries." In other words, Postyschev admits that his campaign in the Ukraine is intended to prevent the recurrence of attempts to bring nationalist aspirations into harmony with proletarian internationalism, as Skrypnik sought to do on grounds of the deepest conviction. His declaration further implies that any movement intended to foster the national individuality of the Ukraine, its art and literature, will henceforth meet with the most rigorous repression, since in his view all compromises lead only to separatism and counter-revolution.

An exhaustive description of all the steps taken by Moscow during its fight against the Ukrainian population would lead us too far. It is not my task to describe this struggle. I must confine myself to the description of those steps which were particularly far-reaching and of direct bearing on the subject under discussion. The most important of these was the purging of the Communist Party of all unreliable elements. This purge was carried out all over the Soviet Union; but it had quite a special object in the Ukraine, White Russia and other districts having non-Russian populations. Postyschev directed particular attention to the elimination of all Skrypnik's adherents. The purge here was simply the execution of a mass sentence on all the "nationally suspicious elements." Any Ukrainian who had the courage to take the line that the country's most valuable possession, its men and women, must be saved from destruction, was expelled from the party and from his post, i.e. from the possibility of earning any livelihood. About twenty-five per cent of the members of the Ukrainian Communist Party were thus rendered destitute; and in April 1933 it became known that some of them had even been arrested and executed. It is claimed that the People's Vice-Commissary for Agriculture, the Communist Markevitch, who had been decorated with the highest Russian order, the Red Flag, had been secretly condemned and shot.

The real object of the purge becomes clear from the following statement contained in the organ of the Central Committee of the Communist Party in the Ukraine, the Kharkov "Communist" (June 2, 1933). The leading article contains this passage: "A number of grave defects in the work of the party in the Ukraine, most convincingly revealed by Stalin at the session of the Central Committee in January, are clear proof that the chief fault of the Ukrainian party organization consists in a relaxation of Bolshevist zeal in dealing with the class enemies. The purge has revealed certain conditions within the party—in the All-Ukrainian Academy of Science at Kiev, in the Wynitsa district, etc.; these, with the presence of nominal Communists of bourgeois sympathies, and adventurers, in the Odessa grain trust and other organizations is proof positive that the relaxation of our party vigilance and zeal has allowed remnants of the *kulaks* and adherents of Petlura to creep into the ranks of the party. Covered by their membership cards they attempt to weaken the dictatorship of the proletariat, to undermine collective farming, and to divert cultural interests into bourgeois and nationalist channels."

In this connection the purge of the party centre of the All-Ukrainian Academy of Science at Kiev offers an instructive example. This, the most important Ukrainian institute, was to have been converted into a bulwark of national-bourgeois "science." All the sworn apologists of Nationalism (there follows a long list of names) had wormed their way into the party and tried to sabotage Socialist reconstruction by falsifying or misinterpreting the theory of Marx and Lenin. Certain Communist leaders, selected by the party to supervise the work of the Academy, succumbed to the insidious work of the Nationalists, who, supported by the reactionary elements within the Academy, were working eagerly to hamper or destroy the work of loyal and zealous members. Equally instructive evidence of the sabotage due to hostile elements possessing the party card was furnished by the purge in the Wynitsa district.

The extent of the purge in the Ukraine appears from a second statement in the same issue of the *Communist*. "In four districts in the Ukraine, the Donetz, Kiev, Odessa and Wynitsa, the purge of the party organizations is in progress. The first results prove the political importance of this measure, whose sole object is to increase and secure the fighting capacity of the party. It is the object of the Ukrainian Party organization not only to strengthen the party machinery, but also to make an end of the eternal lagging behind of the Ukraine in the sphere of agriculture." The purge continued until late autumn, and on October 25 it was reported from Kiev that the Government had published the names of certain high officials of the Ukrainian Communist Party, Zaslavsky, Karatchevsky and Rybak, who had had the courage openly to protest against the ruinous system of taxes (deliveries in kind) employed against their countrymen. They were immediately relieved of their posts and accused of Trotskyism and counter-revolution. Numbers of other officials had to follow them.

Always the same! Whether in White Russia, the Ukraine or

elsewhere, as soon as murmurs of protest are heard among the starving masses, when, despite all violent measures of the Ogpu, the agitation increases, and even local Communists take up the cudgels for their countrymen's rights, the cry goes up that the unity and peace of the Soviet Union are threatened by separatists and saboteurs. The local Communists, however, resist expulsion by Moscow's "Political Sections," which are generally controlled by men despatched by Moscow to the local centres.

The systematic consistency with which the activity of the Political Sections—as a first and decisive step towards the suppression of local resistance—was prepared and carried out by Moscow, is shown by a speech by the recently appointed Commissary for Agriculture, Jakovliev, at the Moscow Party Congress. He explained how a special agricultural department, under the chairmanship of Kaganovitch, had been formed at the Central Committee of the Communist Party to organize the special machinery of the Political Sections. Jakovliev admitted that, with the help of the latter, "tens of thousands" had been dismissed from the agricultural organizations alone. The entire system of Political Sections, like the party purge, was intended to effect a radical reform of the political and bureaucratic structure within the Soviet Union, substituting the influence of Moscow for that of the local authorities.

The campaign against the peasants now reached its climax. The decree about the collection of grain had aroused furious resentment, among not only producers but the whole of the local population. Any attempt by the starving peasants to take grain from the fields or to hide part of it, every protest by Ukrainian Nationalists, was crushed: Postyschev, the Political Sections and martial law held the field.

Yet even Postyschev had to admit that the resistance he had alleged to be fomented from abroad was in reality due to the "measures taken by the party to force the country's agriculture into a Socialist channel"; in other words, to Stalin's general agricultural policy. "This period" (i.e. that of collectivization), he stated, "was characterized by an immediate intensification of the nationalist counter-revolutionary activity."

The famine, which was now reaching its climax in the death of millions of persons, had brought even the most loyal Ukrainian Communists to revolt against Moscow and Postyschev. Skrypnik was still alive and was in a position to make a last stand. Indeed, Moscow and Postyschev were fully aware that the victory was still incomplete so long as Skrypnik held his post at the head of the devoted Ukrainians.

The clash between Postyschev and Skrypnik, the hand-to-hand fight, took place on June 10, 1933, the day on which the Central Committee of the Communist Party of the Ukraine met at Kharkov. For the last time the proconsul from Moscow, backed by the entire power of the Soviet Union, and the champion of the Ukrainian people, who on this occasion was appearing in this capacity and not as the exponent of Communist ideas, stood face to face. But the issue was already decided. Postyschev had the task of publicly denouncing Skrypnik as an enemy of the State and as the cause of every difficulty, in order to justify his expulsion. Skrypnik's mission was to express, however vainly, the protest of the Ukrainians against the ruin of their land, the death of their countrymen and the suppression of every cultural movement in the Ukraine.

He was the first to speak. The text of his speech has not been published and is not likely to be. But Postyschev's reply has been reported in the Soviet press and affords a clue to Skrypnik's arguments. He seems above all to have denied the assertion that disaffected Ukrainian Communists were acting as enemies of the State and tools of anti-Soviet movements, and to have urged that the new situation brought about by the methods of force and exploitation employed against the people could only lead to protests against the policy of Moscow on the part of those intellectuals and Communists now being charged with nationalism. He further showed that the chief reason for the collapse of Ukrainian agriculture must be looked for in the steps taken by Moscow and the suppression of local freedom and initiative by Moscow centralism.

What was Postyschev's answer? He shouted in Skrypnik's face that it amounted to high treason to say things of the kind from a public platform, on which the attention of millions of Communists and non-Communists was centred. It was not the attitude of individuals, he went on, that had altered; the trouble was that the enemies, party card in hand, had been hiding "behind Skrypnik's broad back" to prepare and carry out their destructive work. Skrypnik's argument that Moscow had dissolved the local bodies in order to centralize everything was described as "hostile gossip."

Postyschev then proceeded, amidst the thunderous applause of his adherents, to attack Skrypnik's activities and personality. He claimed that it was Skrypnik's own department, the Commissariat of Education, which contained the greatest number of "harmful counter-revolutionary and nationalistic elements," and that no steps had ever been taken against these "poisoners" and "spies." He further declared that Skrypnik's sins were not confined to his actions, but appeared also in his writings on the national question and on cultural reconstruction, and, indeed, were manifested in the entire administration of his department. Thus, before an applauding crowd of his partisans, he openly poured scorn on one of the founders of Bolshevism and the vice-president of the Council of People's Commissaries of the Ukrainian Soviet State!

Thus Skrypnik was branded from the platform of his own party Congress, and before the whole Soviet public, as a class enemy and as a protector, indeed a leader, of all the counter-revolutionaries and agents of the foreign anti-Communists. Such was the reply to his protests in the name of the Ukraine. His career, of course, was ended; Moscow had delivered him over to public contempt. With him his adherents were condemned, and it was only a logical conclusion when, a few days later, the news of Skrypnik's suicide sped through the world. The report of his death was published at Moscow in a *communiqué* (July 8, 1933) saying that he had become the "victim of bourgeois and nationalist elements," who, under the cloak of formal party membership, had gained his confidence and misused his name for their anti-Soviet and nationalistic aims. Skrypnik had fallen into their toils and committed a series of political errors. When he recognized these errors he had taken his life.

For ten long months Postyschev fought with the starving population of the Ukraine to collect bread and extirpate every national movement. The population replied by the one means at its disposal—passive resistance, which only too often meant death. An Austrian engineer who witnessed these events declared that the attitude of these Ukrainian peasants, who refused to surrender their nationality and their attachment to the soil, revealed a silent heroism.

Skrypnik had been removed and the last obstacle in Moscow's fight against the Ukraine was gone. Moscow could now be as ruthless as it pleased. Further measures were taken which severely restricted Ukrainian autonomy in the legal sphere. Also on July 21, 1933, a few days after Skrypnik's death, a decree was issued appointing one public prosecutor for the whole Soviet Union—the *coup de grâce* to the autonomy of the judicial system. A *communiqué* issued in this connection contains the following passage: "The Central Committee has created the new office of a public prosecutor of the Union, to whom the Ogpu, the militia, and all the organs of justice will be subordinated." Thus by this decree the entire judicial system and even the fate of the individual Ukrainian State officials was made to depend directly on Moscow.

Towards the end of the summer of 1933 conditions in the country, as at Kiev and Kharkov, were terrible. But Postyschev declined to diverge a hair's breadth from the prescribed line. He proudly proclaimed that he did not know the meaning of leniency (in contrast to the People's Commissary for Supply, Mikoian, who had been so shocked by conditions as he found them in Kiev as early as Easter that he had all the army stores handed over to the population at twenty distributing centres). All resistance had now been broken.

But the enforced silence did not really mean the end of the nationalist movement in the Ukraine, nor did it prove that the will to preserve the national individuality had been crushed.

On March 2, 1934, *Pravda* reported that "5,000 different persons" had been recalled from the village Soviets of the Kiev district because "they were unworthy to be members of the Soviets." The same issue reported that in Soviet Armenia two hundred members of the party, including ninety presidents of local councils, had been removed, whence *Pravda* concluded that "everything was not yet in order." The purge, in other words, was continuing systematically, and thousands of local officials were being displaced in favour of more docile elements.

With this end in view the Soviet Government took another important step. In the speech mentioned previously, the Commissary for Agriculture, Jakovliev, mentioned that a special commission existed at Moscow under his chairmanship whose function it was to confirm the appointment of directors, senior agricultural experts, accountants, etc., at the motor and tractor stations of the entire Soviet Union, and that from 20 to 50 per cent of these local officials had already been removed. The Moscow Commission confirms and does not appoint; yet clearly in practice Moscow can interfere in the most important agricultural appointments made by the local authorities. In other words, the right of the autonomous districts to appoint their own officials has become illusory: Moscow despatches its servants into the districts, and it is they who control everything down to the most inferior posts. Often the local authorities oppose the new arrivals, and although passive resistance is their only weapon, the struggle is a hard one. This friction between local officials and the men of Moscow appears from an open letter published in *Pravda*, in which officials despatched to the Turcoman region complained bitterly that they nowhere obtained the salaries due to them, and nowhere work; people told them to their faces: "We did not ask for you, we have our own candidates for these posts." In the long run, however, resistance is unavailing; and the Moscow emissaries penetrate everywhere.

For White Russia the deputy to the Moscow Party Congress, Gikalo, is perhaps the best source of information. According to him, "the fight for the correct prosecution of Lenin's policy in dealing with the nationalities as carried on in White Russia does not differ from that in the Ukraine." Here again the alleged "machinations of noxious elements" have to be checkmated. Gikalo praises the resolution of the Central Committee of the Communist Party adopted in December 1932; a resolution which for White Russia, too, initiated a change in Moscow's policy towards the local population. He pointed particularly to the fact that the resolution contained valuable information about the "alleged national flag behind which certain counter-revolutionary elements and their counter-revolutionary activities were hiding." In the capital, Minsk, a complete reorganization of the Academy of Science and of other institutions, in other words an elimination of every endeavour to preserve national individualism, was carried out, and nationalist elements were expelled from the Communist Party and the Soviet institutions. According to Gikalo, "as late as 1933, while the activity of the party organization was considerable, and the number of workers was large, counter-revolutionary elements succeeded in finding a way into the Soviet administration and even into the party organization." According to him, the fault is due to a diminishing "Bolshevik watchfulness in the face of nationalist counter-revolutionary elements" and to "nationalistic errors" which were suffered to exist within the local party organizations—the familiar catchword. Any manifestation of White Russian individualism is declared to be inadmissible.

What is particularly interesting is Gikalo's statement that the fight against nationalism in White Russia began with what is called "a case of pure nationality politics"—that of the teacher Stepura, who had been locally forbidden to speak Russian to his wife. The case showed that "everything was not in order in the White Russian party organization; when, early in 1933, we began investigations into this matter, we found it necessary to take decisive measures. As in the Ukraine, so here we were too blind to perceive the manœuvres of the class enemy even as late as 1933. Now he has been crushed in a number of fields; but that is not enough."

Particularly interesting is Gikalo's description of "twenty days' experiences in December 1932" (the consequence of Moscow's "declaration of war" in the December decree). The experiences show that "when the Bolsheviks proceed on Bolshevik lines, they know no obstacles. . . . In twenty days more grain was collected than in the previous three and a half months. . . ." By January 1 the plan had been fulfilled 106 per cent, to say nothing of the potatoes, butter, hay, etc., collected. It is easy to imagine the methods by which the grain was taken from the peasants if such quantities could be collected in twenty days in the middle of winter.

Parallel to the collection of grain the famine[1] was accompanied by the fight against nationalist movements, and more especially against the local Jewish minority—of which I shall speak again later.

On April 3 the official Swiss News Agency, whose reports are based on reliable sources, mainly official, published the following item: "It is reported from Soviet Russia that the peasants are once again practising sabotage by slaughtering quantities of cattle. In the Kostjukova district alone more than 15,000 head were recently destroyed. There are similar reports from other parts of Soviet Russia. The Minsk *Orka* explains

---

[1] The famine in White Russia is described by Harry Lang in the Jewish *Forward*, New York.

these phenomena by the counter-revolutionary activity of *kulaks* and White Russian nationalists." Comment would be superfluous. The report shows clearly that the national struggle continues unchanged.

The lot of the Finns within the Soviet State to-day is also particularly hard. It is true that their position is theoretically more advantageous than that of most of the other nations and groups, for at the signing of the Peace of Dorpat Finland succeeded in inducing Russia to make a binding declaration in favour of the Finnish population of Karelia, as well as of the Finns of Ingermanland (near Leningrad). By thus entering the lists on behalf of the Finns who have lived outside Finland for centuries, the latter state was the first to make a hole in the doctrine of non-interference in the affairs of the nationals of another state. Finland is the only state which has succeeded in enforcing the view that it is the elementary right of every nation to intervene on behalf of its kinsmen outside its own frontiers when their lives and means of existence are threatened.

Unlike the pure Finns of Ingermanland, the Karelians are a separate race of Finnish origin, and were promised by the Soviets administrative autonomy and the maintenance of their educational and linguistic rights. Soon, however, it was seen that these concessions were being rendered nugatory by a number of breaches in practice. No arrangements were made for any right of supervision to ensure that the promises were being kept, with the result that the so-called autonomy of Karelia—which in theory is an independent people's republic within the framework of the Soviet State—is entirely subordinate to the dictates of Moscow. Again, a settlement of the frontiers of the autonomous region had been omitted, and the result of the arrangement subsequently enforced by Moscow was that to-day the Karelians constitute no more than one-third of the population of this region. The Soviet regime—according to a fully documented exposé furnished by the Karelian Academic Union of Helsingfors—soon proceeded to

Carrying on everyday conversation regardless of the corpse by the roadside

A child dead from starvation to whom passers-by pay no attention

Body of famine victim lying on the roadside

Another famine victim lying in a field

THE STRUGGLE OF THE NATIONALITIES 129

subject the Karelians and the other Finns within the Soviet Union to a policy of repression and destruction.[1]

In the first place the amnesty provided in the Treaty of Dorpat was not observed, and numbers who should have benefited from it were banished. Next, peasants from the interior were forcibly settled in Karelia, and by 1933 the percentage of these people amounted to 15 per cent of the total. The introduction of collectivization brought with it a hard time for the population, as for others of the nationalities. The peasants, attached though they were to the soil, were banished, and many of them perished. In Karelia, as in the Ukraine, the population had to do forced labour for the benefit of the Soviet economy, with the difference that here their labour was used to obtain wood for export. The cause of the tension and hence of the struggle between Moscow and the inhabitants is here again to be sought in the loyalty of the population towards its religion, its nationality, its family life and its soil. Religious persecution was a particularly severe blow for the Karelians. "Almost all the churches have been turned into meeting-halls or clubs. Persons who light candles at Christmas are denounced as enemies of the State and are doomed sooner or later to banishment."

As early as 1922 Finland felt compelled to bring the question of the Karelian population before the League of Nations, contending that its treatment was not in conformity with the Treaty of Dorpat and should be submitted to the permanent Court at The Hague. The Soviet Union, however, declined to fall in with this suggestion—it did not at that time belong to the League—and declared that the Finnish step was an unfriendly act towards the Soviet Union. Further, it followed

[1] It may be worth while in this connection to recall the "Declaration on the Rights of the Russian Peoples" issued by the Council of People's Commissaries on November 2, 1917. The inhabitants of the constituent republics, including the Karelians, were assured in this instrument *de disposer librement d'eux-mêmes jusqu'à et inclusivement la séparation et l'établissement d'un Etat indépéndant.*

its invariable practice on occasions of this kind and pointed to its constitution, which provided for the self-government of the autonomous states. Now again the claim was made that, in contrast to the non-Communist states, the Soviet Union offered the utmost liberty to its nations and citizens. The Finnish attempt to succour their brethren on the basis of the provisions of the Treaty of Dorpat thus proved a failure. (After Russia had joined the League and had accepted the Covenant no further attempt was made.)

The fate of the Finns settled in the environs of Leningrad, where they form a pure minority, is even worse than that of the Karelians. Since 1931 this body, which the Russian statistics put at 148,000 persons, has been made the victim of a deliberate policy of extermination. With the beginning of collectivization began here, too, the expulsion of the *kulaks*. Later, the inhabitants of entire villages were banished to the Arctic regions; by 1932 the number of persons banished was 18,000, i.e. some 15 per cent of the population of the area. This policy was interrupted for a time when the public opinion of the world began to turn its attention to Moscow's methods, only to be resumed with greater intensity at the end of 1934. The Finns have made the interesting discovery that whenever Moscow has succeeded in settling its relations with the outer world, either by the conclusion of treaties or by other means, the policy of internal repression is followed with renewed vigour on the strength of the new security afforded by improved external relations. To-day the Finns of Ingermanland are faced with utter destruction.

Why this is so may perhaps be seen from an event related by refugees whose veracity there is no reason to doubt. In 1931, when the Finns first began to be banished in large numbers, some hundreds were collected at a station some miles from Leningrad under a strong military guard. When the train left the station these people, as well as the local inhabitants who had gathered to bid them farewell, began spontaneously to sing

Luther's famous hymn "A strong castle is our God"[1]—the Finns of Ingermanland being Lutherans, whereas the Karelians belong to the Orthodox Church. As a result of this action the troops immediately fired volleys on the demonstrators, for this hymn is considered the visible sign of a Christian and hence of an anti-Bolshevist mentality.[2]

The remaining, mainly agricultural communities living in Russia—Estonians, Latvians, Lithuanians, Poles, Czechs, Bulgarians and Rumanians—are in much the same position as the Finns.[3]

A separate description of the fate of each of these groups would be a mere repetition. The archives at Warsaw, Riga, Tallinn, etc., contain authentic evidence of this process of destruction, and with their help the tragic fate of each group could be separately described. In dealing with the topic of the fate of these nationalities I will confine myself to that of the most important, the Germans, who numbered about two millions at the beginning of the war and who, to-day, like the Finns, possess an independent State existence, at least in theory, in the shape of the German Volga Republic. To this extent their position is like that of the Finns. The fate of the Germans in Russia at the same time throws light on the fate of all the Western settlers in Russia, who, like the Estonians,

---

[1] "*Eine feste Burg ist unser Gott.*"

[2] In June 1935 *Hufvudstadsbladet*, of Helsingfors, published the last message from its special correspondent who stated that the complete breakdown of the educational system in Karelia had caused Moscow to send a commission of inquiry to Petrozavodsk. It had become known, *inter alia*, that various schoolchildren had been frozen to death during excursions through the neglect of the teachers. There was also said to be serious friction between disappointed Finnish Communists who had returned from America and the local rulers. At the instance of Moscow a number of the most influential local officials were said already to have been relieved of their functions.

[3] While the members of these groups are less numerous than the Finns and the Germans—instead of millions only hundreds or tens of thousands—nevertheless these smaller national groups living in Russia represent considerable percentages of the totals of the various nationalities. Thus the Estonians in Russia constitute 10 to 15 per cent of the whole Estonian race.

Latvians, Czechs and others, used to live in distinct and prosperous settlements in the centre of Russia, most of them east of the Volga.

The German Volga Republic is in the same position as Karelia and most of the other independent or autonomous regions of the Soviet State inhabited by these nationalities. On paper they possess a considerable degree of autonomy, while in fact control rests with the delegates of Moscow. Administratively the Volga Republic is covered by the decree of July 28, 1918, which placed the Germans of that region under the control of the newly formed Commissariat at Saratov (later renamed Marxstadt). The decree provided the basis for the domination and tyranny of foreign elements. This applies especially to such important matters as the contribution, confiscation and requisitioning of grain, for which this decree provided the "statutory foundation." From now onwards these matters were handled solely in co-operation with "proved Communists," who had been despatched to the Volga region for the purpose of these expropriations.[1] The decree was thus the opposite of that issued on July 23, 1763, by Catherine II, in which the German colonists settling in the Volga region were granted autonomy.[2]

It should be particularly emphasized that the decree of 1918 opened the Volga district to the activities of Communist emigrants from Germany, Austria, Hungary, Latvia, etc., i.e. to people who naturally hated everything that the Germans settled on the Volga venerated—religion, family, nationhood. There is thus a profound gulf between the adherents of Bela Kun, Liebknecht and Stutchka who, exiled from their own countries, found here a new sphere for their activities, and the

[1] See In Kampf und Todesnot, by Johannes Schleunig.

[2] In this connection it should be pointed out that the Germans settled along the Volga and in South Russia on the strength of definite assurances and privileges granted by the Russian monarchs. Thus, while their protection is not guaranteed by provisions binding in international law, the Russian State—which is at least important from the standpoint of principle—did bind itself constitutionally.

German peasants, who had been settlers in the region for generations. Naturally enough Comrades Petin, Reuter, etc.— German and Austrian emigrants who were at the head of the recently founded federal republic—did all in their power to destroy the entire national life of the local population, using as a pretext the federal constitution or the cause of local autonomy. I cannot speak here of the sufferings of the population during the first great famine of 1921-2. I would merely point out that the conclusion of the Treaty of Rapallo brought no alleviation to the Germans settled in Russia, because the Reich did not consider it necessary to champion their vital interests. Things became particularly difficult at the beginning of the process of collectivization, which here again meant a campaign against soil, nationhood and religion. Of the mass banishments and the fate of the victims we possess excellent accounts by reliable eyewitnesses.[1] These are historical documents, and they fully establish the systematic extermination of the banished and persecuted persons, especially clerics of every denomination. The process of collectivization and all that went with it placed the German settlers, totally deprived as they were of the yield of their harvests, in a desperate position. Faced with disaster, thousands of German peasants made their way to Moscow, believing that there would be help for them in the German motherland. On their arrival at Moscow they besieged the German Embassy, and finally 5,000 of them were saved, i.e. were allowed by the Soviet authorities to proceed to Germany. All these are well-known facts. What is perhaps less familiar is the fact that the rest of these people— the majority—trusting the assurances of the Soviet Government and the advice of the German Government, returned to the Volga region, where almost all of them were exterminated some time later through banishment and in other ways.

It is certain—Pastor Kern's notes make this quite clear—

[1] Cf. *The Whited Sepulchre*, an authentic account of Church persecution in Russia, by Pastor A. Kern, edited by Carlo von Kügelgen. The Lutterworth Press, London, 1935.

that world public opinion was not informed about the persecution of men and religion in Russia, and that even in Germany the public, after the 5,000 colonists had migrated, took no interest in the fate of the others. Thus the Soviet Government, which had been fearing a spontaneous ebullition of world opinion, was confirmed in its view that the public and the Churches of the West would remain blind to the extermination of the Christians and Churches in Russia; and that there was therefore no need to make any change in policy.

The last chapter in the tragic history of the German Volga settlement begins, as in the Ukraine and elsewhere, with the famine of 1933 and 1934. The development was just as elsewhere. Quite lately—probably as the result of the worsening of the relations between Germany and Russia—the execution of innocent peasants began, whose only fault it was that they had received support from relief organizations abroad. Banishment and sentences of death removed the remaining German pastors—some thirty clerics out of the three hundred formerly resident in the German settlement.

Similar events have been going on in the German settlements in the Ukraine and in the Northern Caucasus and in Trans-Caucasia. Here also the German remnant has been subjected to systematic persecution and is faced with annihilation.[1]

[1] Since the spring of 1935 the position of the Germans has further deteriorated. In June the *Berliner Tageblatt* published an alarming account by an expert on conditions in the Volga district. According to this version the desperate peasantry refused *en masse* to continue working in the collective farms, whereupon the district secretary of the Communist Party, Shafransky, found himself compelled to give way. This step was cancelled, however, by the Central Executive Committee of the party at Moscow, and the Commissary Shdanov, the successor of Kirov, was despatched to restore order in the German Volga Republic. There were collisions between the peasantry and the Ogpu troops under Shdanov's orders. The Central Committee of the party at Moscow issued a decree on June 24, 1935, which dealt exclusively with developments in the region of Saratov, and which clearly indicated that there was considerable disagreement between Moscow and the local authorities. The decree criticized measures taken by the local administration, the practice of mass reprisals and other steps "which are among the main causes of the continual desertions from the collective farms."

So much for the fate of the Western nationalities settled in the Union. I now turn to the fate of the nationalities and groups settled in the east.

The description by the delegate for Kazakstan, Mirsoian, strongly resembles that given for White Russia by Gikalo. The blame, in this instance chiefly for the disastrous decline of cattle breeding, is attributed to the machinations of enemies of the State and the weakness of the party organization. The severity of the famine, which was mentioned also by Mr. Muggeridge early in 1933, when it was mentioned that 25 per cent of the inhabitants had become its victims, appears from Mirsoian's statement to the effect that "emigration on a vast scale" was taking place as late as the end of that year. Blame for the decline in stock-rearing was also laid upon the Cossacks and *kulaks*, against whom the campaign was consequently directed.

The case is similar in Usbekistan, with the difference that the Pan-Islamite movement, embracing all the Mahommedans of Central Asia, plays a part here. At the Congress the delegate for this district, Ikramov, began his speech by saying that nationalist elements were active not only in the Ukraine but also in Usbekistan, and that their activity was due to the fact that all hopes of separation from the Soviet Union had failed. They were now gathering their last forces to prevent the work of building up a socialist order (*Izvestia*, January 30, 1934).

The developments in the Caucasian Republics of Armenia and Georgia call for separate treatment. A significant light is thrown upon Stalin and his loyalty to the ideal of Communist internationalism by the fact that, although Georgian by birth he attempts to crush the nationalism of his countrymen with even greater ruthlessness and consistency than that of other groups.

The fate of the Georgians is a particularly melancholy chapter in the Kremlin's policy with regard to the nationalities. On May 26, 1918, the Georgians, unlike the Ukrainians and most of the other peoples and nationalities, were enabled to found an autonomous State outside Russia. In this foundation every party, but more particularly the groups of the Left, participated. On May 7, 1920, the State was recognized by the Soviet Union and a treaty was concluded, Article 2 of which says: "Russia undertakes to refrain from any interference in Georgian affairs." On January 27, 1921, the Georgian Republic was formerly recognized by the Supreme Council of the Allies, embracing Great Britain, France, Italy and Japan. At that time the relation between Georgia and the Soviet Union, and the relation between the former and the Allied Powers seemed to have been settled. There was thus a parallel to the fate of the Estonians, Latvians, Lithuanians and Finns, who, recognized alike by the Soviet Union and the Great Powers, could proceed to develop their own nationhood.

As early as February 1921, however, Georgia was occupied by Russian troops and thus became a victim of the Moscow regime. From this period may be said to date the systematic suppression of every manifestation of Georgian nationalism, which united in resisting the action of the Kremlin. The Powers and the League protested against this illegal proceeding, and on September 22, 1922, a resolution of the Assembly was accepted which directed the attention of the Council to the question. Meanwhile there were insurrections in Georgia which were violently suppressed and which involved the deaths of thousands of Georgians: members of every occupation and social class were "liquidated," i.e. executed, in numbers. The number of persons deported amounted to 20,000. In various parts of the country there was prolonged faction fighting, and when this was ended every branch of national life began to be impermeated with the Moscow spirit.

A rigorous policy of national persecution was thus pursued by Moscow earlier and more vigorously in Georgia than in any other part of Russia. Georgia affords an example in which the various stages and methods of national persecution can be observed; what happened in Georgia was repeated in all the other autonomous regions. The first stage consisted in the persecution of all national elements in the schools, the administration, the theatre, etc.; the second in the infiltration of Cheka (Ogpu) agents into all circles and groups, down to and including every single family, and in the arrest and execution of elements for any reason considered unreliable by Moscow; and the third, in the annihilation of local nationalists by various economic measures.

In Georgia, as elsewhere, a fearful campaign was carried on in the name of collectivization against the *kulaks* and all individual peasants. Under the slogan "Down with the *kulaks*" the best and most capable men could be eliminated. But in Georgia the entire peasant population resisted collectivization so vigorously that Moscow was at times compelled to make concessions, which, however, were never more than temporary. Guerilla warfare and even regular battles became the order of the day. The Georgians in the Red Army refused to march against their countrymen, and in 1930 martial law had to be proclaimed throughout Eastern Georgia. Here, however, as in the Ukraine and elsewhere, the famine provided Moscow with a new means of removing what it considered undesirable elements within the population.

As in all districts where the nationalists possess churches of their own, the anti-religious campaign in Georgia was a particularly severe blow to an independent national life. As with the Germans in the Volga district, with the Finns and Estonians in the north, and the Mahommedans in the east, so with the Georgians there was too close a connection between national life and the Church and religion. Thus it was that the Georgian clergy tried to the last to champion the cause of their countrymen and co-religionists. The head of the Georgian Church, the patriarch Ambrosius, resolved in 1921, well knowing the consequences of his step, to address a letter of protest to the Conference then in session at Genoa. In this letter the patriarch attempted to draw the attention of the delegates to the hopeless position of the Georgian people under the occupation. In 1922 the patriarch was accused at Tiflis of having misinformed European public opinion of the position in Georgia, was found guilty and was sentenced to nine years' penal servitude.

In 1924, when the persecutions in Georgia had reached their climax, the League Assembly was compelled once again to deal with the position. Before any resolution was adopted the matter was dealt with by the Sixth Commission. As rapporteur of the latter, the Canadian delegate, Mr. MacDonald, was charged with placing the vote of the Commission before the Plenary Assembly. The words used by him in describing the facts, and more especially the latest events in Georgia, give an excellent account of the position. Referring to the Georgian appeal, he concluded by saying: "The sufferings of the Georgian people are intolerable; the terror . . . becomes more and more violent; deportations, imprisonments, tortures in the Cheka prisons, executions, without judgment, of representatives of every class, become increasingly numerous; politicians when arrested are treated like bandits; intellectuals and workmen are alike deprived of the means of work; Georgians who are opposed to the regime find every obstacle placed in the way of their admission to every kind of private, commercial or industrial enterprise, or to the public service; the clergy is persecuted for exercising its religious duties and for having thrown light on the present-day state of affairs; the head of the Georgian Church, the patriarch Ambrosius, has been condemned to several years of imprisonment and is in prison at the moment. . . . Such is the position. I am sure that it will affect all the members of the Assembly. Accordingly, I submit the conclusions of the Sixth Commission with a full confidence in your judgment."

The Assembly thereupon resolved to adopt the procedure followed in 1922, i.e. to submit the report of the Sixth Commission to the Council to enable it to take appropriate steps at the right moment. Thus the *de jure* recognition of Georgia by the Great Powers and by the Supreme Council twice led to a resolution by the plenary Assembly; in this respect the problem of Georgia differs from that of the Ukrainians and the other nationalities. Further, eminent Englishmen and Frenchmen, like Professor Gilbert Murray, M. Herriot, M. Paul-Boncour and the late M. Poincaré, have expressed themselves in no uncertain terms, whether at Geneva or in their own Parliaments, on Moscow's procedure with regard to the Georgians. (M. Poincaré said in the Chamber of Deputies on June 2, 1922: "The French Government could not agree to discuss a question of this nature with the representatives of the Government in power, which has expelled the regular Government from Georgia.")

What made it possible to draw the attention of world public opinion, and more especially of the League delegates, to Georgia, is the fact that the Georgian constituent assembly, at its last session at Batum on March 18, 1921, had adopted a resolution instructing the Government to proceed abroad in order "to take appropriate steps for the restoration and the independence of the country." Headed by the President Jordania, the Government accordingly proceeded to Paris, where it began its labours. Georgia thus differs from the other peoples and nationalities living in Russia in possessing popularly elected representatives abroad, a body comprising all parties and actually including Socialists. Among them there are former deputies of the Third Duma, including Gegechkori, who was one of the leading revolutionary personalities in the old Empire.

The two League resolutions, however, had no practical results. In the autumn of 1934, when the admission of the Soviet Union to the League came up for discussion, the Georgian representatives appealed to the Governments of the various countries and to the League president and delegates. They referred to the two League resolutions and to the *de jure* recognition of Georgia by the Powers, and requested that the liberty of the Georgians might be restored in connection with and as a condition of the admission of Russia to the League. At Geneva it was a Georgian delegation headed by Jordania and Gegechkori which addressed this request to the individual delegates.

At this decisive moment, however, the League was induced, by economic and political considerations affecting a number of states, to shut its eyes to the Georgian claims. The Soviet Union was admitted unconditionally, and this particular transgression, as well as the general policy pursued by Moscow in repressing the nationalities, was thus treated as a fact which must be accepted. There was only one exception—M. Motta, the Swiss delegate—who in his speech protested, amid the applause of the entire Assembly, against the injustice done to the Georgians as well as against the general policy pursued by Moscow in repressing the nationalities and religious freedom.

In admitting Soviet Russia the League completely failed. It failed both in regard to the question of the Georgians' rights and in regard to that of the nationalities, for, in order to remain true to its past policy, it should have required the Soviet Union to recognize the protection of the minorities. It is true that the representatives of the Powers at Geneva stated, without contradiction by the Russian representatives, that the Soviet Union had accepted all the obligations contained in the Covenant. This is not a very precise starting-point; but it may be necessary to make use of it. In this connection it is important to note that the various League of Nations Unions, at their annual meeting in the summer of 1934, jointly adopted a resolution to the effect that the admission of Russia to the League would facilitate the restoration of the Georgians' rights.

The policy pursued by Moscow with regard to the other Caucasian peoples, e.g. the Armenians and the Turks of the "autonomous republic" of Azerbaijan, and above all against the Turco-Tartars in the Volga and Kama region, is similar to that adopted for Georgia. A special treatment of these groups would simply amount to repetition. I will therefore confine myself to a few words about the present hard lot of the Turco-Tartars in particular, the real mainstay of the great Turco-Mahommedan movement towards union and solidarity which has now gripped the many millions of Mahommedans in the east of European Russia and all over Central Asia. If before the war there was not the slightest degree of solidarity between the individual Tartar groups, or between the Turkish-Mahommedan groups in general, it is quite different now. The Turco-Mahommedan union movement is without doubt one of the most important phenomena of the post-war era, and is likely, in the near future, to have a decisive influence on the whole situation in the east.

The two autonomous federal territories inhabited by Tartars —the Bashkir and Tartar Republics—are the principal centre of this movement in the east of Europe. The domination of Moscow's emissaries is even more pronounced in these regions than in all the other parts of the Soviet Union. Almost the whole administrative machinery is, as elsewhere in Russian Central Asia, in the hands of non-Mahommedan elements, and a deep antipathy has sprung up between the population and the intruders—an antipathy which often finds expression even in the columns of the local Soviet press.

Here, too, in the economic field, it is clear that the inhabitants are sacrificed in the interests of Moscow. For example, the people of the Caucasian republic of Azerbaijan were compelled by Moscow to plant cotton instead of the grain they needed to keep themselves alive. In Azerbaijan, as the Soviet press reports, there have again and again been rebellions, bloodily suppressed.[1]

[1] The *Bakinski Rabotchi* of May 26, 1935, reports that sabotage and passive resistance on the part of the population are everyday occurrences. By a resolution passed by the Council of People's Commissaries for the region on May 8, such work as weeding and cutting was supposed to have been completed by May 25. By May 20, however, no more than 2·5 per

But the foreign guests of honour who travel through the Soviet State are always telling us how well off the Mahommedans are. For example, a party of foreign Communists, headed by the Frenchman Cachin, which visited Central Asia some years ago expressed themselves to this effect. The account given by these Communists was attacked by no other than Pierre Rénaudel, who gave this severe verdict: "The agrarian revolution is nothing but a camouflage for a regime of exploitation." This he based on quotations from the Soviet press and the books of the Soviet Russian authors, Ryskulov and Sorokin.[1]

With regard to the position of the Jews in the Soviet Union, there is this to be said. That the leadership and administration of the Soviet State—in trade and industry, in diplomacy, in the press, etc.—is to-day to a considerable extent in the hands of Jews, is a fact which none can deny. Indeed, it can fairly be said that non-national Jewry has played and plays a very large part indeed in the shaping of the Soviet Russian regime; this applies not only to the Soviet Government, but, further, to the activities of the Komintern. But it is just these Jewish circles which play a dominant part in the Soviet State which—comprehensibly—see in those Jews who, unlike them, cling to their nationality, religion and customs, an element which must be destroyed. That is why the Soviet regime is to-day attacking the believing Jews in the Ukraine, White Russia, etc., who are for the most part settled in large communities. I quoted earlier in this book Harry Lang's description of the hard lot of these Jews. I would only like to point out here that even the so-called "Yiddish Institutes" at Kiev, Minsk and elsewhere are simply intended to have a disintegrating effect on the surrounding communities. The function of the Yiddish Institute at Kiev

cent of the total surface had been completed. The issue of May 30 also reported passive resistance on the part of the peasants and mentions collective farms where the fields had been so inefficiently planted that half of the total area had to be resown.

[1] See Rénaudel's preface to Mustapha Tchokai's pamphlet *Chez les Soviets en Asie Centrale*.

as an instrument for opposing Jewish nationalism becomes apparent from the report of a Jewish politician, Herr Karlbach, who visited the institute. The following is Karlbach's report:[1] "I had been following the secretary through the basements and attics where the most valuable Jewish books, periodicals and manuscripts are carefully sorted and arranged. During my visit I had been increasingly pleased to think that in this distant and impoverished region the Government found the money and the energy to ensure that the authorities should allow no book or manuscript to leave the country if it was stated to be of use to Yiddish science. It was satisfactory to find that collectors of Jewish proverbs had become State officials.

"And now we were sitting in the Director's room, talking. I asked how many of the professors at the institute had children and was told seven; I asked how many attended Jewish schools and was told two. I was surprised and said nothing, but one of the professors looking at me, remarked: 'Not long ago Norman Bentwich[2] paid us a visit. He also could not understand it, and asked how it was possible to live *on* the Jewish language and *for* the Jewish language, and yet never think of preserving it for the future or of spreading it. He did not understand that we do not speak Yiddish in the schools and theatres, in order that Yiddish may be spoken, but Russian, because that is the only way of teaching people Socialism. He could not understand why we studied Yiddish philology and noted down every ancient tune, while sending our own children to the Russian schools. But what is there really that is hard to understand?'

" 'What is hard to understand,' I said, 'is this. Whence do you draw the desire and the courage to work for a cause whose death warrant has already been signed?'

" 'We get the courage from the service we are doing to Socialism, just by our work on the Yiddish language. After all, the work we are doing here has a meaning; it is productive, it

[1] *Selbstwehr* (the organ of the Jewish Zionist Party in Czechoslovakia), March 10, 1932.
[2] Formerly Attorney-General of Palestine.

does some good. Do you know what I am working on at this moment? On a Government order. Here it is. . . .'

"He took a sheet from his desk and showed it me. It was a translation into Yiddish of an official form, and the form was a summons before the G.P.U."

There can be no more striking illustration of the real work done by these institutes; which is to suppress every national movement.

I have here dealt with the position of only some of the peoples and nationalities settled in the Soviet Union. But the conditions described exist also among many other peoples and tribes which cannot here be treated in detail. I am therefore justified in asserting that the situation in these areas is the scene not only of a terrible famine, but at the same time of the now openly conducted national struggle.[1]

We are indebted to Postyschev for enlightenment on the future policy of Moscow in the Ukraine, as well as with regard to the various peoples and races settled in the various districts. In a speech delivered late in 1933 he stated that any attempt to harmonize proletarian internationalism with nationalism must make it an instrument of the nationalist counter-revolution and must therefore be most vigorously combated in future. He added that the reorganization of the form and methods of Bolshevik leadership in building up Ukrainian culture must consequently imply "a vigorous and consistent struggle for the elimination of nationalist prejudices."

---

[1] In the late summer of 1935 a decree was issued by the Soviet Government (signed by Molotov and Stalin, which shows the importance attached to it), ordering a "fundamental reform of the educational system in the Soviet Union." It orders, *inter alia*, that curricula, school-books, time-tables, etc., must be standardized throughout the Soviet Union, and that from January 1 a uniform—also identical throughout the Soviet Union—must be worn by all schoolchildren. What is particularly characteristic is that this decree takes the school administration out of the hands of the autonomous Soviet republics and places it under the control of the central authorities. Arthur W. Just observes in an article on "Education in the Soviet Union" in the *Rigasche Rundschau* of September 27, 1935, that all pretence of the nationalities possessing intellectual freedom is now abandoned.

What is the meaning of Moscow's programme as set out by Postyschev? It means that Moscow has definitively adopted the new course with regard to the nationalities and has abandoned the "rotten compromise" of the first period of Russian nationalism. The attempt to enforce the sociological ideology of Lenin while feigning recognition for national individuality has been given up, and a policy has been adopted which must inevitably be accompanied by far-reaching consequences. The new programme means war to the knife on all the national movements, whether among the Ukrainians, the White Russians, the Caucasian peoples, the Germans, the Finns or the Jews. Whether the struggle is carried through with the whip or with the velvet glove is simply a matter of expediency.[1]

But this decisive change in the Kremlin's policy towards the nationalities has yet another cause. The autonomous Soviet republics and districts which were set up along the frontier from Finland to the Black Sea for propaganda purposes have proved a disappointment. The correspondent of the *Kölnische Zeitung*, who has lived for many years in Moscow, has dubbed these the "Irredenta Republics," whose propagandist value he states to have been disappointing. Instead of appealing to the peoples and nationalities across the frontier, these pseudo-national regions along the western fringe of the Soviet Union have turned into centrifugal factors—a severe disappointment for Stalin, who, as Commissary for the Nationalities under Lenin, played a leading part in their formation.

It is a matter of course that in these circumstances the

---

[1] Later utterances of Postyschev's indicate that he is encountering serious difficulties in carrying through his policy in the Ukraine. The *Wisty* of Kiev (March 6, 1935) reports him as saying in a speech before the party committee that cultural life in the Ukraine must be "Ukrainianized" in order to take the wind out of the sails of the Ukrainian nationalists and separatists, who had won over the masses by declaring that Moscow was Russifying the Ukrainian Soviet Republic.

In another speech (*Pravda*, June 1935) he appeals to the Communist writers of the Ukraine to join in spreading abroad accounts of the achievements of the Communist State.

K

attitude adopted by Moscow with regard to the famine, or rather, to the possibilities of exploiting it—I refer now to quite recent events—should in the course of time have undergone a change, and that the Kremlin should see in the famine a positive relief, and even an actual support for its campaign for the ultimate triumph of Communism. To put it in plain English: Moscow now has a direct interest in the destruction of a large part of the generation now living in the Ukraine and in other autonomous districts.

The nationalities of these districts, especially the Ukrainians, are thus engaged in a struggle for their existence and for the salvation of a part of their national being. But they are wholly at the mercy of Moscow and can do nothing to defend themselves. They have to look on in silence while their harvest is taken away, and the very existence of the famine is denied when foreigners are ready to intervene. The majority of these nationalities—Ukrainians, White Russians, Caucasians, etc.— in any case have no state of the same nationality capable of appealing on their behalf. And even where there are such states, their existence is of no avail, because they are unable to do anything for their kinsmen in distress; considerations of their political and economic relations with the Soviet Union compel them to confine themselves to remittances or food parcels, which in any case are no more than a drop in the ocean, if they do their recipients no actual harm. On the contrary, one cannot avoid the impression that the authorities in Berlin, Helsingfors, Warsaw and Riga have resigned themselves to the destruction of their kinsmen in the Soviet Union.

Since the end of 1934 Moscow's systematic policy of destruction as applied to the nationalities has become even clearer. After the assassination of Kirov, representatives of the local peoples and nationalities who had nothing whatever to do with that crime were sentenced to death and executed in the Ukraine, White Russia, Usbekistan, etc. Indeed, there is no doubt that the Government exploited Kirov's assassination in order to take measures against the nationalities as "enemies of the State." Almost daily reports were received from Kiev, Minsk and elsewhere telling of the condemnation and execution of dozens of local inhabitants. In the period when all these things were happening, the Foreign Minister, Litvinov, delivered his famous speech against the individual terror before the Council at Geneva—a speech which remained unanswered by any member of the Council. Yet the events which took place late in 1934 were no more than a prologue to the measures introduced in the following year to exterminate the various nationalities—especially those of the west.

One cannot but gain the impression that the intention is completely to eliminate the nationalities settled in the west.[1] It is a favourable opportunity, since there are many states desirous of entering into political partnership with Russia; and in these states public opinion is occupied with hymns in praise of Moscow and its role as a factor for peace in Europe.

In order to bring about this annihilation, Moscow has recently adopted a novel method, which consists in the evacuation of entire national groups, or rather of the members of these groups settled along the western frontier.[2] This policy is carried out from the Bessarabian frontier in the south as far as Karelia in the north. The simple reason adduced is that the presence of members of alien nationalities, such as Germans,

[1] It should be emphasized that the national groups of western origin, who are almost in their entirety on a high cultural level, are much more severely hit by the Soviet nationalities policy than many of the ethnographical units living in the east of Russia.

Moscow is now endeavouring to destroy the remnants of religious life among the Germans in Russia. Many clergymen have been banished to the far north—usually for ten years—and Pastors Seib and Deutschmann were actually sentenced to death on trumped-up charges; but, in view of the indignation expressed in foreign countries, their sentences were commuted to banishment to Siberia.

[2] Early this year a great number of the Finnish inhabitants of Ingermanland were arrested and transported to remote parts of Russia, and this is still going on. It seems to be the Soviet's wish to purge Ingermanland of its Finnish population.

Finns, Poles, etc., would be a danger in a war. This is a measure which, if applied to Central Europe, would have the effect of exterminating the greater part of all the minorities, most of which are settled along the frontiers. The unhappy exiles are taken to remote districts, where nobody troubles about them.

To carry through this policy of elimination of the nationalities, Moscow employs lately a method of a quite particular kind—the evacuation of all peoples, or rather of certain groups of them, from the border zones on the West to remote parts of the Soviet Union. This is carried out from the extreme south to as far north as Karelia so thoroughly that there now exists from north to south an evacuated zone—a kind of vacuum—varying from a width of ten miles in some parts to as much as fifty miles in others. All this is done with the simple explanation that the presence of these members of foreign nationalities —Finns, Germans, Poles, etc.—cannot, in view of the possibility of a future war, be tolerated in these border territories. Here we are confronted with a policy which would be extremely dangerous if it were applied to national minorities in general. By its help the greater part of all national minorities in Central Europe could be eliminated, as most of them occupy border territories.

The unfortunate exiles are sent by the Soviet authorities to distant parts of Siberia, where nobody troubles about them and where they perish in masses—a method of elimination which is extremely easy for the Soviet to carry out.

Instead of summarizing the contents of this chapter myself, I will quote the opinion on this subject of an observer of Soviet Russian conditions for many years—Mr. W. H. Chamberlin. In his book *Russia's Iron Age*, he says that nearly half the population of the Soviet Union consists of "non-Russians," whose attitude towards the Soviet regime is determined above all by the policy of the latter in dealing with the nationalities. The hostility to Moscow in the Ukraine and elsewhere is not due to "the suppression of the language" of the nationality in question, and certainly not to "racial Chauvinism," but far more than anything to the starvation and economic ruin of the population as a result of collectivization. As for the vaunted freedom and independence of the local Soviet republics, he declares that the head of such a republic is entirely dependent on the instructions and the dominating influence of the Soviet Government. The conduct of the delegates of Moscow in the non-Russian areas he characterizes by comparing them with Skrypnik, for years president of the Ukrainian federal republics. "This old revolutionary," he writes, "was not so hard-hearted as many of the young men whom Stalin sent into the Ukraine with instructions to raise the last bushel of corn there; in fact, to carry out collectivization even at the cost of a famine. . . ."

Mr. Chamberlin sums up his judgment as follows: "The Soviet Government, along with the other Powers which adhered to the Kellogg Pact, has renounced war as an instrument of national policy. But there are no humanitarian restrictions in the ruthless class war which, in the name of Socialism, it has been waging on a considerable part of its own peasant population; and it has employed famine as an instrument of national policy on an unprecedented scale and in an unprecedented way."[1]

These comments of a distinguished writer, whose authority is undisputed by friend and foe, require no elaboration.

So it is that in the middle of the twentieth century, at a time when influential Soviet statesmen are praising the Soviet Union as a factor making for peace, a systematic war of destruction is proceeding in the interior of Russia—a war carried on not with artillery and machine-guns, but by banishments, executions and famine. I think I have shown that this war is directed in particular against the members of the various nationalities, millions of whom have already been sacrificed to it.

[1] *Christian Science Monitor*, May 29, 1934.

CHAPTER IV

MOSCOW'S ATTITUDE

WHAT has the Soviet Government done in the face of the catastrophe within its borders? It has kept silence; it has simply denied the existence of the famine; it has not even attempted to ameliorate it by rapid distribution of the grain available for export among the starving population. More than that, by exporting part of the grain wrung from the peasantry, Moscow has contributed to increase the number of victims of the catastrophe. To find an explanation of this at first sight wholly incredible fact, it is not enough to study the economic embarrassment and internal conflict which I have dealt with in previous chapters, nor to examine Moscow's general attitude to the question of famine and famine relief. We must also look at the root motives which dictate Moscow's policy.

First, there is the general attitude of Communism, and more especially the value it sets on human life. It is the Bolshevist view that the one ultimate ideal is to lead mankind to the earthly paradise, and that the way to realize it is to realize the Communist ideal of Society. So long as an economic order destined to last for ever is achieved, the death of millions becomes insignificant. It follows from this general assumption that human life in Bolshevist eyes has little, if any, value: man is an economic factor, like labour in the abstract, and nothing more.

It would be a different matter if the population necessary to maintain the economic system were endangered; in this case the Government would do anything to avert such a threat. But the fact is that the Soviets possess a vast human reserve. M. Herriot begins one of his articles by stating that the population is increasing so rapidly that it grew from 147 millions to 161 millions during the five years 1926–31. The theory of the growth of the population and of the huge reserves of human labour has in all probability ceased to be valid. Since 1928 the rate of increase has steadily declined. In that year the increase amounted to 3,800,000, in 1929 to 3,300,000, in 1930 to 2,900,000, in 1931 to 2,800,000, and in 1932 to 2,500,000. In any case, the rulers consider that a loss of 10,000,000 or even 20,000,000 persons causes no serious harm to Bolshevist economics.

This fundamental Bolshevist attitude to human life, this view which regards human beings as economic factors, implies a similar attitude to human suffering. Compared with the realization of the Communist ideal, the life and death of the individual is a matter of indifference; why, therefore, trouble about his personal conditions, diseases and sufferings?

The practical results of this theory are described by an American doctor of Danish extraction, Dr. L. O. Jensen, of Oregon, who recently returned from a stay in Russia. In a newspaper interview[1] he was asked: "Were you admitted to the hospitals in Russia?"

"Yes," Dr. Jensen replied, "everywhere, and what I saw was dreadful. The doctors think nothing of amputating arms and legs without using any anaesthetic. If the patients cannot stand the pain, they die—Soviet Russia has no use for the weak and the feeble; as for the aged, no trouble at all is taken about them; they are simply left to die. It was almost more than I could bear to watch these operations being performed without local or other anaesthetic. I am a surgeon of long standing, but there were cases where I was physically sick. It is impossible to imagine the horrors of such an operation. In these days human lives are of slight value in Russia; indeed, human beings are the cheapest commodity of all."

It must also be remembered that Moscow considers the triumphant industrialization of Russia as the necessary foundation of the Communist world revolution. As things are at

---

[1] *Extrabladet* of Copenhagen, July 25, 1933.

present, this mechanization can be carried through only at the cost of agriculture. It may involve the death of millions; but in the eyes of the Soviet rulers this simply does not matter. This attitude also finds expression in the ruthless brutality with which the Government cuts off imports even of the first necessities required by the peasantry. There is, too, the fact that most of the victims of the famine represent primitive or unskilled labour. And of unskilled labour the Soviet authorities even to-day have such reserves that the deaths of millions do not sensibly reduce them.

Governing circles have consequently only to work out a simple sum to arrive at the conclusion that not even the slightest sacrifice of a material kind on behalf of the threatened peasants is justifiable, if what would be sacrificed is needed for the maintenance of the industrial plan, etc. Indeed, granted the necessity of realizing the Soviet ideal, such a sacrifice of material values, at a moment when the Soviet plans are in the gravest danger, would be an act of culpable irresponsibility. For in this way some millions of lives would be saved—but at the cost of endangering the "historic experiment" embodied in the Russian economic structure.

This view is well characterized by statements made by a Soviet official called Sklar to an American Communist, Andrew Smith, who recently returned to the United States after a three years' stay in Russia.[1] Sklar said: "Suppose 6,000,000 more people die from hunger, what of it? It is still worth the price of Communism. . . ."

This explains not only why grain is being exported at a time when numbers are dying of famine, but also why Moscow is infinitely more anxious to preserve and even increase the number of draught oxen than to render aid to a suffering population. And, indeed, from the point of view of Russian interests, the real catastrophe is not the mortality from starvation, but the unexpected loss of draught oxen due to

[1] *New York Evening Journal*, May 29, 1935.

collectivization; for, while there is a superfluity of unskilled human labour, there is an enormous shortage, despite agricultural mechanization, of draught cattle. The Soviet press stated that up to the middle of February no more than 50 per cent of the tractor repair plan had been fulfilled. This is another blow for Russian State economics: and it is a blow which strikes at the roots, not only of the regime, but of Bolshevism as a whole. The regime must, therefore, have a greater interest in finding fodder for draught oxen than in saving starving people. The Soviet press devotes columns to the question of draught oxen and the problem of increasing their numbers. *Pravda* announced on February 22, 1934, that the Russian cattle stocks were to be increased shortly, "partly by way of purchases of cattle." In other words, quantities of grain which might save innumerable lives will be exported and the foreign exchange thus obtained will be used to buy and import cattle.

Possibly the methods of Moscow in dealing with the factor of unskilled labour are illustrated even more strikingly by an example not from the agricultural south, but from the far north. This was in the winter of 1933, when all available timber stocks had to be exported as quickly as possible to save the economic system.

On February 1, 1933, the *Pravda Severa*, the Archangel Soviet organ, published a Moscow decree which may certainly be called a historic document. It openly declared that timber exports were a capital element in the "exchange battle" and hence in the fulfilment of the second five-year plan; further, that the deliveries of timber had been wholly inadequate in the northern districts, and that consequently there would be, from March 7 to 10, a "militant mobilization of all workers and all collective farm and individual peasants"; in other words, of the entire population of the northern districts. This movement was to be called—note the slogan—"Stalin's timber crusade."

The decree laid down that everyone was to proceed to the

forests with his own horses, and that twice the old number of woodcutters and three times the number of horses were to be mobilized. "The daily standard work of each cutter," the decree says, "must amount to double the number of trunks cut down, and each horse must yield a maximum of transport labour. This can only be done if every woodcutter does his duty from early morning till late at night; if every moment during the day is spent wholly and entirely in work." But what is most characteristic in this decree is the statement that the "first duty" of every peasant and worker in the north was to "fight" for the fulfilment of the export programme, so that non-fulfilment of this duty and evasion of the obligation to cut wood would be considered "direct sabotage." The penalty for such "treachery" would be, for collective farm peasants, banishment from the collective farm; as for individual peasants, the local Soviet was to take immediate steps to make them feel the consequences of their action.

Members of Communist organizations detailed for work in the forests were instructed to keep a sharp look-out for the machinations of class enemies and counter revolutionaries— for if "treachery" occurred it must be due to these. What did this mean? Malcolm Muggeridge, from whose account in the *Manchester Guardian* I have taken these details, rightly points out that the entire population of a district has been condemned to forced labour, under threat of being treated as class enemies in case of inadequate compliance.

The degree of compulsion applied in collecting grain from the peasantry in the agricultural districts has been described elsewhere. Here I would merely refer to a particularly characteristic measure. This is the order prohibiting the peasants from leaving the collective farms. They are thus deprived of their liberty of movement—in other words, tied down to the collective farms.

And yet this decree was issued in the name of an idea and in order to realize the ideal of harmony between men and peoples. To answer the question whether the decree is mere falsehood and hypocrisy, I must now deal with the one power at present controlling the fate and fortunes of the Soviet Union; the sole force responsible for the existing economic order with all its attendant phenomena, including the numberless deaths. This force is Stalin. Among living men, including all his fellow-dictators, he is perhaps the most striking phenomenon; for, while his life is devoted to the realization of the Communist world order, he appears to be insensitive to every human emotion standing in the way of the realization of what is, theoretically, a grand conception.

To appreciate the part played by Stalin in the Soviet Union, and beyond it, in the play of international relations, we must first grasp his dominant position among the 160,000,000 inhabitants of the Soviet Union. Times have changed since Lenin, and to-day there is no one to share Stalin's power. He is the culminating point of the whole vast pyramid, an absolute autocrat, controlling the lives, fate and happiness of the officials who are personally subordinated to him—and they all are. There was a time when the old guard of Communists might be described as a kind of order; the members of this order were grouped around Lenin, and at that time there was a kind of comradeship between them. All this is over now. Resistance, or even the expression of a personal opinion, spells destruction. In consequence, all those who once played an independent part in the Communist Party at Lenin's side have been removed, or else just continue to exist in complete subjection, entirely dependent on Stalin's will.

Yet this change in the system is not, in my opinion, the result of personal ambition on Stalin's part. There is inevitably a vast difference between the opinion held of Stalin by his friends and by his enemies. A London Sunday paper recently published a series of articles in which a former Communist and colleague of Stalin, Kakabadze, dealt with his life and character. Mention was made of Stalin's alleged debaucheries and excesses. I do not think that this description is correct. At the present day Stalin is carrying an immense burden of work. From morning until night he is struggling to maintain the Communist economic system; and assuredly he has neither time nor inclination to waste his time in debauchery. His friends, on the other hand, describe him as the embodiment of courage, will and iron resolution; hymns of praise are intoned in honour of his energy and devotion to an idea. In my opinion, no one can understand Stalin—and everything that is happening in Soviet Russia—who does not take the trouble to find out what his principal aims are, and by what motives his actions are directed.

In spite of opinions freely held in the west, it must be recognized that after Lenin it was Stalin who was the first to grasp that the existence of millions of peasant properties inevitably meant the fiasco of the Communist order in Russia.[1] And it was he who alone had the courage and the almost inhuman ruthlessness to stick to his views and undertake the sudden transformation of the old type of peasant economy, despite the inevitability of sacrificing human lives in the process.

At that earlier time no other than Trotsky flung at Stalin the reproach that his policy meant "the military-feudal exploitation of the peasantry." (This was recalled in Bukharin's speech at the Moscow Communist Congress, January 28, 1934.) Nevertheless Stalin decided upon this policy; for he believed that it was essential for the realization of the Communist order in Russia, a fact which must be borne in mind by those who would grasp the considerations underlying Stalin's economic plans dealt with in the first chapter of this book. The fact is that he realized earlier and more clearly than others that the Soviet regime was faced by a crisis; the Lenin type of Socialism, implying collectivization at whatever risk, had to be carried

---

[1] Recently, during his speech at the Moscow Communist Congress, Stalin declared, like Lenin, that "the predominance of small peasant properties in the country involved the danger of a split within the Communist Party." (*Pravda*, January 30, 1934.)

into practice if Communism were to remain the foundation of the Soviet State. In a letter of recantation which must produce a deep impression on any reader, one of Trotsky's oldest and most obstinate adherents, Sosnovsky, recently admitted[1] that Stalin smashed the collegiate constitution of the party in order to make himself the sole ruler of Russia, and that it was he alone who could have carried through the collectivization of the peasants. "We revolted against both," Sosnovsky wrote; "to-day we see that, but for Stalin's action, the party and the system would now be ruined. I therefore capitulate—" (to summarize the last part of the letter) "and I am one of the last to do so: I surrender because, unlike others who did so before me, I need not disguise the fact that our view has become bankrupt at every point. I ask for pardon."

Now what is the ultimate ideal of Stalin, this unquestioned ruler over the territory and population of a state embracing one-sixth of the entire world? It is to bring about Communism in industry and agriculture; to embody the "pure doctrine" of Lenin, despite all sacrifices, despite human hecatombs, despite fearful distress and unceasing toil inflicted on millions. But this can only be done if the giant industrial concerns already erected survive to form a new and stable foundation for Russia's industry.

This is Stalin's general line, pursued and determined with full and rigorous consistency by Stalin and Stalin alone. Other leaders of the Communist Opposition, headed by Trotsky, objected, because they were firmly convinced that the vast difficulties of agricultural communization and the attendant struggle with the peasantry would prove unsurmountable in practice. It is significant that to-day, when the Soviet regime remains unshaken in spite of famine and numberless deaths, these men return penitently to the fold one after another and openly confess their error. At the same time they rejoice at Stalin's victory, since it has proved the capacity of the Soviet

[1] *Pravda*, February 27, 1934.

system to survive every blow. This proves that these men's original protests were not inspired by fears of the consequences of agricultural collapse, famine and the like, but by apprehension that the Soviet system might not succeed in meeting such shocks. From this standpoint it appears reasonable that Communists of every shade of opinion should now be speaking of Stalin's historic victory, and that it was possible for the delegates at the Moscow Communist Congress, at the moment when the most dreadful distress was prevailing in various regions of the country, sincerely to describe the results of Stalin's policy as the victorious communization of industry. Significantly enough, not a single word was said at the Moscow Congress about the question of the famine and its attendant phenomena.

Admittedly many of these praises gave the impression that their authors were officials anxious to curry favour with the dictator, the master of the lives and fortunes of every Communist in Russia. On reading a report of any session of the Moscow Congress, one is amazed at the inflated language in which all speakers without exception saw fit to laud Stalin. Even those ignorant of the Russian language can obtain some impression of this adulation when they look at the printed speeches and see Stalin's name recurring constantly in enormous black type. Such an attitude becomes intelligible if it is remembered that the last party purge in the autumn of 1933 "eliminated," i.e. expelled, nearly 20 per cent and in some regions nearly 25 per cent of all party members. One appreciates that certain delegates must have appeared to render their public account before the dictator with internal tremors.

Michael Kolytsov, the eminent Soviet journalist, describes how one delegate after the other mounted the rostrum, each well knowing that while he was speaking he was being weighed in the scales. How much ability had such-and-such an official displayed while leading his troops in the fight for Socialist reconstruction? How did he organize his comrades and how did he conduct himself? Had he contributed any valuable addition to Bolshevist successes? Had he failed, or had he actually diminished these successes through slackness, irresolution or weakness?

In such circumstances it is not surprising that a man like the Commissary for Agriculture, Jakovliev, whose position was already undermined at that time, should have ended his speech with the words: "Our cause is headed by the great leader, Stalin. Like Lenin he carries the Soviet State past every difficulty to the Socialist world order: he prevents any Communist from indulging in overweening ambitions. And, like Lenin, he forges the Communist Party into the strongest instrument of our advancing movement. In this we must see the surest warrant for the overcoming of all hazards." Yet even these words of praise failed to restore Jakovliev's shaken position, and he was soon afterwards removed from his office.

It is even more interesting to see how one of Trotsky's chief adherents, Rakovsky, extols Stalin's personality in his letter of recantation. This document, published in *Izvestia*, says: "Stalin embodies uncompromising Bolshevist ideology, organized discipline and harmony between Communist words and deeds. Together with the entire Communist party and the working class I repeat that only a leader possessing the uncompromising ideology, political vision and iron will of a Stalin could enable the land of the Soviets to solve the vast difficulties of Socialist reconstruction."

It may be admitted that Rakovsky is right to this extent—that nobody except Stalin would have had the courage and resolution to hold fast to his ideas and methods in his struggle with economic problems, even at the cost of sacrificing millions of innocent persons. It may, too, be assumed that the words of another delegate at the Moscow Communist Congress, Khataevitch, the representative of Dniepropetrovsk, expressed the views of many important people well aware of the critical economic position of the country. The delegate said: "In this concentration of material resources and of the will and energy of the masses in the fight for the five-year plan, it is Comrade Stalin who leads the army of fighters for Socialism, conducting them with resolution, calm and deliberation up to a clear-cut issue. And," Khataevitch added, "the workers in the Ukraine have had special occasion during the past year to appreciate these qualities of Stalin's. . . ."

The words of these Congress delegates really say all there is to be said about the part played by this sinister man, whom no human emotion can deter from a resolution once taken. In view of the ten million dead lying in the common graves of the Ukraine, the Northern Caucasus and Western Siberia, and of the successful overcoming of all these "difficulties," Communism has every reason to see in Stalin the saviour of the Soviet system from a collapse which, but for him, would have been inevitable.

It would be quite another matter if Stalin and his unique experiment were to be judged from the standpoint of the Russian population and the country's industry in general. In such a case the victory of 1933 would have to be judged very differently. But Stalin has another aim besides uncompromising communization of Russia—the Bolshevization of the rest of the world. Stalin has clearly recognized, and recently stated, that a Communist Russia in a bourgeois world would in the long run be an impossibility. One cannot but thoroughly agree with this view, and recognize that Stalin steadily pursues this second aim, too, if only for the reason that, in Stalin's view, Communism has not yet thoroughly established itself in the Soviet Union.

A leading article in *Pravda* of January 30, 1934, quotes Stalin as saying: "Can it be claimed that we have eliminated every trace of capitalism from our economic system? No, it cannot be claimed. Still less can it be asserted that all remnants of capitalism have been eradicated from our mentality. And this is so because people's understanding develops slowly as compared with economic development, and also because the

Body of famine victim lying by freshly dug grave
ready for burial

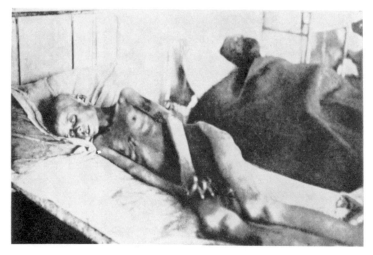

Famine victims in hospital

Body of famine victim in a field, stripped of clothing by passers-by

capitalist surroundings remain, whose aim it is to maintain and to promote the outworn capitalist influences in the minds of the dwellers in the Soviet Union. Against such a danger we Bolshevists must keep our powder dry."

It would be underestimating Stalin's personality to assume that this uncompromising ideologue would abandon his steadily pursued line of action just at this critical point from any opportunist considerations or political expediency—for the sake, perhaps, of a newly acquired friend. It seems simply grotesque when well-known representatives of European and American capital still maintain that the work for revolution in other countries is now purely theoretical, and that in practice Messrs. Stalin, Litvinoff, etc., have thoroughly adapted themselves to the views and the claims of their bourgeois friends. It is true, of course, that when necessary the work of preparing revolution is carefully hidden from the eyes of business acquaintances; but once the situation allows the mask to be dropped, as happened after the disorders of February 1934 in Austria, Moscow's activities are clearly revealed. The Moscow press openly reports collections for the victims of the Austrian revolution and tells how the proceeds were sent to Austrian Communists and Socialists.

The Soviet press even states that these sums were remitted to Austria to prepare for fresh struggles not so much in the Socialist as in the Communist interest. Precautions adopted when dealing with major Powers are neglected when dealing with a minor Power like Austria, and what is more or less concealed elsewhere is here proclaimed quite openly.

It must in fairness be conceded that the Soviet regime and press at present display astounding frankness in admitting the activities and aims of the Third International in various countries. Thus Sosnovsky's letter of recantation, mentioned above, contains the following reference to the co-operation between Communism in Russia and in other countries. "Even if the world revolution should be delayed, our victory is assured, provided that we are guaranteed decent relations with the peasantry for the next ten or twenty years. Admittedly the Soviet Union would have been spared many difficulties in the past and present if Germany were ruled by a government under Comrade Thaelmann and not by the hangman of the working classes, and if England, instead of being administered by that hybrid between jackal and fox,[1] were governed by the fraternal English Communist Party. So much is obvious. But though the capitalists remain in power in those countries, the experiences of the first and second five-year plan demonstrate that even if the world revolution is delayed, we are assured of an amazing growth of Russia's resources; and this growth will accelerate the coming of revolution elsewhere. Assuredly, too, the victory of the proletariat in other countries will improve the outlook in Russia for the perfection of the Socialist structure. This in turn will allow us to give liberal support to the new Soviet Republics abroad."

Sosnovsky concludes by declaring that if the "various types of opportunists" had remained in power, their principles would have ruined the regime, so that it was a piece of good fortune that Russia possessed a strong and determined ruler like Stalin to control her policy. In this direction, too, Sosnovsky concludes, there would be neither compromise nor withdrawal so long as Stalin remained at the head of the State.

Anyone believing that Sosnovsky's words should be regarded as merely theoretical should be told that the same issue of *Pravda* contains the following references to contemporary world-revolutionary questions and to Russia's participation in them. First there is a sympathetic report on "unrest in the Australian navy," due to bad food and inhuman working conditions. *Pravda* comments thereon: "Following on the recent disorders in the British battle-cruiser *Hood*, this disaffection brings fresh proof of the growing class-consciousness of British sailors."

[1] When this letter was written, Mr. Ramsay MacDonald was Prime Minister.

On the same page is a report on conditions in another bourgeois country in the shape of an account of the trial of fifty-six Communists at Lutsk (Polish Volhynia), who are alleged to have been beaten and otherwise maltreated. The leading article, entitled "Vienna, Paris and London," contains the following significant passages: "Despite the different conditions prevailing in Austria, France and England, there is a close connection between the revolutionary events in these three countries. The widest proletarian masses are in ferment there; the idea of revolt is ripening in their consciousness. Recent events (the demonstrations by the unemployed in London) have shown that the masses regard with distrust the agitation of the Labour Party and are commencing to adopt the platform of the revolutionary struggle. The Communist Party in England is not very numerous; still it numbers some hundreds of thousands and is setting itself the task of exerting an organized influence. In England, too, the proletarian struggle is beginning to grow."

The celebrations in commemoration of the fifteenth anniversary of the Komintern in March 1934 showed the aims pursued by Stalin and the Third International in supporting and organizing revolutionary movements abroad. At that time the Soviet press published an article by M. Sorkis, bearing the significant heading "Laws of History and Laws of Artillery," and having the underlying idea that the masses everywhere in the world can follow one path only, that of bloody and resolute fighting, of revolutionary assault, of battle on behalf of the Soviet power. According to Sorkis this fight should be directed equally against "Social Democrats and opportunists within our own ranks"; for this fight against opportunism is like that between proletariat and bourgeoisie—a necessary stage in the development of the bourgeois State. Hence the task is everywhere "uncompromisingly and consistently" to prepare the outbreak of revolution.

Now what guarantee does Sorkis imagine to exist for the

success of this policy? He sees it in the fact that to-day the Third International has a real leadership, "calm, modern and logical leadership." "Under Stalin's guidance the Komintern is educating everywhere a new generation of proletarian leaders and fighters on Stalin's model."

So Stalin is not only the absolute lord of the Moscow Government and of the Communist Party of the Soviet State, but, as leader of the Third International, he is also in charge of a staff of newly trained local fighters, who one and all—for this can be the only meaning of the reports contained in the Soviet press—receive direct instructions and support from Moscow. Their chief task is to prepare the inevitable and bloody revolution in their own countries, and, by achieving the victory of Communism in the rest of the world, to free the Soviet Union and its trade and industry once and for all from the ring of bourgeois states which surrounds them.

Such is Stalin's logical conception, which treats the work of communization in Russia and in the rest of the world as a whole, one and indivisible. According to this view Communism in Russia can be saved from collapse only if the iron ring of bourgeois states can be broken; and this is possible only if the Soviet regime remains intact in Russia, whence it can provide nourishment for the whole movement.

A remarkable achievement of the Third International was its work in Germany. It there succeeded in organizing a large part of the population under its direction and in making far-reaching preparations for a Communist revolution. The Communist movement had been the only one before the Nazi revolution, with the exception of the National Socialist movement, to organize wide circles of the German people. How strongly Moscow had counted on the "fraternal government of Comrade Thaelmann," as Sosnovsky calls it, to seize power in Germany, is apparent from many recent Moscow commentaries and from the observations published in the Moscow press when Dimitrov arrived on the conclusion of the Reichstag fire trial.

Since the revolution in Germany the efforts of Moscow have been concentrated primarily upon France. This is entirely consistent with the Communist principles and line of action. During the years following the conclusion of the Treaty of Rapallo, Moscow consistently strove to organize wide masses of the German people in preparation for the Communist revolution, despite friendly relations with official Germany. Now to-day similar principles are being applied in dealing with France. While the Governments, the industrial organizations and the military authorities of both countries are in friendly collaboration, Communist agitation is carried on with all possible vigour and thoroughness.

The question arises whether these methods are compatible with Moscow's assurances of the friendly intentions of the Soviet Government. Many of Russia's enemies think that they are pure hypocrisy, and that Russia with her powerful armaments is simply preparing an armed attack, or, as Sosnovsky calls it, "the bloody assault." This view seems to me untenable. On the contrary, I believe that the Soviet Government sincerely desires peace, indeed urgently requires it for the realization of its plans.

It should be mentioned in this connection that Moscow's method of preparing revolutions in various states abroad was radically altered a number of years ago. In my opinion this change was largely due to the failure of the military *Putsch* at Tallinn (Reval) in December 1924. Since then the Soviet State as such has declared its intention of maintaining friendly and peaceful relations with all the bourgeois states, while the work for the realization of the ultimate aims of the Soviet is carried on exclusively through the Third International and its agents in the various countries. In this way Moscow is enabled to play the part of the champion of peace in Europe.

In this connection it may be well to state that *Humanité*, the French Communist organ, replying to French interpretations of the *communiqué* published in connection with the festivities and speeches on the occasion of M. Laval's visit to Moscow, roundly declared: "The world revolution is and remains the aim of Communism."

I have been compelled to dwell at length upon the ideology and the aims of the Soviet regime, because only a clear understanding of these will enable us to see why recent Russian developments could not have been other than they were. Moscow's, or rather Stalin's, ideology and aims inevitably led to the present Russian economic policy as described in my first chapter. Just as inevitably this policy led to convulsions in various districts, which in turn compelled the regime, if it wished to preserve its existence, to begin a ruthless war against all its enemies, including those in its own camp.

Mr. Muggeridge has admirably insisted on the inevitability of the struggle which Moscow is to-day compelled to carry on in various directions. He finds that what he calls the modern forced labour in the grain fields of the south and the forests of the north is not due to the evil intentions of a few individuals, but is an unavoidable consequence of Russian ideology when translated into action. The dictatorship of the proletariat led to the Communist Party; the latter to that of the political bureau, and this in turn to the dictatorship of Stalin and the ideas which possess him. According to Mr. Muggeridge, these guiding notions can be realized only if embodied in the life of the entire population. But the majority resists, whence the necessity of subjugating it by force. The atmosphere in which this struggle between the champions of the guiding idea and the peasantry is carried on is described by Mr. Muggeridge as fear of force, fear of the loss of the bread ration, fear of being expelled from one's domicile, fear of denunciation to the police. Tyranny and fear dominate everything.

In Sosnovsky's letter of recantation, quoted earlier, he

writes: "What would have become of the party if it had pursued the path of our alleged democracy and left the selection of leaders to electoral caprice without the firm hand of the Central Committee?" What, he asks, would nationalists in the Ukraine and the Northern Caucasus, and the Pan-Islamite movement in Asia, have done in such a case?

These observations admirably characterize the present position. Stalin is at the head of the pyramid, waging a relentless war against all opponents of his person and his regime. To subdue all resistance within and without the Communist state, a firm and, above all, a single will is required, employing all other forces and factors as merely executive organs; in other words, as simple tools—whether high or low is immaterial. With the help of these tools—Litvinov, Kaganovitch, Ordjonikidze and the rest—a single and consistent line of action is maintained, even if it is necessary to have recourse to foreign capital to complete the work of reconstruction.

Stalin now worked with all his power to preserve the Soviet Union as a Communist "cell" for the rest of the world. This meant the preservation of the Communist structure of the country without admitting any bourgeois elements whatsoever. It is only if we remember this that we shall understand how Stalin could come to take the desperate step of suddenly collectivizing the entire agriculture of the Union.[1] "Nep" had led to a temporary improvement of the position, or at any rate to a breathing space; it had strengthened the position of private enterprise, thus threatening the structure and the supporters of the Communist order. If "Nep" had retained the supremacy, private enterprise would in the long run have remained victorious over Communism. This Stalin clearly perceived, and in order to preserve Communism in Russia he was willing to risk Russia's very existence—to allow the State to perish rather than permit non-Communist elements

---

[1] Stalin was interested not so much in the agricultural as in the sociological and political aspects of the problem.

to re-establish themselves as masters of its economic life and later in its culture. Only this explains the courage with which Stalin embarked upon collectivization. Further, it was only because absolute power was and is centralized in Stalin that he was able to keep in subjection hostile and disaffected elements, and to preserve the system from collapse, despite the enormous economic, national and other difficulties. Even so, he was able to secure victory only by a brutal struggle carried on daily and even hourly against all elements regarded by the Soviet regime as unreliable or merely as not reliable enough. The dimensions of this struggle can be seen from the fact that Stalin's annual purge of the party has on occasions swept away as many as 20 per cent of the party members. I have shown elsewhere that this purge is largely intended as a measure to defeat nationalism in various parts of the Soviet State. Within the Communist Party the purge is only part of the struggle carried on to-day by Stalin against the real or supposed enemies of Moscow.

Ever since the Bolshevists seized power, the standpoint of Moscow has been that any compromise with non-Bolsheviks is impossible and that its existence demands the extermination, as far as possible, of all who hold non-Bolshevik views. The extirpation of the enemy began at once. It was carried on by direct methods for years, the elements in question were arrested, banished or executed by the organs of the State, mainly by the Ogpu, or, as it is now called, by the State Security Police. At first it was solely the Ogpu—the all-powerful Soviet Russian secret police—whose work it was to keep "class enemies" in subjection. It is no longer necessary to describe the manner in which it fulfilled its task, but even its more than summary methods were found by degrees to be too costly and too cumbrous. Another direct method was then adopted, which consisted in banishing undesirable elements as *kulaks* or "enemies of the State," without trial, to do forced labour in the forests of the north or in Siberia. The fate of these persecuted and banished *kulaks* will always form one of the most terrible chapters in Russian history.[1]

Thanks to such methods it became possible to turn the persecution of these unreliable elements into an important economic measure; these modern slaves naturally became the source of the cheapest labour for the Soviet Government. With the help of the banished *kulaks* the exports of timber, etc., could be enormously increased, and at the same time those dumping prices made possible, which at the time created a sensation all over the world. A most striking illustration of this combination of "punishment" and economic exploitation is to be found in the banishment of thousands of Ukrainians and others to the north-west of European Russia to complete the canal from the White Sea to the Baltic. This was a magnificent piece of work, and Moscow has utilized it for propaganda in every direction; but its completion will always be associated with the destruction and the sufferings of banished "enemies of the State" from the Ukraine.

The so-called "special transfer" of peasants from the south to the Far East and elsewhere, where they worked for the State, falls under the same heading. Formally, at least, this measure differs from the banishment of the *kulaks*; for in this case the transfer was effected simply in order that the peasants should be enabled to work in regions where land and opportunities awaited them. In reality, however, the fate of these settlers was no better than that of the persons who were banished to the north.

Latterly, however, the struggle has attained gigantic dimensions, partly by reason of the developments among the nationalities described elsewhere, and partly through the rise of Stalin's personal dictatorship. The Moscow regime is now employing a new and effective method of getting rid of its enemies— destruction by indirect means. This is based upon the peculiarities of the Russian class and rationing systems. This is the

[1] Cf. *Das übertünchte Grab* previously mentioned. Also *In Wologdas weissen Wäldern*, by Alexander Schwarz: Altona, Hans Herder.

decisive factor, the explanation of which is the key to a proper understanding of what is happening in the Soviet State, and the opportunity it affords the Soviet regime of exploiting the famine in the struggle against its enemies.

In the Soviet Union, that classless state, all ranks, titles and social distinctions have indeed been abolished. But the old distinctions have been replaced by new and much greater ones. To put it shortly, they consist above all in the fact that a limited number of privileged persons are given sufficient food, while the rest are undernourished or in some cases have to starve. This contrast dominates the life of the population to-day, from the Black Sea to the Arctic and from the Baltic frontier to Siberia.

Even M. Herriot, in Odessa, was struck by the fact that in the summer of 1933 there were different categories of shops or of bread-card holders in the Russian towns. He found that there were the following different kinds of bread-shops: (1) the co-operatives, (2) the Odessatorg, etc., which sold food at high prices but without bread cards, and (3) the Torgsin, which sold to foreigners and others bread which had to be paid for in gold roubles or in foreign currency. (Natives also were allowed to buy food in the Torgsin shops for gold.)

M. Herriot thus distinguished between three different methods of obtaining bread and other necessary food supplies. Even this cursory observation indicates the principles on which the whole Soviet system is based. The chief of all Soviet principles is that it is the business of the State to maintain the supporters of the regime by the system of State rationing or even to give them food in plenty, according to their usefulness to the regime; but at the same time to restrict to a minimum of food those who are not particularly useful or positively harmful to the regime. The category of the privileged—i.e. of the well-fed, for everything depends on food nowadays—is contrasted with the suffering masses far more acutely than in the old Tsarist Russia.

The contrast between these two classes has recently grown in intensity. Walter Duranty mentions that 1934 was a turning point in social life. He describes how dance halls and jazz bands are springing up everywhere in Moscow, Leningrad and other cities, where the Communists indulge in dancing and flirtation like the detested bourgeois of the Western world. The big hotels, formerly reserved for foreigners, have now become the meeting places of the Communist public, which spends the hours until the early morning eating, drinking and dancing. All are well dressed, and Duranty thinks he can see the coming of a new age of gaiety and cheerful living in the Soviet Union.

Other foreign observers who have been able to observe the night life of the Communist aristocracy at Rostov-on-Don and elsewhere have reported that the most acute misery and distress prevailed within a few yards of these haunts of pleasure. They came to the conclusion that this new orgy of amusement was partly a consequence of the latterly increasing corruption among wide circles of the official world. This corruption, and the attendant illegal revenues which many Soviet officials now enjoy, were strikingly revealed in the great trial at Kiev, which ended with sentences of death or long terms of imprisonment for numbers of leading officials in various local economic organizations. This re-emergence of social activity is not, as Duranty thinks, a result of improved conditions; it is merely an indication of the growing gulf between the elect and the mass of the non-privileged. It should be remembered that a desire to impress the outer world with the growth of a bourgeois system in the country has induced the Government to foster the growth of society life and night life, with Paris frocks, jazz music and other attributes of modern sophistication.

Two worlds face one another to-day in the Soviet Union, separated by a deep gulf. The privileged govern, administer and control industry, agriculture and trade. They may be described as the supporters of the State system, that vast apparatus which lives at the expense of the rest of the population. It would be a mistake to include all State officials within this privileged group; it embraces only the members of the higher categories, while minor officials, such as station-masters and the like, live in the utmost distress like the public generally.

It goes without saying that the privileged group may be subdivided into several subordinate categories. The more essential a functionary is to the economic and political order of the system, the higher is his rank in the hierarchy of the privileged, at the head of which stand the rulers themselves, members of the G.P.U., of the central organizations, of the higher command, and the like. Shades of difference may be distinguished in the rationing even of these members of the highest categories, a fact confirmed by every foreign observer returning from the Soviet Union. Thus we hear that members of the army are treated less well than those of the G.P.U. and that officials of the Commissariat of Foreign Affairs and certain other privileged departments of State occupy an exceptional position compared with other officials in the capital.

The following account of the rationing of the various categories of the population is based in the main on information supplied by a Swiss workman who, on his return after a long stay in Russia, communicated it to the *Neue Zürcher Zeitung*. Since the autumn of 1933 there has been no substantial change. The most exalted circle consists of those entitled to so-called Kremlin rations. Kremlin rations are so liberal that ration cards alone amply suffice for all needs; the prices which have to be paid at the various distributing centres are so low that 75 roubles a month is quite enough for one person. The Soviet aristocracy has further so-called food coupons, allowing it to eat in the metropolitan restaurants; the price of a coupon is 1·60 roubles, while the same food would cost 25 roubles if sold free of control. Besides high Soviet officials the privileged class also includes certain stars of the Moscow theatres, some of whom, as the correspondent of the *Paris Soir* recently reported, lead lives of luxury as mistresses of the Commissaries. They have cars of their own, and are loaded with jewels and costly furs.

The second place within the highest category is filled by the G.P.U. They are given good and cheap food and some of them have their own canteens. The third class consists of the garrisons in the capitals. While not so well looked after as the first two classes, the army's rations are adequate, at any rate in the big towns visited by foreigners. In the smaller provincial towns food is always, and uniforms generally, very poor.

The next class of the privileged consists of the industrial workers in Moscow and Leningrad. Rations are smaller, and the factory kitchens are dearer than the communal kitchens of the G.P.U. A plateful of soup with some macaroni and a small piece of meat costs 1·65 roubles. Workmen's rations in the provinces are considerably worse; here there is a definite shortage of food.[1] Yet the workers' position is excellent compared with that of other employees, such as draughtsmen and clerical staff. The lowest class in this category is occupied by the peasants in the collective farms, some of whom belong to the group living on the margin of subsistence.

The foreign specialists constitute a separate and privileged category with regard to food and pay. Their standard of living simply does not compare with that of their Russian colleagues.

[1] *Pravda* of February 18, 1935, reports an incident illustrating to the full the arbitrary treatment to which the non-privileged classes of workers are subjected. This account relates in cool and detached language how the workers in the canteens of the Isakogorsk works had protested because there was a cockroach in the soup, whereupon the secretary of the party committee of the Sosnin works punished them by compelling them, under penalty of dismissal, to eat a soup consisting entirely of cockroaches. The account in *Pravda* shows that the workers were compelled to submit.

Experts agree in reporting that the food rations (*payok*) of industrial workers in the provinces are often so small that the workers frequently have to buy a part of their food in the extremely expensive State shops.

Special mention should also be made of the members of the model collective farms which form the foundation of Russia's agricultural propaganda for the benefit of foreign journalists and other eminent visitors. They occupy a privileged position, and have to do most of the talking at the Moscow congresses of the collective farms.

The same Swiss workman has interesting facts to relate about Russian wages and salaries. Factory managers and high officials receive 500 to 1,000 roubles a month; officers 500 to 800; high Communist officials 400 to 800; engineers, agricultural experts, architects and managers 350 to 600; teachers at high schools, inspectors, foremen and technicians 200 to 400; draughtsmen, doctors, school teachers and dentists 100 to 150. Cabinet makers, tool makers, etc., earn 300; electricians, carpenters, turners, 240; bricklayers, painters, etc., 180; locksmiths, fitters and lathe hands 120; textile and leather workers 90. In many of the provincial towns workers are paid 50 to 60 roubles. Rates are not uniform, and many factories, especially those outside the big towns, pay less than the show places.

It must be borne in mind that the rouble has a different purchasing power according to its owner. At Moscow the father of a family may earn 400 roubles a month as book-keeper in a trading concern. His daughter is perhaps a shock brigade worker in an engineering office and is paid 150 roubles. But her 150 roubles are worth more than her father's 400, because her cards are cheaper and she has access to privileged distributing centres, so that she has to pay only a fraction of what her father will have to pay at the ordinary co-operative shops.

Much has been written about the variation of prices in Russia; I will confine myself here to a few examples. A kilogram of meat bought against ration cards costs on the average 3·18 roubles; without ration cards or bought at uncontrolled prices in a State shop, it costs about 30 roubles. The corresponding prices for bread are 19 kopecks and 4 to 8 roubles; for butter 7·30 and 45 roubles; for sugar 2·60 and 15 roubles; and for potatoes 25 kopecks and 3 roubles. Thus, while a Communist or Ogpu official pays 3·18 roubles for a kilogram of meat against his ration card, a provincial worker, whose card entitles him only to bread and meat, has to pay 25 roubles for a kilogram of meat. The same applies to all other foodstuffs, so that a workman would pay 477 roubles for foodstuffs which would cost the Ogpu officials 100 roubles. A high Ogpu official obtains a decent lunch at his club for 1 rouble, while the workman has to pay 1·65 for a poor dish of soup. The same applies to clothing, boots and all other necessaries, including rents: everywhere the classes of minor importance to the State are neglected, while the "State-preserving classes" enjoy numerous privileges. No wonder foreign observers, who consort only with the privileged categories, do not perceive this fact, and conclude that there is no hunger and no distress in Russia.

We have, then, on one side the recipients of the ample Kremlin rations, the industrial workers with their more modest rations, and the local Communist organizations (which often form a transition group), and the members of the show collective farms; on the other the great mass of starving, miserable people.

These "non-privileged" classes include above all the majority of the peasants, as well as certain categories of minor officials and employees in the provincial towns. These are so ill-nourished that many of them have lost all desire to live. They receive too much to let them die, not enough to live.

So it is that two to three million "State supporters" live as in an island of plenty surrounded by an ocean of hunger and misery. Renegades are banished from the blessed island and are cast out into the sea of the starving. Hence the ghastly discipline which is the foundation of the Soviet State.

The contrast between the life of the privileged classes and that of the masses, and between Government promises and realities, has been described by Basseches in a Moscow report published in the *Neue Freie Presse* (November 17, 1933):

"Russia is still in distress. I can still see in my mind's eye hundreds lying in the railway stations of the Northern Caucasus and the Urals, underfed, often miserably clad, waiting for days and weeks to find a seat in the train. The regime promises new trains, new lofty stations. But hunger has yet to be overcome in the Ukraine. Tremendous efforts are needed to supply millions of people with the barest necessities.

"But Moscow's propaganda posters promise that next year will see the fulfilment of every wish, even the most fantastic. Therein lies their political importance. That is the new political line of the Soviets. The Russian is tired; he would prefer bread to macadamized roads and butter to mammoth locomotives. The State complies, and produces this decorative propaganda to show that the dictatorial regime is at length going to attend to the subjects' personal needs. The red poster showing a macadamized road will perhaps be replaced tomorrow by a huge red canal lock with a smart steamer going through it—an allegory of the Stalin canal, the new waterway between the Baltic and the Black Sea.

"As yet every dwelling in Moscow displays a collection of bell-pulls and brass plates to show that in every flat where formerly one family lived each room now shelters a numerous family. But the propaganda posters promise impressive blocks of flats. On May 1 the city was decorated with accounts of what the heavy industry has done and what was achieved during the five-year plan."

This account, together with the details given earlier in the book, shows that the Soviet Government is enabled, by means of the system of rationing and the compulsory collection of grain, to inflict the severest injury on any groups of people incurring its displeasure, if not actually to annihilate them. No special individual persecution is necessary. The way in which this "indirect method" is applied to the peasants in the provinces has already been explained in detail; so that it now remains only to refer to the ill-treatment and even extermination of undesirable categories in the towns. The Russian food-rationing system is such that outwardly everything is in perfect order. Individuals are allocated to certain distribution centres and are required to comply with their regulations. The essential point of this system is that the various distributing centres are the only places where persons attached to them are legally entitled to obtain supplies. Persons attached to one distributing point have nothing to do with the members or supplies of another. They are thus more closely bound to their own community than, in earlier times, were the members of any guild or profession. Each commissariat and every great Soviet organization has its own distributing centre, which observes the utmost reticence towards outsiders with regard to the quantity of its supplies.

The people in the towns who are worst off are naturally those who have no licence to work or permission to reside. These unfortunates are automatically doomed to starvation. Their fate is a particularly tragic one. The strictly regulated system of rationing enables the authorities to make the whole population completely dependent on the regime; a "regulated situation" prevails which in effect is the essence of tyranny. No protests avail against inclusion in any given category. The individual has to remain satisfied with the amount of food which the regime considers proper for his category, and if this is insufficient it is his function to accept the inevitable, to vegetate in hunger, or to die without protest. For a protest would be evidence of a class-hostile spirit or of hostility to the Soviet regime.

How far the privileged categories in the Soviet Union differ from the more comfortably situated elements in the "class states" is another question. The general economic decline of Russia has led to a standard of living which by non-Communist standards is extremely low even among the

M

privileged classes, whose chief advantage it is that they can satisfy their food requirements more completely than others. Few people regularly enjoy what would be an ordinary meal by Western or Central European standards; this would be the acme of luxury in Russia. Messrs. Lang, Muggeridge and others have described how a present of food suffices to induce any Russian to talk.

Persons unable to obtain goods by means of cards, i.e. those not belonging to the categories having a right to the issue of these cards, are consequently forced to buy quantities of food in the open market at speculative prices. If the salary or wages are inadequate—and these are settled by the State and its officials—the person in question cannot even purchase a minimum of food, to say nothing of clothing and other essentials. Thus the members of certain categories, e.g. the *lyshentsy* —members of the ex-bourgeois groups—are exposed to malnutrition, hunger and even extinction without any special measures of persecution or penalization having to be employed against them. This state of things has become worse since the bread cards were abolished and the bread became dearer for many who had hitherto obtained it on the card system. In the provinces similar results are obtained by giving privileged treatment to members of the old collective farms and by forcibly collecting the harvest from the bulk of the producers.

Since 1933 things have grown worse than ever. Although the harvest had been good, the supplies of grain available were so scanty that the numbers of those who could obtain sufficient nourishment had to be further decreased. At the same time Moscow thought it detected a growing menace from the "class-hostile elements" and nationalists in various parts of the country. More rigorous measures were taken against these groups. Moscow argued—and in my view was bound to argue— that the food shortage was a heaven-sent opportunity to be exploited in this struggle. It was now possible to settle once and for all with the real and imaginary enemies and to exterminate them more systematically than before. The famine now became a political weapon.

Early in 1933 the extent and suddenness of the famine had come as a surprise, and elements of the population perished whose disappearance was not considered to be in the interest of the Government. In future it was intended to proceed according to plan, and to utilize the famine in order to exterminate —especially in the agricultural districts—those groups which the Government regarded as the natural enemies of the official views on the questions of the nationalities, religion, family, etc.

In connection with the famine and with the radical change in the Russian policy with regard to the nationalities, Moscow now began a struggle whose extent it is impossible to gauge. It was recognized that not only the Ukrainian population, but also the inhabitants of the other districts, were offering an obstinate resistance. Hence Moscow became convinced that almost the entire older generation, including leading circles in the local Communist Parties, felt the appeal of pre-Communist ideas such as religion, home and nationhood. All these persons were regarded as being practically class enemies, for Moscow saw in them irreconcilable enemies of the Soviet State and the "proletarian internationalism" which it preaches. It now became possible to deprive certain groups of producers, above all the individual peasants, and even the population of entire districts, of the minimum necessary for existence, i.e. by not leaving to the peasants the necessary grain or not restoring it to them (as was done to the members of many collective farms). In this way the individual peasants were completely eliminated; either they entered the collective farms in so far as they were allowed to, or they died of starvation. In addition to the elimination of the individual peasants a rapid purge of "class-hostile elements" within the collective farms was undertaken in order in all circumstances to preserve the remnant of collective farm peasants. In 1933 comprehensive measures were taken to separate the "harmful elements" from the "reliable collective farm peasants," to expel the former and to leave them to starve, but to help and save the latter and carry out the full agricultural programme with their aid.[1]

These statements are based on reports published in the Soviet press. As an example I may quote events in Western Siberia as reported by the political departments of that region.[1] A report of the political section of the motor and tractor stations furnishes unique evidence of what is going on not only in those parts but all over the Soviet Union. It begins by stating that the political sections in Western Siberia were simply following instructions given by the Central Committee of the Communist Party. The work done by these sections consisted and still consists in purging the collective farms of elements belonging to other classes. In 1933, 7,494 persons were expelled from the collective farms of the sixty-three motor and tractor stations as belonging to this category. Of the heads of the collective farms from 40 to 50 per cent were expelled. The report went on to say that there were still collective farms which were "defiled by anti-social elements, and that the work of cleansing them continues."

What does this statement mean? It reveals the methodical work being done to free the collective farms from the burden of undesirable elements and to transfer the thousands thus expelled into other categories, where they are left to their fate. Everything is done, on the other hand, to assure the subsistence and future of the remaining docile members, and measures in that sense are continually to be read of in the Soviet press. Reports are often published vehemently reproving officials who fail to treat the collective farm workers as they ought to be treated. Further, a distinction is made between the collective farms as such, i.e. between the privileged show collective farms and the rest.[2]

[1] Cf. *Pravda*, March 11, 1934.

[2] By a resolution adopted at the Moscow Congress of collective farm representatives (March 1935) the distinction between the old, i.e. the "show" collective farms and the non-privileged collective farms is very clearly

The means by which even members of the collective farms can be "legally" deprived of their harvest is described by *Pravda* of March 17, 1934. It reports that on a collective farm in the district of Shpoliansk the payment for work done was not made to the members in kind as it should have been; on the contrary, the management calculated the value of the grain in money and told the men that they might buy grain from the farm for these amounts. The result, according to *Pravda*, was that the accountants of the Kondratenko collective farm credited a worker with 737 roubles for 910 working days where his actual claim should have amounted to 3,722 kilograms of grain and 365 roubles. The difference of 372 roubles was nowhere near enough to make up the deficiency in grain. The *Pravda* report showed in any case how the members of the collective farms can be deprived of their minimum of food by perfectly legal accounting methods, the bread ration being simply calculated at the high official prices.

Other collective farms are dealt with in other ways. There is a decree in existence ordering that in future no steps shall be taken to secure supplies to the *prikhlebateli*, i.e. the village doctors, minor officials and rural intelligentsia in general. This again is an unpopular category because many of its members belong to the older generation or else support local nationalism. Rudzutak's account at the Moscow Communist

revealed. According to the new agrarian statute adopted by the Congress every single collectivized village community will in future have the entire land of the collective farm in question made over to it for all time. This means that the privileged collective farms are assured in perpetuity of their present extent and their present membership. New members—i.e. individual peasants applying for membership—need not be admitted, and these have no choice but to form new collective farms under particularly unfavourable conditions, the best and most fertile soil having long ago been given away to the old collective farms. How great is the difference in the situation of the different collective farms can be seen from the fact that as early as 1924 there were some which distributed 25 kilograms of wheat per working day, while there were others whose figure was no more than 1½ to 2 kilograms. There can be no doubt that the new statute will bring about new and wide class distinctions among the rural population.

Congress of 1934 fully explains the official attitude with regard to these *prikhlebateli*. He said: "Another question is the abnormal burden placed upon the machinery of the collective farms by various parasites who have nothing to do with the work of the collective farms, but are paid work-days, i.e. in kind." Rudzutak went on to explain that he referred to postal officials and employees of the road administration and transport institutes, etc. This explains a report recently published in the Soviet press according to which sixty station officials from Kazakstan and the lower Volga had escaped to the Donetz region, to eke out an existence there as workmen. The alleged reason was that the wages they were to receive were higher, but no doubt they fled simply to escape starvation.

As for the non-privileged categories in the towns, their treatment consists in a more intense application of the possibilities for the destruction of undesirable elements which the rationing system puts into Moscow's hands. How deliberately and systematically it goes to work is best proved by the passport decree (referred to in an earlier chapter) which was enforced in the summer of 1933 in various towns, a measure which is probably unique of its kind.

The main object of this measure was to regulate the "liquidation" of expelled persons. It provided that all inhabitants of the towns in question whose passports were not renewed were to proceed to a place at least sixty miles distant from the town. Thus at one stroke the towns were freed of the unemployed, of the *lyshentsy*, expelled persons, etc. The authorities had no longer to fear that the sight of them might produce an unfavourable impression on foreign guests of honour. What happened sixty miles away was another question; even if they died of starvation the towns were rid of them. Shortly after its promulgation the passport decree was extended to another twenty-five towns and to the western frontier zone, to a depth of sixty miles, as well as to new factory plants,

State farms, and tractor and motor stations. The towns in question include Moscow, Kiev, Odessa, Minsk, Rostov, Stalingrad, Baku, Gorky (Nijny Novgorod), Magnetogorsk, Sebastopol, Perm and Cheliabinsk.

All inhabitants who were refused passports had to leave within ten days and were not allowed to return. These hundreds of thousands of unfortunates had no recourse except migration to a place not barred to them, where they had to apply for a new passport. It is significant that the execution of the new passport regulations was entrusted to the central militia administration of the Ogpu. It is easy to imagine what a tragedy this regulation meant for countless people.

I described in the last chapter the disastrous effect of Moscow's policy on the various nationalities in the country. It would be wrong if the impression were conveyed that this policy of destroying entire groups within the population were directed exclusively against the nationalities. The Moscow Government adopts similar measures against all those groups within Russia proper which resemble the nationalities in remaining loyal to the concepts of religion, family, nationhood, etc. Take as an example the measures for the extermination of the Kuban Cossacks.

A former member of the staff of the *Moscow Daily News*,[1] an American called Sanger, who was in a position to follow events on the spot, mentioned how after the sanguinary revolt of these Cossacks in 1932, tens of thousands were sent into banishment. Most of those who were left died of starvation in 1933. The chief crime of the Kuban Cossacks was that they resisted the forcible collection of grain.

Mr. Witting Williams, also an American, who travelled extensively in the south, wrote that the events taking place in the Kuban mountains were the result of a political plan. The Cossack population was being mercilessly starved; almost everything was being taken away and the Cossacks were

---

[1] A newspaper published in English in Moscow.

dying in masses. As the result of this policy whole communities of Cossacks were exterminated: for instance, the Kuban Cossacks have practically ceased to exist.[1]

What the intentions of the Soviet Government in this respect are is clearly visible from a speech[2] delivered in May 1934 to a conference of judges and other administrators of justice by Krylenko, the Soviet Commissar of Justice. He referred to rumours circulated, as he said, by "wiseacres," that the time had come for a certain relaxation in the rigour of the Soviet punitive organs, and said then literally: "That would be a great mistake; the class war must continue and must even be intensified. The enemy classes had been shattered, but individual class enemies still existed. We have not shot them all, we have not caught them all, we have not destroyed them all physically. Many toilers came under the influence of class enemies and were upsetting the plans. They also must be handled by punitive organs; we must educate by compulsion."

These words of the Soviet Commissar of Justice speak volumes. They show that in spite of the use of famine to eliminate "class enemies" the Soviet has by no means given up their older methods.

The statement of Krylenko shows clearly that the direct persecution of individuals, "undesirable" in the Soviet view, is still carried on with the help of Ogpu and other political organizations. In view of the gigantic dimensions of the struggle, the older methods no longer suffice. Stalin's decision to start the collectivization of Russian agriculture led inevitably to the famine, to Moscow's struggle against the nationalities, and to the employment of famine as an instrument of national policy.

---

[1] The *Osservatore Romano* (August 1934) records the following significant utterance of Stalin: "The Cossacks have a middle-class mentality. I have no doubt that they will take the first opportunity of rebelling against us. We must exterminate them as a class and a caste, and even their memory must be destroyed."

[2] Published in *The Times*, May 11, 1934.

These are all links of one chain. The famine which in the beginning overwhelmed the Soviet as an unforeseen catastrophe, was gradually transferred into a kind of disciplinary institution—"organized famine."

Moscow's aim is clear: the present generation, in so far as it remains loyal to the principles of nationhood, religion and family, is to be exterminated, to clear the way for the conquest of the rising generation. The young are to be uprooted and set free from old-world influences, that they may be won over to the ideals of a world proletariat—unencumbered by God, nation or family. This is Moscow's self-imposed task to-day: for this is held by the Kremlin to be the sole means of realizing the victory of Communism. To achieve this object it is essential first to destroy the old generation which still believes in God and nation. This explains the fanatical hatred with which Moscow—despite the denials of its friends and agitators abroad—is obliterating the remnants of religious life and exterminating the clergy of all denominations in the country. It would exceed the scope of this book to describe the measures by which Moscow seeks first to uproot and then to win over for its own aims the growing generation by first destroying the foundations of family, religious and national life. But what is at stake is not the youth of Russia; it is much more than that. If Moscow really were to succeed in inspiring the growing generation with a lasting hatred of religion, family and nationhood, the very foundations of Western civilization would sooner or later be endangered.

CHAPTER V

PROPAGANDA METHODS

THE question will be asked: Why is the existence of the Russian famine so unknown to the public of the world outside that its existence can be disputed or actually denied? How is it possible that in the twentieth century—an age of wireless, aeroplanes and the like—millions of persons can die and the fact remain unknown or at any rate be a matter for debate. The question demands an answer, the more so since a reply would explain the indifference with which the world in general and the Western democracies in particular regard the fate of those who are perishing in Soviet Russia. I must, therefore, deal briefly with the entire system of the news service on Soviet Russian affairs and the unique work done by Moscow in order to influence it.

The task with which the Soviet regime is faced at the moment is a heavy one. The hated bourgeois world, which is indispensable for the maintenance of the Russian economic system, must be induced to co-operate with the Soviet State or even to support it politically as well as economically; and this at a moment when, under Stalin's leadership, Moscow is compelled to take steps to break through the ring of non-Communist states by undermining them and fomenting world revolution. Simultaneously, the present struggle to maintain the Communist economic system makes it necessary to prevent disturbances from without and above all to ensure the political and economic support of the outer world for this transitional period. If the systematic preparation of revolution abroad is Moscow's first principle, its second must be to take account of foreign public opinion.

It is a task of Russian foreign policy and of the Third International, both under Stalin's guidance, to ensure that official and unofficial policy can proceed in conformity with these two principles. Hitherto this has consistently been done. While Communism and class war were being organized abroad, no toil and trouble were spared to achieve propagandist successes and to win over public opinion to support the Soviet Union and to ensure friendly co-operation with it.

Before dealing with the methods employed by Moscow to this end, I must recall a fact which is generally neglected but which is of prime importance for the success of Soviet propaganda. Russia is a vast country and is unique in its geography, its ethnography and in the backward state of its communications. The distances in Russia, and the remoteness of certain regions from the centres, are unparalleled in Europe. I myself, in the years immediately preceding the war, travelled through the most distant parts of the Russian Empire, partly in connection with my studies, and later in the execution of a special economic task in the interest of my own homeland. I was struck even then by the remoteness of the provinces from the capitals and by the ignorance prevalent in the great centres about conditions in the countryside. Beyond the Volga, a few miles from Kazan or Ufa, there was already a different world Opened up by no railways, it could be reached in winter only by sleigh routes.

Even before the war foreigners could admire the cream of Russian culture and art in Moscow and St. Petersburg and remain wholly ignorant of the everyday life in the provinces. Visitors coming to Petrograd and Moscow, Kharkov and Kiev, have naturally but vague notions about conditions in the rural districts. It is this peculiar nature of Russian geography and of Russian communications which forms the foundation of the propaganda exerted to influence foreign public opinion. Foreign guests of honour, and journalists and "Intourist" travellers in general, are practically confined to the two capitals and a few provincial centres. Other districts are inaccessible because of transport difficulties, lack of accommodation and other reasons.

Thus it suffices if the capitals, a number of provincial centres and the stretches along the main roads are adapted to foreign "invaders": a few miles away there is no need for any change.

The secret police—and this was also true to a certain extent before the war—takes care that when visitors stay in the capitals or in the provincial centres they learn practically nothing from the local population. They are left under the illusion that they can move anywhere at any time and have access to the inhabitants in order to obtain any information they may desire, and to a certain extent the illusion is based on fact. Visitors can do as they like; the system at present employed by Moscow does not consist in any open restriction of *their* liberty of movement. It operates not upon the visitors but upon the local inhabitants, whose every word and movement, while in contact with visitors, is strictly controlled. The presence of an Ogpu official in the humble role of a hotel servant or an "Intourist" clerk is enough to remind the inhabitants of the consequences which may follow any careless word spoken to, or, indeed, of any contact with, a stranger. The unhappy inhabitants would risk their liberty and even their lives if they explained their dreadful position to a visitor; and it is not from them that information can be obtained. Even from leading professors at Leningrad (Petrograd) and Moscow and members of the Academy of Science, just as from representatives of the local population, the foreigner will always hear what the Ogpu and its agents want them to hear. If anyone tells them any other story, his fate is sealed.

Another means employed to prevent news of the real position from being spread abroad and creating alarm there is the procedure employed—quite apart from the control of the Russian press—in dealing with foreign correspondents stationed in Moscow. Practically these have freedom of movement only in the capitals, the provincial centres and along the chief lines of communication, where any local inhabitants dealing with them are subject to the same control and, if necessary, to the same persecution, as those who come into contact with foreign tourists and guests of honour. Further, any reports sent to the papers abroad are subject to direct or indirect censorship and also to an unrelaxed pressure. Pierre Berland writes as follows on these methods as applied to the famine[1]: "The silence of the press on this subject is one of the most astonishing phenomena of present-day Russia. There is a kind of conspiracy of silence on the food situation, the disastrous nature of which is an open secret. The official censorship dominates the telegraph and remorselessly mutilates the despatches of foreign correspondents, allowing only comparatively harmless expressions like 'grave supply difficulties' and so on to pass muster. These expressions may perhaps mean something to those who know Soviet Russia, but are pure euphemisms as applied to the real position."

The pressure exerted goes so far that in cases where foreign correspondents living in Moscow report something which the authorities consider inadmissible, they are immediately and mercilessly expelled. For material and other reasons, a number of the journalists living in Moscow are anxious not to lose their posts in that city. (Moscow is doubtless a very good post for many of them from the material point of view.) Among the foreign correspondents there are some who have already been expelled once and who have had the greatest trouble in getting the expulsion cancelled.

It is not that the reports of the Moscow correspondents are untrue[2]; but they neglect, or at the most mention only in passing, the unfavourable aspects of Soviet life—on the principle "one step forward, two back." They never see any occasion to give the undesirable phenomena the same attention which they devote to Moscow's supreme achievements.

[1] *Temps*, July 18, 1933.
[2] Cf. facts recorded in this connection by Malcolm Muggeridge in his *Winter in Russia* (London) and by W. H. Chamberlin in his *Russia's Iron Age*.

It should be added that in cases where the Soviet Government desires to prevent foreign correspondents from obtaining first-hand information about the position, it simply prohibits them from moving outside Moscow.[1] But it is confirmed on all hands that Moscow is a positive Eldorado compared with the rest of Soviet Russia, and this is especially true with regard to living conditions for foreign journalists and diplomatists. And even if a Moscow correspondent obtains the Kremlin's permission to travel in the provinces, he is invariably confined to the routes and to the provincial centres specially designed for tourist traffic. Naturally enough, reports of such journeys are restricted to impressions from sleeping-cars and dining cars—for example, on the famous route from Moscow to the Caucasus via Kharkov and Rostov, or the lines to the big provincial centres.

By the side of this group of journalists who are compelled to pass over the gloomy side of Soviet realities with vague allusions, while reporting in full detail the record achievements of the regime in art, music and science, there is another and a deliberately misleading group who do not hesitate to spread untruthful reports about Russian conditions.

Another method which Moscow is now compelled to adopt in order to prevent the truth from being known abroad is the elimination of the last permanent foreign eyewitnesses of events in the south, e.g. by the dissolution of the *Drusag*, and by refusing to renew the contracts of foreign specialists. Apart from all this, all foreigners visiting Russia are more rigorously treated, for it is thought undesirable to have a repetition of the incidents of 1933, when men like Malcolm Muggeridge, Harry Lang and Gareth Jones succeeded in evading the vigilance of their guardians.

The chief measure, however, is to refuse permission to leave the country to Soviet citizens desiring to visit relatives abroad. Attempts to escape are treated as crimes: the inhabitants of the Soviet Union are like mediaeval serfs tied down to a definite territory.

[1] A decree to this effect was issued in the summer of 1933.

The general impropriety of these methods is well illustrated by the way in which Moscow dealt with those *Drusag* employees who were of German race but not of German nationality. When the company was wound up, and hundreds of these employees had suddenly lost their positions, *Drusag* offered these officials a chance of emigration and of fresh work. Moscow, however, decided that, apart from German nationals, no *Drusag* official was to leave the country. Most of the former *Drusag* employees, who are rebuked for having worked for a foreign undertaking, are now exposed to the hardest of lots —some, indeed, to extinction. The point is—and this illustrates another of Moscow's methods—that the Russian Government can thus exercise a kind of blackmail over the former *Drusag* employees who are now abroad; for it is assumed that they will, at least for a time, be reticent in revealing the true position in the south, if only to save their former colleagues from reprisals. This, as has been generally known for years, is one of the oldest and best-proved of Moscow's methods. Fortunate exceptions are made only when the Government's need for foreign exchange becomes urgent; then, characteristically enough, certain Soviet citizens are allowed to leave the country. In such instances an operation takes place which in reality is simply a modern trade in human beings. For a sum of £100 or £200 or even more, Soviet citizens are handed over to their relatives through the intermediacy of "Intourist"; but these are only a few elect persons, while all others, even if they have promises of work or support abroad, have to continue under the system of "modern forced labour," as Mr. Muggeridge calls it.

Since the famine has become so much more acute in Russia, there have been an increasing number of cases where members of the Russian services, particularly of the air force, have fled abroad and have given accounts of the position in Russia. In order to prevent escaping officers and officials from spreading such reports the Soviet Government has had recourse to a measure exceeding everything done in recent times in the way of reprisals against Russian citizens. Early in June 1934 a decree was issued containing the official proclamation and legalization of reprisals against the hostages mentioned above, i.e. the relatives of refugees. Thus it is now possible in Russia that people who may have had nothing to do with their relatives' offence (this is expressly stated in the decree) may be condemned to exile or penal servitude up to ten years, and in cases where they are suspected of complicity, sentenced to death—or, rather, as there can be no real judgment—to retaliatory vengeance. Here for the first time principles are proclaimed in a penal code which, if it were not in the Soviet Union, would rouse the indignation of all Europe. It is interesting that a few days after the decree was issued, a flying officer who had escaped from Russia, G. Krawts, gave an address in Paris in which he declared that he had seen the Kirghizes in the Orenburg district dying of starvation. It is unlikely that after this latest decree any more officers of the Red Army will be found to risk the lives of relatives by escaping abroad.

But more important, perhaps, for Moscow is the solution of the second problem—how to create, in every State and every part of the world, a favourable view of the economic and cultural development of the Soviet Union. The task demands hard and systematic work; optimistic reports have to be produced in a steady stream and spread by the most various channels. There is no doubt that Soviet work in this field will always be reckoned a masterpiece. In particular it should be noted how correctly Moscow is able to appreciate the economic selfishness and the permanent conflicts of interest which prevail in the ruling circles of the capitalist states. It must be accounted a psychological masterpiece on the part of Moscow that it knew in advance exactly how far it could go in dealing with the public of these countries. Nor did it overestimate the capacity of the capitalist world to swallow the most primitive and transparent propaganda so long as it appealed to self-interest.

Collecting corpses for burial

These families boarded a train and went to Kharkov to demand food, which they did not, however, receive. When the train was opened they were found to have died from hunger on the return journey

The last journey

Moscow knew, and indeed openly stated, that as soon as these other states perceived political or, above all, economic advantages, however transitory, all regard for more lofty ideals, e.g. the fate of kinsmen living and dying in Russia, would cease to have weight.

The principle of Moscow's propagandist methods is always the same: to broadcast record achievements and to create the illusion that the general development of the country conforms to these records and thus approximates to the ideal state aimed at by Communism. And, indeed, everything possible is done to create the impression in the bourgeois world that, "despite inevitable difficulties and obstacles," the realization of the desirable state which the Communist theory promises the nations of the world is already approaching. In its endeavours Moscow propaganda is favoured by the extraordinary suggestive force exerted by Communist theory on many just and high-minded persons all over the world, quite apart from the fact that certain industrial interests in many countries—actuated exclusively by selfish private considerations—are only waiting to catch up and spread the Bolshevist slogan that business with Russia brings ample profits to all countries taking part in it.

The chief preliminary condition for the success of the pressure so actively exerted on world public opinion is that Moscow, simply to attain its end, has no regard for truth, real facts or any ethical considerations. Stalin and the Kremlin know one principle only: "The end justifies the means"; and in the present case the end demands that economists, statisticians, officials and others shall calculate and represent as true whatever is demanded of them. The whole Soviet apparatus is the servant of this task which the Kremlin has dictated.

The Government, correctly estimating the credulousness of the non-Communist world, believes it possible to publish facts and figures which contain extraordinary exaggerations. The Bolsheviks say to themselves that this method almost

N

always secures its object, if only because even the sceptics who discount the figures and calculations of the Soviet institutions still have an impression that "the truth lies somewhere in the middle." It may be said that to have created this impression is one of the greatest successes of Soviet propaganda. M. Herriot claims that his observations of the situation in Russia, containing a denial of the existence of any famine, exemplify the view that "the truth lies somewhere in the middle," contrasting them with the extreme views of other witnesses. Indeed, it can be said that the thesis of "the truth lies somewhere in the middle" is to-day exploited by practically every propagandist of Soviet Russian achievements. A most striking example of the disregard of truth in making calculations for a special purpose is the recent harvest statistics. But it is not only statistics whose function it is to create the illusion that Russia is a land of great achievements and successes. Much more primitive methods are used for the same end. Thus grandiose plans are launched to build unique hospitals and civil institutions, and these serve as propaganda material before a stone has been laid. The following is a striking example. On March 18, 1934, *Pravda* contained an interview with Comrade Sadovsky, the director in charge of the construction of the Institute of Experimental Medicine in Leningrad. The director had now gone to America, accompanied by an impressive staff, to travel about with gigantic plans for the building of this institute. The report says that in New York the commission met the world's greatest specialist for hospital buildings, the Government commissioner for hygiene in New York, Dr. Goldwater. This expert was consulted on the plan. Dr. Goldwater thereupon stated that he could render an opinion "with enthusiasm and appreciation." There were no private persons, no organizations, however powerful, and no governments which could construct an experimental medical centre to rival that of the Soviet Government. Never before had there been a building of such dimensions. After printing this opinion, the paper added that the doctor had signed a contract according to which he was to be consulted while the building was in progress, and that he would go to Russia in the summer.

The Soviet Government also makes use of industrial exhibitions abroad. The object is to display really striking exhibits, which produce in the astonished visitor the impression that the efficiency of Soviet industry and the quality of the products of Soviet industry by far exceed the highest expectations. Such exhibitions have for years formed the centre of attraction at various European fairs—at Riga, Königsberg, Leipzig and Marseilles. Moscow always achieves its object; the impression is produced that Soviet industry in all its branches is quite extraordinarily efficient. Yet it is the same industry whose vast and systematic mass production of *brak* (shoddy goods) led to the issue of the decree for the punishment of the officials responsible by exile to Siberia.

As an instance of the effect such exhibitions have on wide circles, I may quote the recent Soviet exhibition at Marseilles. M. Herriot, the Mayor of Lyons, was so much affected that he made the following declaration in the Soviet press:[1]

"Brightly illuminated, attractive, decorative, and even exciting our envy, the Russian stands are daily visited by numerous groups of attentive and interested spectators. All are favourably impressed by the raw materials and manufactured articles shown, which demonstrate the achievements of the new Russia. The mass of goods exhibited is incontrovertible evidence of the industrial activity of a powerful country. A tour of the Russian exhibition is an education in facts and ideas which lead to the most valuable useful conclusions. We feel that this country is not among the victims of the economic crisis, now raging all over the world, and that it is making vast endeavours to increase its production, to expand its consumption, to open

[1] Significantly enough this declaration was published throughout the world by the official Russian telegraph agency under the heading: "A manifestation of the economic power of the Soviet Union."

new markets, and to develop economic possibilities, in order to win the leading position in world industry."

M. Herriot went on to say that the Soviet held this exhibition in order to "prove the possibility of such an exchange as that having for foundation the Franco-Russian trade treaty signed on January 11th." The problem of this exchange is, according to M. Herriot, clearly set forth, "and all that matters now is to find men of goodwill on either side able to solve the problem." M. Herriot concluded by saying: "For my part I have made no secret of the fact that I support a rapprochement with the Russian people in every sphere; they are a people for which I feel a genuine attachment and which I salute yet again."

Another part of Moscow's economic propaganda consists in giving commercial advantages of a temporary kind to certain states in order to suggest to the public that things in Russia have now reached a stage where an exchange of goods with that country would be of the greatest advantage to its traders. The advantage derived by the Kremlin from the fact that all its economic decisions are centralized, whereas this is not the case with its foreign competitors, will be appreciated.

Yet it is evident that a propaganda intended to produce in the outside world the impression that economically, socially and culturally the Soviet Union is well on the way to realize the ideal Communist State cannot rely wholly on invention, exaggeration and hypothesis. It can be successful in the long run only if it can, to some extent at least, take its stand upon actual concrete performances.

I pointed out that during the Tsarist period numbers of foreign visitors formed wholly fallacious judgments. They were deceived by the existence of two different worlds. Now, as then, Moscow and Leningrad, together with a few provincial centres, are the seats of artistic and cultural institutions which reach a respectable standard in such fields as the ballet, theatre, music, painting and, above all, science.

In view of these achievements foreign visitors can honestly speak of the high cultural development of Russia. But the crucial point is that these achievements are in no sense a clue to the real social and cultural position of the bulk of the population. On the contrary, the latter is quite disproportionately backward. The cultural achievements of the capitals are simply a mirage; they characterize a *milieu* in which a small circle of the elect lives its own life quite apart from the misery and distress of the population. Incidentally, it may be observed that the principal achievements in science, the theatre, the ballet and art in general are for the most part the work of the same men as before the Revolution.

Apart from these performances in the field of science and art, the propagandist activity of Moscow also makes use of its giant industrial undertakings of model works, like the Dnieprostroi dam, the Magnetogorsk plant, of the super-Soviet farms, and the like. These undertakings are no evidence of any healthy economic progress in the country. On the contrary, they are artificial creations erected with a vast expenditure of State funds and with the assistance of the best foreign specialists. The question whether they would pay and what their budget would look like was never elucidated or answered. This is another element assisting the regime in its propagandist activities, since it is in a position to present to the admiration of the outside world and of foreign visitors not only scientific and economic achievements, but also the "show monsters" which have been erected in different parts of the country, above all the Dnieprostroi dam. The cultural institutions in the capital and these special giant undertakings are the main foundation of the unique propaganda which is being methodically and most successfully pursued by the Soviet Union with the assistance of guests of honour, tourists and journalists.

It is possible to sum up by saying that Soviet Russian propaganda, in so far as it aims at creating a favourable view of the cultural, social, economic and artistic progress of the country, is based on a combination of imaginary statements and generalizations drawn from certain exceptional performances on which no inference as to the general position should be based. The resultant impressions are spread among all the states of the outer world, both orally and in writing, and through a number of different channels.

The most important of these is the press which is at the disposal of Moscow. The activity of this press should not be confused with that of the Moscow representatives of the bourgeois press; I am speaking of the numerous Communist or pro-Soviet papers abroad, which stand directly or indirectly in the service of Moscow propaganda. Such papers appear in every language. The most important are those which, while not ostensibly of Communist leanings, do the work of the Third International under the guise of anti-Fascist propaganda.

The Russian press has to bear in mind the fact that its readers have a certain knowledge of conditions within the Soviet Union; they know, for example, that there is such a thing as a famine. Those British, French and other papers who are of a pro-Communistic tendency have, therefore, among others, the task of conducting the whole campaign against those eyewitnesses who testify to the truth in Russia, quite irrespective of what Russian readers may know. It is the task of these papers to attack critics of conditions in Russia—in quite different ways, as the local conditions dictate—sometimes by apparently objective argument, at other times by mere abuse.

There is a far-reaching division of labour between the Russian press in the country and the Communist organs supported directly or indirectly in New York, Basle, Paris and elsewhere. Statements and opinions which cannot be upheld in Russia on account of the local population are left to papers abroad; and the same applies to views which Moscow prefers not to publish in its official press in order not to injure its political relations with the Western Powers. In such a case the Communist papers abroad proceed to action.

For example, the Russian press has for years observed complete silence on the question of the attitude of the outer world to foreign aid in the matter of the famine. The obvious reason is that the population of the agricultural districts, who cannot well be told that there is no famine, must not be allowed to learn that endeavours to help them are being made abroad, or, indeed, that the outer world is aware of their plight. It is intended that the population shall believe that the outer world takes no interest whatever in their unhappy situation. Here again the organs controlled by Moscow have to take the field— for example, against members of the international relief organization—by methods of controversy, denunciation and innuendo. This printed propaganda makes use of pamphlets and agency reports as well as of newspapers.

But it is oral propaganda which continues to be the chief and growing instrument of Moscow's activity. The work is done by spokesmen who may be Communists proper or else pacifists, anti-Fascists, etc. Since the West has recognized Soviet Russia, and the latter State has established friendly relations with a number of countries, new possibilities have opened for Moscow's propaganda. As an instance I may quote the campaign carried on by the German Communist, Willi Münzenberg, with a number of other Communists of different nationalities, in the summer of 1934 in the United States. With the slogan "For Peace and against Fascism"—a slogan which in itself has nothing to do with Communism—Münzenberg and his friends succeeded in holding mass meeting in all the cities of North America; and the camouflage was so successful that these activities were supported by numerous bourgeois people and papers. Münzenberg's speeches, however, did not so much deal with the advertised subject—the dangers of Fascism—as with the praise of Communism and with an explanation of how a Communist revolution might be brought about in the quickest way. Münzenberg's activities show how successfully Moscow's emissaries can camouflage themselves by substituting the "fight for Peace and against Fascism" for the struggle on behalf of the Bolshevist world revolution. But it also shows how easy it is for Moscow and its emissaries to deal with non-Communist circles and how slight is these circles' power of resistance.

This kind of oral propaganda is not confined to Moscow's official spokesmen. The Kremlin has also succeeded in enrolling numerous auxiliaries who have succumbed to the fascination of Communist ideals. It is specially skilful in exploiting for its oral propaganda a number of personal interests. Thus the Kremlin has for years been spreading Communist principles in various professional bodies, under the cloak of an appeal to common professional interests.

For example, Moscow has been trying to induce certain professional groups in Russia to attempt to exert propagandist influence on their colleagues abroad. In March 1934 *Izvestia* reported the fiftieth anniversary of the all-Russian theatrical union. It pointed out that this was the oldest Russian union of "stage-masters" and communicated to theatrical workers a resolution of the union in which the following declaration was addressed to their colleagues all over the world:

"The seventeenth Communist Congress has worked out a concrete plan to prevent the exploitation of men by men and to bring about the final dissolution of the remnants of capitalism in economics and in human consciousness. . . . All lovers of art are asked to watch the proletarian revolution and to join their voices to that of the Communist party in their country in order to support the latter's propaganda on behalf of the Soviet power and of the revolutionary overcoming of the crisis." "We know," the appeal concludes, "that the way to a rich and happy life is barred to-day by the ruins of the old world which has been blown sky-high." The comrades all over the world are then promised support in their fight. The passage in *Izvestia* proves that the latest Communist Party congress has resolved not to confine itself to official State propaganda, but to attempt to influence given professional groups abroad as well, seeing in such a method a valuable means of influencing bourgeois circles.[1]

An important part of Moscow's oral propaganda is carried out by high Soviet officials, who appear in public and formulate the principles of this propaganda in a number of effective catchwords. One of the most conspicuous spokesmen of the Soviet regime who have this task to fulfil is the Commissary for Foreign Affairs, Litvinov, who has proclaimed the achievements of Soviet Russian industry and the prosperous development of the Soviet State in general in a manner hitherto unsurpassed. I mentioned above that the emissaries of Moscow have the power, in accordance with the principle that the end justifies the means, of totally disregarding the facts of the moment. Litvinov possesses this faculty in a striking degree. At a time when numbers had been executed in consequence of the assassination of Kirov, he did not hesitate to protest in a public session of the League Council against terrorism in certain non-Communist bourgeois states (it is true that he confined himself to individual terrorism), in order to put on record the hatred of the regime for terroristic methods.

When the Soviet Union joined the League he sang the praises of Moscow's policy in dealing with the nationalities, and even went so far (this in the League Council) as to attack the disturbers of the peace among the nations, without a fear that such words, coming from the champion of a Government whose principle it is to work consistently towards a revolution in the non-Communist states, were bound to excite astonish-

[1] The question, what success has attended this personal propaganda, is well answered by a number of observers in the United States. They claim that at many universities (e.g. Chicago) a large proportion of teachers and undergraduates inclines towards Moscow and its doctrines. This observation may frequently be made in certain circles of those countries which are remote from Russia

ment. Litvinov, who has an exact knowledge of the mentality of leading circles in the bourgeois states, rightly argues that while things are as they are no one will oppose him, much less contradict him, either in the Council or at any other international meeting. The result is that his statements about the policy and achievements of the Soviet Union, and his protests against the terror exercized by certain quarrelsome bourgeois states, are published by the press of the entire world.

When Mr. Eden visited Moscow, Litvinov actually went to the length of having "God save the King" played at the banquet given in his honour, although everyone knew that the Tsar Nicholas II, a first cousin of King George V, was murdered with his entire family by the express orders of the Government, among whose chief members was Litvinov. The fact that Litvinov listened to the National Anthem standing led the press to conclude that here was yet another indication of Russia's adaptation to the bourgeois world, and were even prepared to see in this event the proof that Moscow had given up its old Communist aim of world revolution. Litvinov's attitude had clearly gained a notable success for Moscow and Moscow's policy.

Special attention should here be drawn to what has latterly proved the most effective method of Russian propaganda. I mean the exploitation of the personal evidence furnished by foreigners, guests of honour, "Intourist" travellers and others who have spent a few days or weeks in the Soviet State, on the strength of which they lay claim to "a knowledge of local conditions."

The propaganda carried on with the help of foreign guests of honour, tourists and journalists, is pursued in accordance with an exact plan of action. It is based upon the institutions in the capitals and in the "show giants." Indeed, it would be hard to produce better evidence for the favourable development of economic and cultural life in Russia than that afforded by the British, American and other travellers. These people spend a few days at Leningrad and Moscow, and perhaps at Kiev and Rostov-on-Don; they are profoundly impressed by all the achievements they have seen in the sphere of the theatre, of art, of industrial reconstruction and of model farms, and when they return home they duly spread the news of the amazing cultural and economic developments in Soviet Russia.

I mentioned above that in all the vast territory of the Soviet Union only a few towns and only the main traffic routes have been adapted by the authorities to the requirements of people travelling for purposes of study. To see, much less to study, all the rest is wholly impossible. As to the towns and routes mentioned above, they have been prepared in every respect for their foreign visitors. They possess, what is not necessarily true of all Russian towns, more or less habitable hotels, which incidentally are meeting points for Ogpu officials; in other words, secret or open centres for the supervision of foreign visitors. The hotel servants without exception are in the service of the local Ogpu, and this is true also of those inhabitants, especially certain ladies, who enliven the restaurant and cocktail bars of these hotels on given occasions. But the hotels are never visited by the local population, if only because their prices are adapted to foreign purses. Yet, although the prices are far beyond Russian means, the hotels are uncomfortable and poorly-furnished; indeed, when M. Herriot stayed in a hotel at Rostov the bed of the local Ogpu chief had to be put at his disposal—a fact of which he is probably unaware to this day.

No sooner has the foreign visitor crossed the frontier than he is taken over by political agents who supervise him from morning until night under the guise of special guides, "Intourist" officials, hotel employees, agreeable ladies, and so on. Their attention, however, is devoted not so much to the visitors as to those inhabitants who for any reason come into touch with them, so that these are well aware that they risk their neck if they make any rash remark. In any case, of foreign visitors to Russia, not one per cent, or one in a hundred and fifty, can speak Russian. (Persons who formerly lived in Russia are almost without exception refused a visa.) It follows that visitors are completely dependent on their guides and hosts; there is an invisible wall between them and the populace, and they have not the faintest notion of the conditions under which the latter live. Furthermore, the local population is in a permanent state of mental depression and has a feeling of personal inferiority, the result of hunger, malnutrition, continuous worry, the general dreariness of existence, and not least fear of tyranny and persecution. The result is that even if they could, without attracting notice, establish contact with the foreigners —those members of a higher and happier *milieu*—they would on principle avoid them. Instead, the foreign visitors are regaled from morning till evening with the special sights and the record achievements—all this according to a fixed plan. The same objects, such as the Dnieprostroi dam, are shown again and again.

As the inhabitants avoid contact with the strangers, and the few who approach them know the part they have to play, the visitors do not even suspect that they are being kept at a distance from the life of the people. This is true also of foreigners who stay in Moscow privately, i.e. not in a hotel. During a debate following a recent lecture at Cambridge a young student stated that he had travelled to Moscow out of curiosity and had taken a comfortable room with a Russian lady, where there were ikons on the walls; he added that his landlady went to church every day. He should be told that in the whole of Moscow, apart from members or friends of the Ogpu, there is not a single person who has rooms free to let to foreigners, still less anyone regularly going to church—in other words, no one ostentatiously vaunting his non-Communist opinions.

Certainly foreigners who go to Russia see much that is valuable in the fields of art and science. The mistake they make is in supposing that life and economic conditions in the Soviet Union can be fairly assessed from the small number of objects used for the purposes of foreign propaganda (and mostly also of national defence). How the regime succeeds in exploiting these impressions of foreigners is shown by the following instances. A year or two ago a French professor of agriculture visited Russia. On returning to France he published a report in the *Action Agricole* which was immediately telegraphed to *Pravda* and printed on the front page under the headline: "We have been left behind by Russia." (See *Pravda*, January 30, 1934.) The report contains this passage: "I was greatly impressed by the research institutions, the many experimental stations, and the high standard of work done. The results obtained do credit to Russian scientists. They are numerous and in some respects even sensational. To sum up, we have been beaten by Russia." There is no reason to doubt that Russian experimental stations and scientists, who had an international reputation before the war, are capable of important achievements. The point is that such statements are made without any hint that these institutions occupy a special position in their respective branches, and without a word being said to show that, as things are to-day, these exceptional achievements cannot exert a decisive influence on the development of Russian industry—which is borne out by hundreds of admissions in the Russian press.

It is hardly surprising, then, if a party of prominent English people like Mr. G. B. Shaw and Lady Astor, who cannot speak a word of Russian, should be roused to positive enthusiasm by the achievements, the special celebrations, and the attention paid to them generally. The members of this group and certain other tourists duly wrote a letter to the *Manchester Guardian* (March 2, 1933). This declaration was coupled with a direct criticism of the state of affairs in the non-Communist world.

Mr. Bernard Shaw's signature is the first beneath the solemn declaration published in the *Manchester Guardian*, a document which protests quite vehemently against all state-ments about forced labour, famine, etc., in the Soviet Union. I lay stress on this declaration because, in my view, this manifesto, issued by a number of eminent visitors at a time when the severest famine and distress prevailed in wide regions of Russia (a fact reported on by special correspondents of leading English papers who made their own local investigations) is the clearest evidence of the success of that branch of Russian propaganda which is based upon foreign guests of honour and their "unbiased opinions." (What is striking about this declaration is the special tone, the histrionic note, with which the position of the Russian workers, the new spirit and the pleasure taken in work are praised as compared with conditions in the non-Communist world. This is quite contrary to the admissions contained in the Kremlin's own decrees.)

There is something profoundly tragic in the way in which visitors to Russia treat the populace; for most of them have no idea that their conduct is harmful, nor, above all, do they realize the effect of their attitude. Travellers arrive in Moscow, Leningrad, Kharkov or Kiev. They take a lively interest in artistic achievements, social experiments, in the theories and catchwords of the rulers; but in one thing they take no interest—the fate of the unhappy people at whose expense these unique, unprecedented experiments are undertaken. Even the initiated almost seem to hold the view that the fate of people in Soviet Russia no longer concerns the world, perhaps just because it is inevitable.

The same reproach may be levelled in particular against the foreign journalists who year in and year out have admiringly described the construction of the giant concerns without troubling—as was their first duty—to investigate and reveal the human aspect of these grandiose experiments, and the burden and distress which they inevitably brought on the population. Often one had the impression that the travellers, experts and specialists treated Russia like a kind of experimental chamber.

They were interested in everything but the most important thing—the fate of the people as such. These hard words must be used, if only to show why I feel that these travellers, despite their ignorance of Russian and many other obstacles, ought surely to have felt enough human sympathy and sense of duty to attempt to discover the truth about the effects of these experiments on the people themselves.

The most effective part of propaganda by the spoken word is probably the remarkable work done by Moscow's wireless broadcasts. It may fairly be claimed that Russia is to-day the only state which has succeeded in making its wireless programmes serve the work of propaganda wholly and exclusively. It is true that this has become possible only because, unlike most other states, Russia completely controls the activities of the stations in the country; in other words, it can exploit them for the purposes of its propaganda without taking anything else into consideration. This is the only explanation of the fact that programmes in the Western European languages, which hardly anyone in Russia speaks, predominate. By employing British, French, German and other announcers, the fullest allowance can be made for the mentality of listeners abroad, and millions of British, French, Czech, German and Polish listeners are exposed to psychological pressure by their own countrymen.

The essence of Moscow's wireless propaganda is the spreading of invented or distorted information, more especially with regard to conditions in Russia. In dealing with foreign countries, with many of which the Kremlin maintains friendly relations, the wireless chiefly deals with the unfavourable aspects. These are then cleverly contrasted with the achievements of the Soviet regime. All this, if skilfully prepared, produces effects which often have an extraordinary suggestive power on distant listeners. The degree of solemnity or the reverse in which these reports are given out is invariably adapted to the contents.

As an example, I will describe a single programme, viz. that of Christmas Day, 1934. On the evening of this day, when millions of workers, of course, had time to listen in to the Moscow station, the programme was broadcast in several languages, being continually interrupted by the ringing of the Kremlin bells and the singing of the Internationale.

The order of the items was as follows. First there was a report from Kiev in German on the achievements in agriculture in the Ukraine, a report calculated to rouse envy at the extraordinary prosperity of the Ukrainian peasants. The *leitmotif* of this address was that Russia, unlike the bourgeois countries, knew neither hunger nor unemployment, and that the population was steadily progressing towards wealth and contentment.

The next item was in French and consisted in a paean in favour of Moscow, the metropolis of the world proletariat. Reference was made to the ambitious plans for the reconstruction of Moscow, and especially of the districts surrounding the palace of the world proletariat (i.e. the Moscow Government buildings). Mention was made of the sacrifices which the population of Paris, living in dirt and darkness, had to make in order to enable the Paris building plans to be realized—these, unlike those in Moscow, had cost vast sums in compensation to owners. Praises of the Moscow underground, as always, occupied a prominent place in the address. This glorification of Moscow as a world metropolis ended with a comparison between the achievements of the Russian theatre and the misery of bourgeois theatrical life; this was based on the brilliant successes achieved by the Russian delegates at the theatrical congress in Rome in contrast with the bourgeois delegates.

The Western listeners thus having been prepared by the glorification of Russian achievements, and some of them perhaps having become duly emotional as a result of the Kremlin bells and the Internationale, the Moscow station produced a masterpiece of propaganda by allowing this praise of Moscow to be followed by a description of crime and criminal statistics in the United States. Exact statistical information was furnished to demonstrate the fearful extent of criminal activities in the New World. Murder and robbery! Millions upon millions of dollars stolen! Thousands and thousands living a life of crime, organized gangs supported by the police! The sons of millionaires, full of sensual lust, and only waiting for the time when they can become criminals! It was indeed a picture of horror and degeneracy which was unfolded before the Moscow listeners. All this—that is the fundamental idea—did *not* exist in Soviet Russia.[1]

Similar items, long or short, are broadcast in foreign languages almost daily. There is always the same skilful contrast of light and shade—of light in Russia and shade in the bourgeois countries—which has a suggestive effect on the many listeners all over the world. This method of contrast can therefore be described as the very essence of Moscow's wireless propaganda. Almost daily the utterances of foreign statesmen are quoted, expressing themselves in laudatory or even enthusiastic terms about conditions in Russia as the result of their personal observations in Moscow.[2]

Moscow's wireless methods as here described are typical of all the Russian programmes which are broadcast in Western languages. Since the completion of the great Russian transmitting station Moscow has been in a position to address thousands of persons in the West, in America, and indeed in the whole world. In Germany, Austria, Switzerland and other German-speaking countries many people listen in to the

[1] The present state of crime in Russia can be learned from a plain account by Dr. Basseches in the *Neue Freie Presse* of April 28, 1935. He says that the police columns, which had been omitted for years in the Soviet press, had to be re-introduced. "It is found," he says, "that even official figures admit that there is a great deal of crime. There is so much crime that radical means have to be employed to overcome it."

[2] Among them are often very prominent politicians, such as M. Pierre Cot, whose remarks in the *Œuvre* were broadcast on February 19, 1935. "The only country," he said, "which knows no unemployment and where agriculture and industry are making continuous progress is the Soviet Union, the country of the will to peace."

German programme from Moscow, if only from a feeling of curiosity. The wireless enables Moscow to enlighten the bourgeois world on the Soviet achievements and revolutionary innovations, e.g. in the matter of marriage, sexual ethics, classlessness, etc. In the wireless propaganda service the Soviet regime undoubtedly has one of its most effective methods of creating the impression in the widest circles abroad that the Soviet Union, despite all difficulties, is approaching the ideal of the classless state.

The more friendly are its relations with the Western states, the more effectively the Government is in a position to exploit another instrument of its propaganda—namely, the cinema. There is hardly another instrument so suitable for giving the ' inhabitants of the bourgeois states an idealized picture of developments and conditions in Russia. Here the leading artists of the Soviet Union are able to use their talents to convince the outer world of the idealism and the achievements of the State. Thanks to their masterly technique, and the great ability of the producers and actors, some of these films have made their way all over the world.

Here, too, the two fundamental tendencies of Russian propaganda can be clearly traced: on the one hand the great achievements of Russia are described; on the other, the sub-human conditions in the bourgeois states are depicted. This latter tendency does not find full expression to-day owing to the desirability of cultivating good relations with the bourgeois world. The sound film called *Sailors of the King*, announced some time ago, which was supposed to show the wretched conditions under which the men of the Royal Navy had to live and work (the film was planned to show a mutiny in a vessel of the Navy), has apparently not been completed, or at any rate has not been shown abroad. The Russian standard film, the *Chelyuskin*, confines itself to comparing, quite *en passant*, a failure of the American aircraft industry with the remarkable achievements of Russian aircraft construction. It emphasizes—characteristically, only in the Russian language —that an airman using an American aeroplane crashes while landing on the ice near the *Chelyuskin* camp, while two other pilots using Russian machines make most excellent landings.

To-day Russian films are mainly used to glorify work and the conditions in the country. Thus in the summer of 1934 an evening was devoted to Russian art in one of the smartest Paris concert halls. It had been announced that a "completely objective" series of photographic documents on Russian conditions was to form the main part of this exhibition. And what was the Paris public told about the real facts in Russia? They were shown excellent pictures illustrating the youth of Russia devoting itself to sport and showing how the Bashkirs have learned to read and write. But the film was primarily designed to glorify the technical achievements of Russia, like the giant works and the Dnieprostroi dam. Mechanization as such was meant to illustrate the victory of Communism. Not a word, of course, was said about the victims.

Thousands and millions of people who follow enthusiastically the artistic pictures of the Soviet films imagine that what they see represents everyday conditions in Russia.

In connection with the successes achieved in the sphere of the cinema, a few words should be said about another method of carrying out optical propaganda. I mean the art of producing and circulating posters dealing with the musical week at Leningrad, the "Intourist" tours and all kinds of subjects. As late as the winter of 1934 effective posters could be seen in various places, e.g. in the Vienna trams, suggesting the sending of "presents" to friends and relations in Russia. The Moscow artists have far outstripped those of the non-Communist states in the art of achieving powerful effects by means of posters.

In this connection I may point out another instance which shows the absolutely unique manner in which the Moscow Government knows how to make a virtue of necessity, and even how to exploit Torgsin remittances for Russian citizens in

distress on behalf of its prosperity and progress propaganda.
The press (*Pravda*, May 20, 1935) stated that a religious
union in America had remitted some hundreds of dollars to
the Jews of the villages of Osarichi and Kalinkowichi by order
of two emigrants, Simon and Mendel Heim. These people had
formerly been "*kulak* exploiters," and the money was meant to
be distributed to their "starving countrymen." (The inverted
commas are the newspaper's.) "The impudent offer of these
former *kulaks*," *Pravda* declared, "caused profound indignation. At a meeting of the workers of both places it was unanimously resolved to return the money." It is easy to imagine
with what heavy hearts the suffering Jews carried out this
"voluntary" resolution. But what is most interesting, however,
is the "collective reply"—unanimously approved by the meeting
—which accompanied the return of the money. The reply runs:
"At a time when the proletariat is starving in every capitalist
country, not excluding America, in our country prosperity is
growing every day. In the free land of the Soviet Union, where
the national policy of Lenin and Stalin has been made a reality,
the Jews capable of work are labouring in the factories, the
works, the mines and in the Socialist fields. They collaborate
actively in the building up of Socialism. The 'starving countrymen' about whom you are so distressed are to-day living well
and working successfully."

Thus at a time when the Chief Rabbis of France and Paris
were describing in detail the extreme distress of the orthodox
Jews in Russia, and appealing to world Jewry for help, and
when even the Soviet representatives in every part of the world
had Torgsin posters put up asking for "presents" to be sent to
Russia, the money remitted by American Jews was refused on
account of the progress and prosperity of Russia, or often
handed over to the "Red Aid." Hundreds of pro-Communist
papers throughout the world thereupon published these replies
addressed to the "exploiters" abroad in order to prove the
falsehood of the allegations of distress in Russia. One cannot

help asking what is the object of the request to send "presents" to Russia.[1]

The success obtained by Russian propaganda—wireless, films, pamphlets, etc.—still depends to a certain degree on the art of devising slogans and catchwords to create an impression of remarkable progress and a high standard of living. For example, one of the most frequently mentioned sayings of 1934 was that of Stalin that "the collective farms were to be made Bolshevik and the collective farm peasants made prosperous." On January 3, 1934, the Moscow radio sent out a press notice in German for the benefit of the collective farm papers of the German settlement on the Volga. It ran:

"At yesterday's sitting of the central executive committee of German collective farms of the Odessa region, Comrade Merz reported that Comrade Stalin's watchword, 'The collective farms are to be made Bolshevik and the collective farm peasants made prosperous' has already been made a reality. In 1932 56 per cent of our collective farm peasants had cows; in 1933 the percentage was 89 per cent. Our slogan now is that by May 1, 1934, *all* collective farm peasants of the district are to have their own cows." Comrade Merz further reported: "In 1932 the collective farm peasant received on an average $2\frac{1}{2}$ kilograms of grain per unit of work. In 1933[2] they each received 12 kilos. These few figures," Merz concluded his press report, "show that we have made a reality of Comrade Stalin's slogan." After such figures, it is hard indeed to doubt that Stalin's catchword has been translated into fact!

[1] Here is another example of this propaganda. When a remittance was sent from Austria, three collective farm workers from Bergdorf (autonomous Moldavian republic) replied as follows: "You have come to the wrong address; we are not your 'suffering brethren.' We are led by the Communist Party of the Soviet Union, headed by our beloved Stalin. We have every opportunity of leading a cultured and prosperous life in our Socialist fatherland, and we do not require a single Fascist penny. We reject your assistance, to which we have replied by the rapid realization of the loan of the third year of the second five-year plan. By means of this loan we are strengthening our country and ensuring the future growth of its prosperity."

[2] When there was a severe famine.

Yet after the expiration of the period at the end of which, according to the words of Comrade Merz, every collective farm peasant was to be the owner of a cow (May 1, 1934), Comrade Postyschev had made the following admission (he had just been pointing out that in the district of Kharkov the decline in the number of cattle amounted to 60 per cent and that of pigs to 75 to 80 per cent): "What conclusion are we to draw from the figures given for the Kharkov district? The enemy, of course, will say that they mean the breakdown of the collective farm ideology; but we know that these figures only show the victims of the struggle with the class enemy—the victims of our apprentice period in the organization of the collective farms."

Thus, according to Postyschev, the plan is not by any means being fulfilled; on the contrary, it is not being fulfilled. None the less, Moscow continues its propaganda by wireless and in other ways to show that the collective farm peasants are in a state of prosperity and the industrial workers in a satisfactory position. The same applies to other of Stalin's slogans. Thus he says: "It is our task to double and treble the workers' standard of living and to make prosperous people of all the collective farm peasants. The collective farm peasant should have not only a cow but also a hen, a pig, a sheep and a goat." These slogans were spread abroad at a time when the one care of the peasants of the Ukraine, the Northern Caucasus, etc., was not to die of starvation.

Particularly important among the Moscow slogans is that which speaks of the unique solution of the social problem achieved in the Soviet State. For many years this claim has been the pride of Russia's foreign propaganda. Its exploitation is one of the main tasks of Moscow's court poets—those eminent Russian writers who have placed themselves at the service of Moscow and its aims. They are headed by Maxim Gorki, who is the darling of the Kremlin. These bards adopt a varying technique. Some follow the master and indulge in unrestricted praises of Stalin and the Soviet regime, while others, like Ilya Ehrenburg, mingle their laudations with a little modest criticism.

Gorki lives in a fine house specially built for him in the best suburb of Moscow, where he acts host to the pilgrims from the West who visit him. Romain Rolland quite recently, during a stay with Gorki, sought to obtain confirmation of his own views about affairs in Russia. The Soviet papers published photographs showing Gorki walking in his garden with his guest, or sitting at a table before dishes of the finest fruit. (See *Izvestia*, July 6, 1935.)

Hundreds of papers, wholly or in part under the command of Moscow, proclaim to the world the happiness of the nationalities within Russia and the solution of the nationalities problem. Thus we read in *Pravda* of July 2, 1935, that after the great *physikkultura* (physical culture) parade, in which thousands of Moscow's privileged young people took part, Maxim Gorki wrote a paean in praise of Stalin in the Soviet press under the title of *Joy and Pride*. He expressed himself as follows: "Long live Joseph Stalin, the man of great heart and great intellect, to whom our youth yesterday offered due thanks, because he has given them a happy life." (One cannot help thinking of the terrible moral and physical condition of the *besprizornie*, e.g. the thousands of wandering and neglected children.) "Long live the simple and clear wisdom of our leaders, the first and the only ones in the world who will never send their people to enslave Manchurians, Abyssinians, Chinese or Indians."

Moscow's attitude towards the problem of the famine, foreign relief measures, and the question of the need of relief in the agricultural districts, is an excellent example of the way in which the various instruments of Moscow's propaganda co-operate, and of the determination and ruthlessness with which it forces its view on the world. Since the summer of 1933 a struggle has been in progress between the bodies who ask for light to be thrown on the famine, and, if necessary, help conveyed to its victims, and the Moscow authorities; a struggle which might well be called a fight for truth. Moscow has been perfectly consistent and wholly untiring in defeating these endeavours by all the means at its disposal.

It will be readily understood why the Government could never admit the existence of the famine and thereby the real conditions in the agricultural districts. It had to do everything possible to discredit statements about the famine. This has been a special task of the Commissary for Foreign Affairs, Litvinov, who has admirably fulfilled his task. Thus at the World Economic Conference in London in the summer of 1933 he informed the assembled statesmen of the world that Russia was "the only country in the world unaffected by the economic crisis." Just imagine that when the various countries were already possessed of authentic information about the terrible catastrophe in Southern Russia, the Commissary had the assurance to praise the economic policy and the general conditions in his country, contrasting them favourably with conditions in the bourgeois states. He also declared—for the benefit of those states which were trying forcibly to stimulate their exports—that Soviet Russia intended shortly to purchase abroad goods to the value of a thousand million dollars. The Soviet regime knew by experience that it was impossible to overestimate the credulity of the bourgeois states and the mutual jealousy and conflicts which prevailed among them, and its view was once again confirmed. No one rose to contradict Litvinov.

Even more significant was the attitude of the Soviet delegation a few days later at the London Grain Export Conference. At this conference the Soviet delegates began a fierce campaign for the increase of the export quota intended for Russia from 25 to 85 millions of bushels. Although Russia has latterly shown that she is in a position to export grain even at a time of the severest famine, it was nevertheless obvious that she could not export much, and that the request for an export quota of 85 million bushels was made solely for propaganda purposes. World public opinion was to be made to believe that if such quantities of grain were available for export, the allegation that a famine existed must be a falsehood, a political campaign against Moscow. For nobody would imagine that there was a State which would conduct its grain export trade at the cost of the very lives of its nationals.

Yet there were certain circles in Europe who thought that the Moscow delegates were going too far, and the editor of the Paris *Journal*, Saint-Brice, wrote: "This" (meaning Moscow's protest against the lowness of the Russian grain quota) "is a tragic contradiction. The economic position of Russia is such that the country not only cannot export grain, but might well absorb part of the stocks lying abroad. There is the greatest distress in the Ukraine, the famous black earth lands; and the peculiar thing is that not a voice was raised in London to draw attention to the scandalous contradiction between Russia's claims to export quotas and the distress of the population. The reason is that everyone to-day is dazzled by the mirage of Russian orders and is only too eager to grant the Russian credits."

So much for the Russian attitude in London. Soon after a certain change of tactics became necessary. Late in the summer of 1933 there was a change in the position. A movement began which made it its aim to fight on behalf of the truth and to throw full light on the question of the Russian famine and the possibility of bringing help to its victims. The Vienna *Reichspost* had published an article containing exhaustive revelations of the position in South Russia, and the outlines of a general plan of relief. This plan was, in fact, the beginning of organized efforts to render assistance in the Russian famine areas in the south. The author's words were published in important journals in Switzerland, Sweden, Germany and the United States. A few hours after publication M. Petrovsky, the Russian Minister in Vienna, issued a categorical *démenti*; he also considered it necessary as late as August to describe

reports of the famine as "inventions." But he differed from
M. Litvinov in admitting that "certain economic difficulties"
were making themselves felt even in Russia as a consequence
of the world crisis.

This admission is an indication of the new tactics. Statements similar to that of Petrovsky were also made by the
official *Izvestia*. The paper went further, however, and saw
fit to couple its attacks on the *Reichspost* with a description of
Austria, "a country of hungry beggars living on alms from
abroad." Incidentally, this was the first occasion on which a
new argument of Soviet propaganda was used, when it was
claimed that the *Reichspost* statements were due to "National
Socialist machinations." This is a significant point; for it
indicates the sources of the assertion later made by M. Herriot,
who also claimed that the allegations of famine in the Ukraine,
the Northern Caucasus, etc., were "National Socialist lies and
insinuations." The Catholic and anti-Nazi *Reichspost* was
enabled to put in the right light these new Russian tactics
directed against the attempts to organize relief by pointing out
that Pierre Berland had almost simultaneously published his
report on the Russian famine in the *Temps*. The *Reichspost*
wrote: "The idea that the *Reichspost* of all papers should open
its columns to National Socialist tendencies will be taken at
its proper value by all shades of political opinion. It should
be added, however, that if reports about the Russian catastrophe were due to National Socialist influence, it follows
that this influence is particularly powerful in Paris."

Moscow issued equally unequivocal *démentis* in reply to
Cardinal Archbishop Innitzer's appeal to the world public.
Once again the Moscow press declared that references to the
disastrous condition in the Ukraine and the catastrophe
following the famine were "absolute inventions."

According to a United Press report the Commissariat of
Foreign Affairs even went so far as to state officially that in
Russia "there was neither cannibalism nor cardinals," and that

Cardinal Innitzer's statements about the famine and its attendant phenomena were "pure inventions." A few days earlier Mr. Walter Duranty of the *New York Times* had hastened to repeat the Moscow cry to the effect that most of the pessimistic reports on the Russian position emanated from circles hostile to the Soviet Union. Thus even in the summer of 1933 and before M. Herriot's journey there were clear indications that Moscow and its political friends were following the policy of describing reports about the truth in the Russian famine area as "the fabrications of political enemies."

In the course of the summer the German relief organization, "Brethren in Distress," and other bodies were redoubling their efforts, by collections and other means, to assist Germans suffering from famine in Russia. Moscow thereupon took steps to counter this movement by wireless and other propaganda. The German broadcasts from Moscow and the entire Soviet press began to insinuate that the "Brethren in Distress," an organization embracing all creeds, whose sole activity for years had been to assist Germans in distress in various districts of Russia by the despatch of Torgsin parcels, were working to foment political unrest in the Ukraine and elsewhere. The Moscow radio broadcast daily protesting statements from German colonists, denying the existence of distress and begging friends abroad to desist from sending Torgsin parcels; and press and wireless even went so far as to send out invitations from the German Volga colonists asking Germany to send a number of proletarian children to recuperate on the banks of the Volga. Simultaneously, the Government began to exploit all available methods of propaganda to counter relief activities in the West and with them the corresponding reports of famine.

Despite these activities, a growing pressure made itself felt in various European centres in the direction of rendering assistance, and this was possibly why a number of foreign correspondents followed Pierre Berland's example and determined to make excursions into the famine regions. Moscow simply forbade the foreign correspondents to leave Moscow. Surely such a prohibition applied to the benevolent correspondents at Moscow is more eloquent than all the *démentis* issued hitherto. Foreign eyewitnesses, however well disposed, were not wanted in the Ukraine, the Northern Caucasus and other areas; for the struggle in connection with the new crop had just reached its climax in those regions.

Yet, after August 1933, the controversy over the Russian famine and the necessity of rendering assistance did not abate; one appeal was followed by the next, and in Geneva the members of the League Council began to discuss the problem. It seemed as though the truth about Russia would succeed in prevailing after all.

But at this precise moment the Kremlin brought off a second master-stroke. The former French Prime Minister, M. Herriot, was enrolled among the witnesses supporting the thesis that there was no famine in Russia, and that the famine allegations were merely the manifestation of separatist tendencies fomented by National Socialists. At the same time Moscow ceased to proclaim itself as the pioneer of world revolution, but as an advocate of peace and stabilization in Europe. Thus it succeeded in winning various states for political co-operation and even economic assistance. These new friends did everything possible to prevent any discussion at home of the real position. Yet the questions, what had happened in Russia, and what course things were going to take there, still made themselves heard in the West.

Once again Moscow's never-failing imagination began to work. The work of propaganda had to be adapted to the new fact that the losses of human life unfortunately could no longer be kept quite secret. In autumn, after the new harvest, there is generally and naturally an improvement in the food position in the producing regions, and this fact was used in order to create the illusion of an unprecedented abundance of grain and foodstuffs. In order to achieve this end Moscow had what one is tempted to call a brilliant notion. Overnight the statistical methods of determining the yield were changed, and instead of the actual yield being taken as the basis, the total yield was calculated—as explained elsewhere —on purely hypothetical assumptions.

Thus despite the ruin of agriculture and of cattle-raising on which all the experts were agreed, the figure of 89,000,000 tons was, they claimed, reached for the latest harvest. The "splendid" harvest from now on was to be the watchword, dominating the press, the wireless and the rest, for nearly a year.

The attempt of the Norwegian Prime Minister, Dr. Mowinckel, to raise the question of the Russian famine before the League Council was foiled by the united resistance of a number of states which were interested in political and economic co-operation with Russia. At the suggestion of this body he turned to the international Red Cross Committee. This gave the Moscow propaganda an opportunity to enter into correspondence with the Red Cross and not only to deny the allegations of famine and distress in Russia in no measured terms, but to indulge in a truly Bolshevist jest. On March 6, 1933, *Izvestia* reported that a proposal to remit the sum of 5,000 dollars to the Indian Red Cross for the victims of the recent earthquake was under consideration. At the same time the Soviet papers were full of "the terrible famine among the Indian peasantry." All this was happening at a time when every month thousands of ragged and exhausted refugees from Russia were reaching the Persian and other frontiers.

In the summer of 1934, when prices were rising rapidly in the towns, the fiction of the 89,000,000 tons harvest could no longer be maintained. It had to be admitted that a large part of the coming harvest had been lost. With regard to the outer world, however, the story of great economic progress and favourable prospects continued to be spread.

Nevertheless, the official representatives of the Soviet State continue to deny that there was a famine in 1933. In the summer of 1934, when I was staying in the United States on behalf of the Vienna Relief Committee, and the *New York Times* published a statement by me, the Soviet Ambassador still considered it possible not only to deny the assertions about the famine, but also to suggest that the members of the committee, who, of course, embrace leading representatives of every religious denomination, were "notorious political propagandists." The attitude of the official Soviet representatives is typical of the psychological background of the Soviet propaganda in the non-Communist countries. Any person criticizing the state of things in Russia is forthwith represented as being an agent of the counter-revolutionaries or as the hired servant of the enemies of the Soviet State. Anyone who dares to write or speak about matters disagreeable to Moscow must be prepared for the most venomous attacks on his credibility and his personal qualities both from Moscow and from Moscow's friends and helpers abroad. This is perhaps the most essential explanation of the great and lasting success obtained by the Moscow system of propaganda.

CHAPTER VI

THE TESTIMONY OF MONSIEUR HERRIOT

AMONG Moscow's guests of honour a special place must be assigned to the former French Prime Minister, Edouard Herriot; not only because his journey was a political event of the first importance which initiated a complete change in France's attitude towards Soviet Russia, but also because it was M. Herriot's ambition to give to his Russian journey and to the publication of its results the character of "a visit for purposes of study by an experienced administrator." M. Herriot too desired to be numbered among the prophets. Now his name is known everywhere; he further claims the authority of an unbiased traveller and skilled observer: the result must be that every word uttered by him on Russia meets with attention in the widest circles. M. Herriot's categorical declaration that there was no famine in Russia naturally made the very greatest impression throughout Europe. His duty to weigh his words was equally categorical.

There is, however, yet another reason why I must examine in detail the evidence put forward by M. Herriot: the fact that it was precisely in the year of the severest famine that he made his journey of investigation. His action has had a disastrous influence upon the incipient will to bring relief to Russia which was beginning to make itself felt in a number of countries. Letters published in Swiss papers (in the Berne *Bund*) and elsewhere show to what a degree M. Herriot's evidence hampered and misguided ready helpers. M. Herriot, on his return, not only disputed the existence of any famine in Russia; he went on to say generally that people who talked about a famine could be doing so only in the interests of a definite anti-Russian policy, of separatist tendencies, or the like. Such assertions are apt to make the uninitiated see in a false light any attempts made to help the famine victims in Russia.

I am not here dealing with M. Herriot as a politician. If the statements he made had been uttered from a political platform, I should have no comment to make upon them: the world knows only too well what sort of political dicta are made by statesmen speaking in the interests of their country. But I am now dealing with M. Herriot the traveller and administrator, who made use of his name in international politics in order to publish to the world an amazingly rash judgment upon the Russian famine—a judgment which, whether intentionally or not, constitutes a serious charge against the men and women labouring on behalf of the thousands dying of starvation in Russia.

It is important to treat of M. Herriot's journey for a further reason—because it throws a startling light upon conditions in this age of wireless, aviation and speed records of every kind: an age in which it is possible for millions to die of hunger in the richest agricultural districts of Europe, while the Chinese wall separating them from the rest of the world remains unscaled, and even official travellers in the Soviet Union have failed to observe a trace of the tragedy being enacted in their immediate vicinity.

M. Herriot's expedition took from August 26 to September 9, 1933; and more than half of this fortnight was spent in Moscow. The stay in the south took no more than five days, a mere two days being devoted to Kiev and Odessa—or, rather, twelve hours to Odessa and its surroundings and twelve to Kiev. Half of this period was devoted to official receptions and banquets, and the other half to a series of inspections in exact accordance with a time-table worked out by the authorities beforehand. The inspections were invariably carried out in the presence of a numerous French company and of high Soviet officials.

It is significant that although M. Herriot was supposed to be travelling for information and in a private capacity, he was accompanied not only by French journalists and Soviet

Mass graves of famine victims, in such numbers that they resemble dunes

A great multitude which no man could number

officials, but also by the French Ambassador, M. Alfan. One may fairly ask whether a journey undertaken to obtain the truth about Russian conditions could reasonably require the presence of the French representative accredited to the Kremlin. On August 26 M. Herriot arrived at Odessa in the Soviet vessel *Chicherin* after a "delightful journey." He stayed at the smart, comfortable, ultra-modern Hotel London (these are his own words), looking straight on to the sea. The hotel and the view pleased him so much that he found it hard to believe "all the tragedies that had taken place in this city" (at the time of the civil war). Now, thank Heaven, all that had been changed; "for the last ten years the Ukrainian metropolis had been recovering" from these tribulations. "A walk down the wide, well-paved streets of Odessa give one the impression of a prosperous and orderly city." Such was M. Herriot's view of Odessa at a moment when a large part of the population (just as at Kharkov and Kiev) was suffering the greatest privations or, indeed, actually dying of hunger. At Odessa a State bakery was visited, and M. Herriot wrote: "The work is done with Russian machines, and everything is amazingly simple and clean."[1]

No sooner was the official welcome and inspection over than M. Herriot and his suite, accompanied by the Odessa representative of the Izpolkom and the Gorsoviet, proceeded to visit the Belyaevka collective farm in order to learn the truth about Russian agriculture "by contact with the people." Here M. Herriot was shown all the things praised in his later articles: granaries, farmyards and tractor stations were inspected. A particularly deep impression was produced by the breakfast, "consisting entirely of the products of the collective farm"— surely not a surprising thing on a farm. Having seen the arrangements and working of the collective farm, M. Herriot remarks with satisfaction: "Apart from his work in the collective farm, every worker is entitled to his own house, garden,

---

[1] From an article published in various papers early in February, 1934, e.g. in the Vienna *Neue Freie Presse*.

cow and pigs. At the moment the Government is *even* anxious for each worker to have his cow." It sounds absolutely idyllic in those regions afflicted by the famine.

A few miles away from Odessa and Belyaevka is the site of the formerly flourishing German Black Sea settlements—now a scene of death and destruction. Dozens of letters on this point may be seen at the offices of the "Brethren in Distress" dating precisely from the period of M. Herriot's visit. The contrast is striking. In a later article (*Pester Lloyd*, October 1) M. Herriot confidently declares: "Nowhere did I find a sign of distress, not even in the German villages, which had been described as suffering from famine." According to the latest figures 140,000 Germans died in Russia in 1932–3. The "Brethren in Distress," the Committee of the Christian Churches in Geneva, and other bodies, have reliable information, on the strength of which they have attempted to help the German settlements in the south by sending food; but M. Herriot thinks himself entitled to dispute the existence of famine in these settlements.

After this first great piece of stage-management M. Herriot and his suite had completed their studies of Odessa and the surroundings and proceeded on their tour. There had also been a banquet in honour of the guests. After hearty farewells —it appears that M. Herriot and the Soviet press were equally satisfied—they entered their special coaches and made the night journey to Kiev, the second stage of the visit to the Ukraine. Kiev is, of course, next to Kharkov, the town in the south most severely afflicted by the famine and its attendant phenomena. M. Herriot was now in the centre of the agricultural district of the Ukraine, the best place from which to undertake a serious study of the position. With the help of trained interpreters he might perhaps have obtained in the course of a few days, in spite of all difficulties, a fairly correct picture of the situation and one not unduly coloured by official influences.

But what did the ex Prime Minister and skilled administrator do? The report published in *Pravda* on September 27
is so characteristic of the activities of M. Herriot and his suite,
and throws so much light on the private journeys of European
statesmen in their search for the truth in distant parts, that I
quote it at length.

"This morning M. Herriot arrived at Kiev, accompanied by
his secretary Serlen, and the deputies Julien and Marcel Ray,
former chefs de cabinet of the ex Prime Minister. M. Alfan,
the French Ambassador, also arrived. They were accompanied
by Helfand;[1] the deputy president of the Ukrainian Chamber of
Commerce, Velitchko; the representative of the *Petit Parisien*,
Lucien; the special correspondent of *Izvestia*, Gari; and the
special correspondent of the Tass agency. At the station the
guests were met by the president of the regional Ispolkom,
Vassilenko, the deputy president of the Gorsoviet [municipal
soviet], the agent of the Narkomindel [foreign Commissariat],
Shenshev, and representatives of the Moscow and the local
press. After an exchange of greetings M. Herriot and his
companions proceeded to their hotel, and after a brief rest
went on to the Ukrainian Academy of Sciences."

This was the second grand deception. After the achievements
of Ukrainian agriculture, the visitors are now presented, in
accordance with Moscow's plan, with evidence of the care
devoted to Ukrainian culture and science. The report says:
"On the way to the Academy M. Herriot expressed the wish
to visit St. Sophia's, with its historically valuable mosaics.[2]
M. Herriot was then received at the Ukrainian Academy of
Sciences by a number of members headed by the president
Palladin, who explained the work of the various departments.
A long stay was made at the Geological Museum, with its many
valuable exhibits. Later the Ukrainian model town was visited,

---

[1] A former official of the Ogpu well known for his activities.

[2] This interest in Tsarist church art had presumably not been anticipated
in the programme; hence the *Izvestia* report ascribed this whim to the
historical importance of the mosaics.

where the work of the museum for historical relics in the religious field and the valuable Potocki collection were studied."

Thus, at the moment when the dictator Postyschev was exterminating every trace of Ukrainian cultural individuality, and a few days after Lenin's friend and co-founder of the Soviet State, the Ukrainian Communist Skrypnik, had shot himself, when even Ukrainian Bolshevists were protesting against the starvation of their countrymen, the Pan-Ukrainian academicians were enlightening M. Herriot about the splendid work done to promote the cultural endeavours of the Ukraine. At this very moment the Moscow delegate was speaking openly of the danger inherent in the activities of the Academy and other similar organizations: and a few days after the guests had left Kiev the members of another similar institute were expelled or arrested. At the moment, however, the object was to provide the guest from France with an idea of the development of the Ukrainian cultural movement under the Soviet regime, and even of the care taken of religious relics, while the academicians had to turn out to sing the praises of the Soviet powers as the protector of such endeavours.

M. Herriot was deeply moved. In the book for the Academy's guests of honour he made the following entry: "I have visited this historic building with the greatest interest. I consider it my duty to express my heartfelt thanks to the director and his staff, as well as to the representatives of the Soviets at Kiev, who showed attentions to me which I and my French colleagues will long remember." The Ambassador Alfan was entirely enthusiastic and wrote: "I wish to express my thanks and gratitude. The working population of Kiev, recognizing in M. Herriot a friend of the Soviet Union, who has done much to bring about the Franco-Soviet rapprochement, welcomed him and the other guests on their way through Kiev with applause and acclamations."

Other delights awaited the guests after their study of cultural movements in the Ukraine and the promotion of these by the central authority. The report says: "Comrade Vassilenko, the President of the District Executive Committee, gave a luncheon in honour of the guests." The report is silent as to the menu of the lunch; but Ukrainian cooking has a good reputation, and it may be assumed that during his fortnight in Russia M. Herriot was one of the best-fed people in the country. No unpleasant interludes marred the feast, and none of the guests was reminded that during the summer thousands of innocent people had perished in that ancient metropolis. First-hand reports from foreign observers tell how in the summer of 1933 starving persons were collapsing in the streets of Kiev, and were often buried before they died. The common graves at Kiev speak eloquently of the tragedy which visited that city, like Kharkov, Odessa, Rostov and many other towns during the months preceding the 1933 harvest.

But a climax awaited M. Herriot after the lunch. The Soviet press reports: "During the afternoon the visitors went for a pleasure cruise on the Dnieper in the steamer *Kalinin*." Only those who know Kiev can appreciate the delightful impression given by a steamer trip on the Dnieper near the city; the view of Kiev itself, of the high banks and of the famous Kievo-Pecherskaya Lavra monastery is unforgettable. Nor is it easy to imagine a better way in which M. Herriot and his suite could have spent the rest of their brief visit. It is hardly surprising that the visitors were impressed and put into the right mood to appreciate the demonstrations by the populace which followed. Returning, they entered their cars and visited the sights of the city. "During the drive through the town," the Soviet press reports, "the population surrounded Herriot's car and expressed their sympathy by applause. Herriot was pleased by this unexpected and spontaneous enthusiasm." His inspection at Kiev was ended and his judgment formed. Before the evening he went to the station.

The hour had now come to give to the press a summary of the results of his studies and his competent judgment as statesman, administrator and unbiassed observer of all that he had seen. Within two days of entering the Ukraine he had reached a final verdict.

After a last word of thanks to the Soviet dignitaries assembled at the station the visitors left in their special train for Kharkov. The hero of the day and his companions could rest from their exertions in their saloons. But while they were digesting the impressions of this busy day in the Ukrainian metropolis the express was passing through the very districts where the struggle for food was at its worst during these summer days, when a ragged and starving population had to surrender its crops by order of the Moscow Envoy, and when the military actually had to enforce the collection of the grain. There are authentic reports on this point, and even the Soviet denials are merely a matter of form. But M. Herriot had seen and heard nothing of all this.

The reason why this could be so is that the programme of this journey for purposes of study, or rather this triumphal progress through the Ukraine, did not allow of anything being seen save what the authorities desired to show. A fortunate coincidence, however, led another foreign observer, who certainly could not be suspected of being the mouthpiece of the "National Socialist enemies of the Soviet regime" to Kiev simultaneously with M. Herriot. On the conclusion of the Zionist Congress at Prague last summer Mr. Harry Lang had travelled to Southern Russia to study the position of the Jews. It is to him that we are indebted for the following description of events during and after M. Herriot's stay at Kiev.[1]

"We were staying at Kiev," he said, "at the time when the French delegation was expected, and thus became witnesses of the camouflage practised at the time. On the day before the arrival of the delegation the entire populace was mobilized at two a.m. to clean the streets and decorate the houses. Tens of

[1] The description was given during a lecture before the Jewish Sholom Aleichim Club in Paris.

thousands were feverishly busy giving the dirty and neglected city a European appearance. Food distributing centres, co-operative shops, etc., were closed. Queues were prohibited, *bezprizornie* [i.e. the hordes of neglected children], beggars and starving people suddenly vanished. At the crossings mounted militiamen were stationed on well-groomed horses whose manes were decorated with white ribbons, a sight never before and never again witnessed in Kiev."

"The guests arrived, inspected with visible satisfaction, entered their names in the city's roll of visitors, and went away. That evening the decorations were taken down, the militiamen vanished, the food distributing centres opened and the queues of weary and despondent Soviet citizens formed up afresh. . . . I happened to be sitting in the company of a number of Soviet officials, directors and members of the party, at the moment when the papers were containing M. Herriot's interview, in which he stated that he had seen no trace of a famine in Russia. The faces should have been seen and the angry, bitter laughter heard that rang out when this interview was read . . ."

Early on August 28 the illustrious travellers arrived at Kharkov, which at that time was the official capital of the Ukraine. There was the usual ceremonious reception, after which the visitors were taken to the children's settlement named after Dzerjinsky, the organizer of the Ogpu. This settlement is an institution where the deserted and neglected children, the so-called *bezprizornie*, are looked after, together with youthful criminals. M. Herriot studied the work and condition of these young Communists "in every detail." He began a "long conversation" with the head of the scientific department of the settlement, and attempts were made to explain why deserted children were housed with youthful criminals. The visitors were impressed by the orderliness and the abundance of fresh air and flowers. After visiting all departments they listened to an "improvised" concert by these children and youthful criminals, and once again were "surprised." Perhaps they had assumed that they would receive the saddest impressions of their visit to Kharkov; instead of which they found "music and flowers." (Contrast the description of the position at Kharkov at the time, particularly of the children, given elsewhere in this volume, as well as the illustrations, which all show the state of affairs in the summer of 1933 in and around Kharkov.)

In the afternoon M. Herriot visited the Shevtschenko Museum to study, once again "in detail," the development of Ukrainian culture. Next there followed the inspection of a tractor factory "in every detail"—indeed, this expression is applied to practically every one of M. Herriot's visits and conversations.

Finally there was a meeting with members of the Ukrainian Soviet Government and "representatives of local society." During the banquet M. Herriot conversed with Comrade Tschubar, the President of the Council of Ukrainian Commissaries, on the collectivization of peasants. He took the opportunity to expound his view that neither the reforms of 1861 nor those of Stolypin in more recent times could possibly have improved the hard lot of the Russian peasantry—a view frequently repeated in articles after his return from Russia. To this view of a very complicated and long discussed question he added the quickly formed judgment that "only the Communist revolution could provide a favourable solution of the problem." This sweeping judgment was made at a time when the peasantry of the Ukraine and elsewhere was fighting for mere existence.

M. Herriot was particularly favourably impressed by Kharkov; his later articles expressed the view that it was "one of the best administered of cities." Apparently he did not know that at Kharkov, as at Kiev, starving people were lying in the streets until just before his arrival, and that almost every other house was the scene of dreadful tragedies owing to passport and other Government regulations.

The next day, August 29, was destined to be one of particular importance, for on this day the pride of Russia's foreign propaganda, the works and dam of Dnieprostroi, were inspected. The works are indeed imposing, as all the world knows. Vast sums were spent on their construction, and leading experts from every country gave their assistance. How long did it take M. Herriot to inspect the vast works and its annexes "in every detail"? From 10 a.m. until 12.30 p.m.—exactly two and a half hours, which included a visit to the Socialist Settlement, as mentioned in the French papers. During the whole period M. Herriot took notes, and he declared later: "I personally inspected the Dnieprostroi, and it is a first-class achievement. I was unable to visit certain other important works of which I have seen only plans and relevant figures, e.g. the Uralokusnezk combine; but I see no reason why the erection of the other centres should have met with less success than where I witnessed the result with my own eyes."

It may be admitted that, by an outlay of millions and with the help of leading foreign specialists, important industrial centres have been set up elsewhere also. The question, however, remains how these works are to function in Russian industry as a whole and how they are to be exploited for the benefit of the population. The setting up of the works as such does not mean much; any number of them can be created with the help of international experts and of State money taken from the country's industry. But it may be asked what use has been found for the power furnished by the Dnieprostroi, and this is a question which M. Herriot has not yet answered. The truth, however, has been told recently by foreign engineers, who report on the complete unproductivity of the Dnieprostroi.

M. Herriot thus confines himself to a superficial visit of the works without asking how the output is utilized and whether the show places can be run at a profit, however modest. While he praises the economic advantages of the Dnieprostroi for the workers of the country, it is known from a number of eyewitnesses that thousands of peasants have died of starvation in the immediate vicinity. It is a contrast typical of the Soviet Union and of the two worlds within it; on the one hand the gigantic constructions of the five-year plan and on the other the misery and starvation of the non-privileged classes.

After breakfast on the right bank of the Dnieper, during which M. Herriot compared the Dnieprostroi with one of Mr. H. G. Wells's marvellous cities, the afternoon was devoted to an inspection of the hydro-electric station and a visit to the neighbouring collective farm called International. During this visit an episode occurred that throws a strong light on M. Herriot's expedition and on the naïveté of Moscow's guests of honour, who are taken from one exhibit to the next and admire the technical achievements with open-mouthed amazement. The episode took place while the visitors were watching an electric threshing machine, and is thus described in *Izvestia*: "Edouard Herriot has frowned. A stream of golden grain runs out of the threshing machine. A peasant girl with blooming face catches the grain in a pail and empties it, as soon as it is full, into a container. While she is doing so some of the grain falls on the ground and a boy with a broom sweeps it aside. Herriot goes to the threshing machine. His black overcoat is grey with dust. The French ex-Premier examines the threshing machine without being quite aware of what is wrong, but his parsimonious sense has been awakened. He manifests disquiet, calls for the president of the collective farm and asks for a second pail. Before the eyes of the abashed members of the settlement Herriot, with sleeves rolled up, demonstrates his method of rationalization. He suggests that two pails should be used to prevent a single grain from being lost. . . ."

A proud day for M. Herriot: he had succeeded in suggesting an improvement upon the perfect mechanization of Russian agriculture. And at a press conference in his honour at Moscow he explained in all seriousness to the Russian and foreign journalists: "During my visit to the 'International' I had the opportunity of observing perfected methods of agricultural mechanization," adding that he had been enabled to observe certain shortcomings in the campaign against loss of grain where electric threshing machines are used. "I myself showed the collective farm workers how the continued supply of pails could be organized to prevent the loss of grain in threshing."

Such were M. Herriot's remarks to the journalists when asked what were the strongest impressions received during his inspection of Russian industry and agriculture. At a moment when thousands were dying and agriculture was passing through the severest crisis, as the Bolshevists themselves admit to-day, it was left to M. Herriot to make the grand discovery of how to perfect electric threshing by the two-pail system. The Russian journalists received M. Herriot's remarks with approval. What one would like to know is what the impression was in the famine region when the interview was published in the Soviet press and came to be read by the inhabitants. Perhaps it was the same as that which Harry Lang observed at Kiev when M. Herriot's denial of the existence of a famine in the Ukraine came to the notice of the Soviet officials.

Thus every day brings M. Herriot and his friends, including M. Alfan, a wealth of striking impressions. On August 30 fresh surprises awaited them at Rostov-on-Don. Arriving at one o'clock they proceeded, after the usual official welcome, to the local circus, and found the building filled by 3,500 Boy and Girl Pioneers[1] and collective farm children. As the *Temps* report stated, the regional Congress of delegates of the Pioneers was in progress; the Pioneers were the so-called "light cavalry" in the campaign against wastage during the new harvest. On entering, M. Herriot was met with loud cries of "Long live Herriot and the friends of the Soviet Union."

According to the reports the Mayor of Lyons was much impressed, especially when two of the "dear children" greeted

[1] A Communist organization for children somewhat on the lines of the Scout Movement.

him with eloquent words. Once again he had the impression of a spontaneous demonstration of "Young Russia" displaying sympathy for the great bourgeois republic of France, that friend of Communist Russia, as well as for himself personally as a friend of peace. Much moved, he addressed the children in the following significant words: "I have seen many fine things in your great country, but nothing finer than this vast hall full of children. I am deeply moved. I am fond of children, and shall tell the children of France that the children of the great Soviet country share with their fathers the great work of building up the Soviet Union. I am proud of the attention shown to my friends and me, and I assure you that the consolidation of Franco-Russian relations which you have just mentioned serves the cause of peace, and, still more, friendship between the children of Russia and those of France."

M. Herriot forgot that, on Moscow's own admission, the education of children, from Moscow to the remotest village in Siberia, has but one guiding line, which is to inspire the young with hate and contempt for the non-Communist countries. He also forgot that Moscow does not intend for a moment to alter its educational principles in order to please France or any other country, and that the attitude of young Communists to that quintessence of the bourgeois order, the French Republic, had not been changed in the very least by his visit. In education, as in other departments, Moscow's openly declared attitude in dealing with the non-Communist world remains one of uncompromising strife.

As for the youthful Pioneers, or "dear children," who greeted M. Herriot at Rostov, the reader must know that they were those bodies of regularly organized children whose function it was, during the weeks before the harvest, to prevent the starving peasants, even if they happened to be their own parents or relatives, from filling their stores at night with the grain of which they were in such bitter need. This "light cavalry" was armed and literally let loose upon the starving peasantry. The resulting tragedies, and the rigour with which the "light cavalry" were urged to deal with adults, as also the manner in which the latter were dealt with if proved guilty of grain theft, appears best from cases quoted by *Molot* (the Hammer), the leading Soviet paper in the Northern Caucasus.

The following instance is quoted on August 30, 1933: "The Pioneer Sorokin, who was guarding the collective farm grain, caught his father filling his pockets with grain. He immediately reported the case and his father was arrested."

On July 19 the paper reported from Kislyakovka: "The Pioneers Ania Samobvalova, Manya Luschakova and Mischa Guba surprised the *kulak* Koschka cutting grain in the fields. She had had time to get her sack half full and succeeded in escaping. This happened on July 7. On the 13th the same Pioneers caught her at her home at the moment when she was beginning to thrash the grain. She was told to come to the militia post, instead of which she used insulting language and again attempted to escape. But Mischa Guba stood in her way and the two girls dragged her to the door by her skirt." There follows a description of the struggle which ended by her being brought to the militia post. Eventually she was sentenced to ten years' imprisonment—in other words, to a penalty ordinarily reserved for the gravest crimes.

Even the Red State prosecutors sometimes lose their nerve on these occasions. Thus on July 5 the *Molot* recorded a case from the Stanitza Naurslaya, where another grain thief had been sentenced to ten years' imprisonment. Soon after his wife was also caught in the act. In Court the State prosecutor asked whether it was desirable that she should be imprisoned when she ought to be taking care of her children. Against this view the *Molot* protested energetically, writing: "We want no rotten liberalism when dealing with thieves."

So much for the attitude of the leading local paper. Nothing could better characterize Moscow's attitude: Moscow does not care if the peasants perish by the thousand; what does matter is to save the crops for the needs of the State, the Red Army, the Ogpu employees, the consumers in the industrial centres, and for export. Meanwhile the starving thieves are locked up for ten years and the peasants' children are organized to guard the "interest of the State" against the depredations of a populace doomed to death by starvation. Such is the truth about the light cavalry: perhaps it is superfluous to make any further comment on M. Herriot's address to the "dear children" at Rostov.

In the afternoon M. Herriot was shown another model Soviet farm, that of Verblyud, in the Northern Caucasus. Here a final surprise was prepared. The visitors were to be shown the marvels of technical perfection and the co-operation of every factor in agricultural mechanization. As the Soviet press said, a "threefold demonstration" took place of the technical equipment of this State farm: motor-cars moving at high speed on perfect roads; dozens of tractors and "combiners" in the fields with an aeroplane assisting the work on the wide, black earth areas. It seems that this grandiose picture of Soviet agricultural perfection thus has a certain resemblance (allowing for the march of civilization) to those produced by Prince Potemkin at an earlier age for the benefit of Catherine II. What particularly impressed M. Herriot was the part played by the aeroplane, and on his return he did not fail, when describing Russian agriculture in general and the Soviet farms in particular, to refer to "the use of aeroplanes for sowing purposes, which is a common spectacle in present-day Russian agriculture."[1] Neither the United States nor the Argentine nor any other important agricultural country has used aeroplanes for sowing; this honour has been reserved to Soviet Russia.

During the inspection of this Soviet farm there was an interesting scene when it was found that neither M. Herriot nor the other French visitors had ever seen a so-called "combiner." The managers of the State farm, as Tass reported, manifested their surprise and willingly offered explanations

---

[1] See *Neue Freie Presse*, October 1, 1933.

to the illustrious guests. Mounted on one of these machines M. Herriot took a drive through the fields, an experience which he described as delightful and most original. Before leaving he was given flowers by the collective farm children. The truth about the economic value of the "Verblyud" and the other agricultural giants appears from figures for which we are indebted to foreign experts. They plainly reveal the breakdown of the vast State farms, whose failure is also indicated by the contrast between them and the *Drusag*. This German concession, run on non-Communist lines, was admitted by all the local experts to be an oasis of plenty in the Russian famine zone which, of course, included also the Don region and the Northern Caucasus.

In the evening the usual banquet took place at Rostov. Next day the "Selmash," a Soviet factory for agricultural machinery, was visited; M. Herriot describes it as "running like clockwork." Notice was also taken of the admirable work done by the State for the workers. The actual deplorable position—e.g. as regards the supply of such necessities as tea or tobacco available to the industrial population—has already been made clear.

This concluded M. Herriot's journey in the South. It had lasted just five days, each of which was filled from morning till night by the official programme of welcomes, visits, gala banquets and "exhaustive conversation" with the hosts. It was as if a film were shown to M. Herriot and his companions, beginning at Odessa and going on to Kiev, Kharkov, the Dnieprostroi and Rostov and its surroundings. In one of the articles published on his return M. Herriot protests against comparisons between his expedition and Catherine II's journey in Potemkin's company.[1] "I may fairly claim," he said, "that my journey was very different; I have a regard for truth and say what I think, whether I am talking of Roosevelt's grandiose plans or of the Russian experiments. I have studied a wide field with the unbiassed eye of a trained administrator." Nevertheless

---

[1] See *Pester Lloyd*, October 1, 1933.

—and this is where Moscow wins our grudging admiration—the
result was produced on M. Herriot as on Catherine II. He saw
only what his hosts intended him to see, and remained completely ignorant of what was going on a few miles away.

A new phase began on the seventh day of the expedition.
M. Herriot had now reached Moscow. There was the usual
reception at the station, with the difference that instead of
provincial leaders the first men of the regime, headed by
Litvinov, had come to greet him, and the papers were once
more able to record the enthusiastic reception accorded to the
former French Prime Minister by the Moscow populace.
Here again M. Herriot led the life of a guest of honour,
receiving at the Embassy and attending banquets. His domicile
was in the best rooms of the famous Hotel National, where,
as everybody knows, all the servants and some of the visitors
are employed by the Ogpu. In his honour the ordinarily
deserted bar of the hotel was peopled with well-dressed "representatives of the population" (as recorded by foreigners staying at Moscow at the time). He was received by Molotov, the
President of the Council of People's Commissaries, and dined
with Maxim Gorki. He was taken to see all the show works of
Russia's armament industry. He had continually to give
expression to his enthusiasm, as, for example, during his visit
to the Institute of Aero and Hydrodynamics. "A number of
academicians and scientific experts surrounds the visitors
and gives the necessary explanations," as the *Temps* records.
The visitors were also shown the huge propaganda aeroplane,
"Maxim Gorki," then in course of construction. On leaving,
Herriot wrote in the Institution's Gold Book: "I have the
greatest admiration for this technically remarkable institution,
for the knowledge of the engineers, for the work done by the
executive officials, and for the enthusiasm of the entire personnel. I trust that this Russian achievement may always
contribute to the happiness of nations in the sphere of work and
peace." He also visited the Museum of the Revolution and was

deeply impressed by the precise and conscientious work done at this institution. He even made observations on the greatness of the two revolutionary movements, the French and the Russian, and expressed his readiness to arrange for the exchange of "relics of the revolutionary movement" between France and Russia. The same thing happened at the Marx-Engels Institute, where he waxed enthusiastic at the scientific precision with which the greatest movement in the history of mankind was being studied.

On the following day he insisted on inspecting the Kaganovitch model school outside Moscow, which was visited in the company of high Soviet officials. The arrangements of this school—they are visited by all guests of honour—are excellent. The food was tasted in the kitchen, and M. Herriot described the dishes prepared for the children as wholesome and tasty, a verdict which was duly repeated for days in all the Russian papers and in France. But this was not all. It would have been a modest achievement if M. Herriot's evidence had been used only to spread the news of the efficient arrangements and the good and tasty food provided in the Soviet schools. Something more was wanted, and, full of the pleasant impressions of the moment, M. Herriot was induced to make the following entry in the school's Book of Honour: "I congratulate the teachers of this admirable school and wish luck to the pupils. The principles which are being inculcated are splendid." Thus the former Prime Minister of what the Bolsheviks recently had called the "rotten republic of the French bourgeoisie" had been induced to approve publicly of the principles of Soviet education. Once again the expert's verdict was published in the entire Soviet press and in many Western papers. Everything went according to plan. There were inspections from morning till night, and M. Herriot was liberal in his expressions of appreciation: indeed, compared with his conduct at Moscow, his attitude during the stay in the Ukraine might almost be described as lacking in warmth.

Q

A dinner given by M. Alfan in M. Herriot's honour, to which
a number of high Soviet officials were invited, and a visit to
the opera, concluded the stay at Moscow. For the last time
the saloon carriage was entered and the journey to Latvia
began. At the station the heads of the Government and Moscow
journalists had assembled; for the last time farewell was said
to the true friend of the Soviet Union. But before he left
Soviet territory the programme had arranged for a final deception à la Potemkin: a "milk centre" had yet to be inspected,
for the regime desired to have the honoured guest's confirmation that in this field, as elsewhere, everything was as good
as it could possibly be. How simple a task it was deemed—
after so many facile successes—to mislead the French statesman, is apparent from the explanations about the development
of dairies given by the President of the Central Committee of
the Communist Party, Kalinin. The tale told by this official,
and the faithful way in which it is repeated, is so characteristic
of the primitive methods employed on M. Herriot towards the
end of his stay that I cannot refrain from recounting the
episode. M. Herriot asked M. Kalinin why there was a noticeable lack of milk in the towns, whereupon Kalinin gave an
explanation which M. Herriot passed on at a luncheon given
at the Prefecture of the Rhône Department.[1]

"M. Kalinin," he said, "gave me a very simple explanation
of the position. Actually milk production has very considerably
increased in Russia; but at the same time the social services
have increased so much that the consumption of milk tends to
exceed the production, with the result that regulations had to
be made with regard to distribution." This is surprising
enough. Stalin himself had admitted the disastrous position of
cattle farming (see his speech at the latest Communist Congress);
the bulk of the cattle had perished, and in important towns like
Kharkov and Kiev not even the minimum milk requirements
of the hospitals could be met: and yet Kalinin did not blush

[1] *Temps*, September 16, 1933.

to bring forward such an "explanation" for the benefit of the visitor from France, without even asking himself whether it was consistent with the collapse of cattle farming as announced by the Soviets themselves.

Before the train left the Russian frontier station M. Herriot's most faithful companion, Helfand, took his leave of the French guests. He had been the first to greet them on August 26 at Odessa, was the last to leave them on September 10, and had guided the expedition with the greatest care and prudence. Now Helfand is one of the most influential and best known officials of the Ogpu—a fact of considerable interest, for it indicates that the journey of the French visitors had been under the aegis of the real rulers of the Soviet Union, the Ogpu, from beginning to end and in every detail. Thus it was possible that everything should go so smoothly, that the populace should cheer enthusiastically whenever M. Herriot was seen, and that on no single occasion any evidence should be obtruded of the drab misery of Russian life, still less of the famine. One can imagine with what complacency Helfand on his return to Moscow reported to his chief the satisfactory supervision of the French expedition from Odessa to the Latvian frontier.

From the frontier station M. Herriot sent a flowery telegram of thanks to Litvinov, concluding thus: "Please convey my heartfelt thanks to all your collaborators and those who contributed to make my journey so pleasant and instructive, and also to the peoples of the Soviet Union, whose grandiose work of reconstruction and loyalty to the cause of peace are a subject for enthusiasm." Before leaving the country M. Herriot thus expressed his thanks not only to Litvinov and his assistants, but also to the pacific peoples of the Soviet Union, to the Russians, Ukrainians, White Russians, Turcomans, Caucasians and the rest, of whose conditions he learnt so little during his journey.

The preparation and execution of M. Herriot's expedition must be admitted to be a masterpiece of Soviet propaganda, and any states arranging similar trips for foreign guests of honour could learn much from this collaboration of all Soviet officials in arranging the different stages of M. Herriot's Russian journey.

But the organization of the journey was only a part of the task. The more difficult part remained—the propagandist and journalistic exploitation of the journey at home and abroad; for it was on this that the whole success of the undertaking depended. It was here that Moscow proved almost inimitable.

The exploitation of M. Herriot's evidence was designed to take place in four stages. The two first stages depended upon the Soviet press apparatus, while in the last two M. Herriot himself was cast for the role of unconscious propagandist. The first task was to induce M. Herriot to make brief statements when visiting Odessa, Kiev, Dnieprostroi and other places, on subjects important to the Bolshevists. These were forthwith transmitted to Moscow and thence to the world.

The chief object was to get M. Herriot to deny the existence of the famine and the disastrous position of the Ukrainian population when he was actually in such centres as Odessa, Kiev, etc.; this would be in August, i.e. before the beginning of the League Assembly meeting, and at a time when news of the catastrophe was just beginning to spread in the West and in America and Cardinal Innitzer was initiating the Russian relief work in Vienna. Accordingly the ablest journalists had been sent from Moscow to meet M. Herriot at Odessa, their function being to wait for utterances from the French statesman. Nor did they have long to wait; after the impressive experiences at Kiev Herriot was "ripe" for making statements. His denial of the famine and of the sufferings of the Ukrainians made at the station at Kiev amounted to a striking success for the Soviet regime, and further declarations about the idyllic state of things in the Ukraine were not wanting. Daily the Russian correspondents were able to telegraph to Moscow, with appropriate comment, the written and spoken dicta of M. Herriot, and thence they were distributed throughout the world. The French journalists who accompanied M. Herriot and took part in the proceedings rendered valuable auxiliary service, some intentionally, others unintentionally. Meanwhile the Moscow papers had an opportunity of receiving telegraphic accounts from their Paris correspondents quoting the reports in the *Temps*, the *Petit Parisien* and the rest.

The second stage was reached with the arrival at Moscow. The problem now was to obtain not brief declarations on various aspects of Soviet life but a general judgment on the position, achievements, political aims and philosophic foundations of the Soviet Union. Accordingly a press reception was arranged, at which the well-primed journalists approached M. Herriot with leading questions. The plan was completely successful, and thanks to the interesting impressions obtained at Moscow, M. Herriot was ready to offer such sweeping opinions that the Soviet press was in a position on the same day to publish his final verdict, which was forthwith despatched to France and throughout the rest of the bourgeois world.

How favourable the verdict was appears from the following extracts. Asked by a representative of the *Socialisticheskoe Zemledelie* to offer his opinion on the question of collectivization and of agricultural mechanization, M. Herriot replied that he could bear witness to the vast technical progress made by Russian agriculture. (He also had to admit, however, that he had visited only one Soviet farm and two collective farms.)

He was next asked by a foreign journalist whether the Russian standard of living had improved or deteriorated since his first visit in 1922 (a question expressly referring not to the standard of living of privileged circles but to that of the entire population) and unhesitatingly replied that the standard of living of the Soviet population had improved out of all knowledge since 1922 (*Izvestia*, September 5, 1933). Only when asked how the Russian standard of living compared with that in other countries did he evade the question by remarking that comparisons with the standard of living in states having a different economic structure were difficult, and that mathematical comparisons would inevitably lead to false conclusions. Of course, his hosts would have liked to hear that workers and peasants in Russia had a higher standard of living than those in countries suffering from the economic crisis. But though they were disappointed in this respect it was still a good deal to be told that the standard of living had vastly improved, for news of distress and of the death of vast numbers in different parts of Russia had already begun to spread in various parts of Europe. Once more Moscow had scored.

The same applies to M. Herriot's remarks upon the appropriate wage of workers in Russia. Referring to a statement by Stalin that every man in Russia had to pay in accordance with his work, and was paid on the basis of his performance—in other words that there was a system of social justice, since it was the individual's fault if his labour did not yield enough for him to live on—he expressed his assent, and thus implicitly admitted the existence of sufficient supplies on which to live. M. Herriot, indeed, went on to eulogize Stalin and his views by describing affairs in Russia as a "synthesis of labour." "By this," he went on, "I mean nothing vague or general. By a synthesis of labour I mean that this synthesis is in force with you, that the idea of labour contains everything, and that hence the synthesis of labour is realized in industry and agriculture. In Stalin's words, I see evidence of the sureness of aim and of the dynamics of development in your country."

M. Herriot proceeded to refer to various speeches of Stalin, and ended by saying: "You know that I am no Communist; but I approach foreign ideas without prejudice. These speeches of his bear witness to two of Stalin's greatest characteristics—his intelligence and his courage. And these are qualities which I appreciate above everything."

M. Herriot had thus announced his final verdict before the journalists of Russia and the world. He had confirmed that the standard of living had vastly improved during the last years, that the workers were treated according to the principles of social justice, and that agriculture had been technically perfected; he had rendered tribute before all the world to Stalin's philosophy. On the strength of his local studies and investigations he had confirmed all the future claims for the Soviet system made for years past by the Moscow propagandists in Paris, New York and London. The French statesman's verdict was, of course, published in every paper of Europe and America, except those directly hostile to the Soviet State.

Thus the second stage had been successfully passed. The outcome was that in Soviet Russia, France and elsewhere the press began to discuss the results, conclusions and general advantages of M. Herriot's visit for world peace in general and Franco-Russian friendship in particular. The Soviet press had undergone a complete metamorphosis. Here Radek, the former enemy of bourgeois France and friend of Rapallo-Germany, held the field. In *Izvestia* he praised M. Herriot's "open-mindedness" and his "wish to extend the circle of his ideas." "We shall be happy," he wrote, "if his meeting with our statesmen increases sympathies and contributes to solve the problems touching both countries."

Radek's article was apparently meant for reproduction in the French press, as also appears from the following passage: "Herriot was able to satisfy himself that the 160 million inhabitants of the Soviet Union are full of enthusiasm for the Socialist edifice and are an invincible citadel of peace. The public opinion of the Soviet Union greeted Herriot with the deepest friendliness. The former French Prime Minister has seen the great creative work of the Soviet Union, our life and our labour. He has grasped the meaning of our existence. As a pacifist he has been profoundly moved. In its fight for peace the Soviet Union reaches out its hand to every man of goodwill, and above all to those ready to save humanity from the new tribulations emanating from Imperialism and Fascism."

These words, of course, were meant for external rather

than for internal consumption, and more especially for France, and Radek had the satisfaction of finding them reported in detail next day in the *Temps* and other Paris papers, where they were quoted with appreciative comment. Thus the final French echo of M. Herriot's journey looked like being a triumph for Moscow, and on September 11, 1933, the Paris correspondent of *Izvestia* could report: "Almost the entire Paris press—excluding the professionally anti-Soviet organs [which include the Socialist *Populaire*]—contained favourable comment on M. Herriot's journey into the land of the Soviets."

As an illustration the commentary of the *Petit Parisien* was quoted: "The journey is drawing to its close. It has led to a considerable and advantageous rapprochement between France and Russia. It is satisfactory to think that a brilliant representative of our culture, a statesman whose capacity for enlisting popular sympathy by simplicity and kindliness is universally known, went to Moscow as the spokesman of France.[1] M. Herriot's journey amounted to a kind of 'French week' which may perhaps shortly be continued."

Here there is a reference to the impending official visit to Moscow of the French Air Minister, M. Cot, and the far-reaching political consequences in the form of Franco-Russian co-operation which M. Herriot's visit initiated. It was precisely this political element which was of the greatest importance to many French papers; this perhaps explains why the *Temps*, for example, abandoned its former objective criticisms of Soviet Russian affairs and began to observe silence on inconvenient matters like the famine.

Politicians who visit a country as guests of honour, or more modestly as students, do not as a rule content themselves with brief statements or lengthy interviews at the various stages of their journey; they have the further ambition of achieving a reputation after their return home as experts on the country

---

[1] The view that M. Herriot went to Russia to enlist Soviet sympathies is, curiously enough, expressed by many French papers.

visited. They achieve this—and here the third and fourth stage of the propagandist exploitation are reached—by producing a flood of articles in their own press and that of various other countries and also by enriching the world's more permanent literature, if possible in several languages, on the country they have explored. What will the honoured guest do on his return? Will he continue to act in the desired way, after he has left his hosts? Such is the great question asked by the organizers of these increasingly popular expeditions, the more so since books or articles in well-known papers have a more lasting effect than brief statements made at the time.

At first the prospects for this further stage in the exploitation of M. Herriot's journey were extremely favourable from the Moscow standpoint. While the tour was actually in progress some of the journalists attached to M. Herriot had made an extremely interesting discovery. They telegraphed long reports of this to their papers, so that Jacques Sadoul, the Paris correspondent of *Izvestia*, was able to report on the same day: "The result of Herriot's journey"—so ran the report by M. Lucien to the *Petit Parisien*, which *Izvestia* had got hold of—"will among other things be the publication of a book. M. Herriot has shown us some of the notes taken during the journey. We were surprised to find some of the chapters practically ready for press. Each night M. Herriot had written down his impressions, and in spite of fatigue had spent an hour a day on his book. His capacity for work struck all those who met him."

It is easy to imagine the joy in the Kremlin at this new achievement of the French statesman. Not only had M. Herriot correctly studied and appreciated Soviet conditions "in close contact with the people" during his high-speed but triumphant progress through Russia, but the resulting book was almost finished before the journey was over. It had only to be printed for the world to be able to form an opinion on Soviet affairs on the strength of this popular man's evidence. It can easily be understood that M. Herriot now appeared more valuable than ever to the Soviet officials, and that it was now made a special task to provide information of every kind for his forthcoming book. Statistics on the increase of the crops, the vast growth of population, the huge sums invested, and every other point of interest were provided. The heads of the Soviet State were industrious in furnishing explanations on every point not perfectly clear. The way in which this was done was mentioned above when dealing with Kalinin's statements about the reasons for the milk shortage noticeable in Russia. Nor were simple and plausible explanations wanting for the lack of petrol in the towns, or the situation in the Ukraine. On his return to Paris M. Herriot set forth his views in a large number of articles, delivered lectures and made speeches at banquets, all in the sense which his Moscow utterances had made it easy to foresee; so that, quite apart from his book, his work must have been entirely to the satisfaction of Moscow.

The only point on which the Kremlin miscalculated was the echo provided by the French press to Herriot's journey. Even before his arrival in Paris a controversy arose in the press over the part which he had played as propagandist of the Soviet Union. He was attacked by important papers like the *Matin, Journal des Débats, Candide* and, in French Switzerland, by the *Journal de Genève*. The *Matin* quoted a passage from the *Dictionnaire de la Conversation*, referring to Catherine II's journey with Potemkin as her guide, and the *Journal des Débats* suggested in a leading article that M. Herriot "merely shrugged his shoulders" when facts were quoted against him. "He shrugs his shoulders if people speak of the famine in the Ukraine; but he is in ecstasies when he had a chance of looking at the second greatest industrial undertaking in the world."[1] The same paper made fun of his standing phrase to the effect that the French people wanted peace, and insinuated that it was irrelevant to the question of the Russian famine.

[1] September 19, 1933.

But the fiercest attacks came from his old enemy, the *Action Française*, which even went so far as to suggest certain causes for the attitude assumed by Herriot. It declared in a leading article of September 20, 1933, that Herriot's advances to the Bolshevists were meant to initiate a return to an alliance with Russia, but added that there might be another and more probable explanation. "It is a notorious fact that important industrial and commercial undertakings, especially in the Rhône district and around Lyons, are heavily committed in Russian credits, and it is equally notorious that these credits are frozen. The undertakings in question would like to see their money back and are believed to have asked M. Herriot, as regent of Lyons, to give them his support."

This is certainly a view which cannot be accepted by anyone who has had the opportunity of personally observing M. Herriot's activities for a number of years at Geneva and elsewhere. He can be believed when he says that he has always endeavoured to serve the truth. M. Herriot is an honest enthusiast, and for this reason his part as defender of the Soviet Union, its principles, achievements and policy does not, as might appear at first sight, resemble that of an operetta hero, but rather contains a tragic element. A lifelong searcher after truth, he has suddenly and unawares become the greatest obstacle to the fight for the truth. There can be no doubt that his conduct has made it harder for the truth to prevail in a question which touches the lives of many millions.

The statements contained in his articles and lectures, and in the book published on his return from Moscow, cannot be accepted without contradiction. He makes assertions which not only amount to a laudation of Russian conditions and a denial of all their sinister aspects, but consciously or unconsciously distort the truth and place the responsibility for the happenings in Russia, and more especially in the Ukraine, on the wrong quarters. When he does this M. Herriot enters the field of international dissension-mongering; although even here he is the victim of the figures, explanations and conclusions offered or suggested by Moscow.

The statements emanating from M. Herriot still continue to be printed by various newspapers and are taken as correct by numbers of credulous persons desiring to form an opinion on Russian conditions—more especially on the famine. For this reason I am compelled to deal with two particularly important points in his most recent effusions. The first point is his manner of dealing with the reports of famine in the Ukraine. He begins by declaring categorically: "There is no country about which more nonsense has been written of late than Russia. The primary reason for this consists in political fanaticism; for some Russia is the object of a kind of mystic cult, while for others it is a land of terror." "At present," he continues, "a regular propaganda campaign is in progress aiming at the dissemination of a belief in famine in the Ukraine."

Now M. Herriot cannot be conceded the right publicly to deny the existence of famine in the Ukraine and to represent it to be "propaganda by political fanatics." His assertions that on the present occasion when "travelling through" the Ukraine "in various directions" he saw "nothing of the kind" (contrary to his experience ten years previously) are meaningless. To-day we know that during the five days of his triumphal progress through the Ukraine M. Herriot took part in a number of banquets, receptions and inspections arranged in his honour, and that on his visit to one Soviet farm and two collective farms he had an opportunity of admiring the technical achievements which he was shown, including the use of aeroplanes for sowing. But he did not take the trouble, as a serious investigator, on whom the eyes of the world were fixed, should have made it his duty to do, to follow up the visible traces of one of the greatest human tragedies of the present day, a tragedy which had reached its climax in the days preceding the new harvest, immediately before his arrival. Such an investigation would have meant leaving his special coach, escaping his Moscow guides, and putting an end to the whole official mystification which was practised upon him during his five days' visit, hour by hour, from morning to night, over a stretch of nearly 2,000 miles. He did not do this, no matter for what reason, and he has therefore no right to pose as an experienced administrator having made serious studies on the spot, and so to mislead a numerous public in the various states of the world with erroneous opinions proclaimed as unchallengeable truth. Nor has he any right to base what he says on the authority of such German experts as Dr. Otto Schiller, whom he cites on more than one occasion; or if he quotes him on certain special questions, it is his duty to inform the public that the conclusions reached by Dr. Schiller in the "thorough and critical investigations" to which M. Herriot refers are diametrically opposite to his own on the subject of Russian agriculture. When M. Herriot speaks of the dreadful experiment of collectivization applied to the Russian peasantry as though the Government were confining itself to the abolition of the *kulak* system, or, as he calls it, "of the landowners who make other peasants work for them," it is a matter of opinion. When he describes the ideal conditions in the collective farms and Soviet farms which he visited, that also is his own affair. But when he arrogates to himself the right to describe the famine as the outcome of political fanaticism or of a campaign of propaganda, then it is in the interests of truth and of the innocent victims of the famine to rebut his judgment and to condemn the irresponsible methods by which it was reached.

The second point on which I must join issue with M. Herriot is his claim that the Soviet regime is a model Government, "an international system allowing for the dominance of the various races and allowing the various peoples an intellectual expansion for which they are particularly grateful," a system in which, as he further claims, "the sacred rights of the minorities" are realized.[1] Elsewhere there is a variation on this theme, and his

---

[1] *Pester Lloyd*, October 1, 1933.

views are summed up in the following terms: "Thus, by an apparent paradox, a fundamentally internationalistic regime is combined with a regime of nationalities allowing for the intellectual expansion of the various peoples."

M. Herriot makes this statement on the strength of his observations in the Ukraine—the only part of Russia which he really visited, apart from Moscow—and with explicit reference to his former declarations on the position of the Ukrainians. At the time when he arrived at Kiev the death of the Communist Skrypnik, a former political friend of Lenin, had become common knowledge. Postyschev had delivered his notorious Kharkov speech, and the entire country was trembling under the campaign then being initiated by Moscow and being carried out by Postyschev against the nationalistic movement among the Ukrainian population and against the hundreds and thousands of Ukrainian Communists who, like Skrypnik, were demanding the recognition of the national and cultural individuality of their people. It may be mentioned that similar campaigns were carried through in White Russia, Kazakstan and other parts of the Soviet Union. M. Herriot, meanwhile, was proclaiming that the demands of the centre and those of local nationalism—in the present case, the claim for nationalist or intellectual expansion in the Ukraine—had been harmonized in actual fact. But here again we must insist that a visit to the Ukrainian Academy of Science at Kiev (an institution which immediately on his departure became the object of Postyschev's most insistent attentions), a talk with Comrade Tschubar (whom Postyschev entrusted with the post formerly held by Skrypnik) and other conversations with exponents of the Moscow regime give M. Herriot no right to "instruct" world public opinion on the position in the Ukraine.

But there is another and more regrettable aspect of M. Herriot's proceedings. Embarrassed by the controversy on the Russian position and especially on the famine in the Ukraine, he made the following statement in a lecture given in the

Vichy Casino (*Journal des Débats*): "*La famine russe, qu'on agite comme un épouvantail, n'est que le produit suspect de la propagande hitlérienne.*" And in another connection he plainly declares that the Ukraine was not so much endangered by hunger as by separatist machinations enjoying the support of German National Socialism. (It should be mentioned that M. Herriot sees in the National Socialists, especially in Alfred Rosenberg, the wire-pullers behind Ukrainian separatism, while Postyschev suspects the Polish aristocracy, Sir Henry Deterding and others.) If M. Herriot's claim were true, it would mean that the numerous Communist officials in the Ukraine who have nationalist tendencies, and thus supported Skrypnik against Postyschev, did so from no love for their own nation, but were the agents or victims of others who remained behind the scenes. In view of the tragic struggle now in progress between Moscow centralization and the various peoples living in the Soviet Union and anxious to preserve their individuality, it is perhaps unnecessary to insist on the arbitrariness of M. Herriot's interpretation of present events in the Ukraine. Of course there will always be interested parties willing and ready to exploit every current of feeling and every divergency of view. Such elements may be observed at work in a great many different countries. But to believe that real convulsions within or between the nations can be initiated by the work of "agents" or "propagandist machinations" implies a complete misconception of the real conditions in most European countries, and reveals an entire misapprehension of the problem of nationalities.

How deeply M. Herriot, in making such assertions, has entangled himself in a net of hypotheses and suppositions is shown by the fact that he accuses the *Vozrojdenie*, an organ of the right-wing Russian *émigrés* appearing in Paris, of attacking him because it is in the service of the National Socialists, on the ground—as he states, "for the benefit of the unprejudiced reader"—that the paper derives its news from

Berlin and from National Socialist circles. The claim that under the patronage of Berlin there is collaboration between the Ukrainian separatists and the Russian *émigrés* must seem wholly grotesque to anyone aware of the violent antipathy between the latter (the right wing of whom has Tsarist or Great Russian sympathies and does not even admit the existence of a Ukrainian people) and the former.

And finally, even papers which cannot be suspected of being under National Socialist influence or of being anti-French vigorously oppose M. Herriot's thesis. Thus the *New York Herald-Tribune* (October 22, 1933) expresses doubts of M. Herriot's reliability, and goes on to say that it is peculiar that he should have noticed things during his brief visit to Russia which even the Ogpu had failed to notice. Impartial observers, the paper added, had found that there was famine in the Ukraine, but had found no traces of National Socialist propaganda. M. Herriot's claim, therefore, must be either a sensational "stunt" by a talented amateur writer or else a testimonial to the efficiency of Communist stage management.

M. Herriot is indignant at the alleged "campaign of defamation" initiated by Russian *émigrés* and other interested parties, but is apparently not aware that his own account of the causes of recent developments in the Ukraine is a defamation of wide circles of an entire people, uttered at a moment when this people, deserted by the entire world, is fighting desperately for its future, for its nationhood, and perhaps for its bare existence. In their opposition to M. Herriot Ukrainians of all shades are united for the first time in many years. At a time when humanitarian efforts were everywhere being set on foot with a view to rendering assistance to the victims of the Russian famine, a former French Prime Minister and statesman of international repute adopts in the most decided manner the thesis of the Moscow rulers—all the reports of the Soviet Russian famine are imagination or invention! It will readily be understood that this attitude of M. Herriot, as we said at the opening of this chapter, was bound to react disastrously on the existing readiness to help. This revulsion of opinion was plainly expressed in a number of European and American papers and periodicals. The utterances of M. Herriot are to this day a serious embarrassment to all those who, moved by humanitarian considerations, are fighting to spread the truth and bring help to those now starving in the Soviet Union.

CHAPTER VII

THE OUTER WORLD AND THE SOVIETS

THE tragedy in the famine areas—this cannot be denied—went on with the silent toleration of all the Powers represented in Moscow. To explain this almost incredible fact I must enumerate the chief factors at present determining the relations of the Soviet Union to the rest of the world. The general remark that world public opinion has been insufficiently informed about the catastrophe does not dispose of the question.

In the countries interested in trade with Russia, and, indeed, in every state represented in the Soviet Union, there were wide circles which were thoroughly informed about developments in South Russia. Indeed, I do not hesitate to assert that the Embassies, Legations, Consulates and trade delegations in Moscow were possessed of authentic material, fully documented reports, eyewitnesses' accounts and photographs illustrating the catastrophe.

The Foreign Office of one of the Western Great Powers was so well informed about the Russian famine and the position in general as early as the spring of 1934, that the officials foretold to me the railway collapse which actually took place in 1935. Another Foreign Office—that of one of Russia's neighbours—has a special room containing nothing but documents bearing on Russian conditions, photographs relating to the famine, and so on.

Why, then, was nothing said? I have shown above that Moscow was compelled to deny the existence of the famine. This meant that the Government was obliged, as far as possible, to prevent the discussion of this problem in the states with which it had diplomatic or economic contact, since any such discussion might have prejudiced relations with the Soviet Union. At present the real or imaginary political and economic interest of the non-Communist states is judged to be incompatible with any light being thrown on Russian conditions, let alone any consideration of the question of famine relief.

Why is it that, despite the Communist regime, and despite the fact that Moscow scorns all the ideas regarded as sacred in the West—religion, family and patriotism—good relations with Soviet Russia are considered so valuable by the Western states that they simply close their ears when the Soviet Union loudly proclaims its intention of introducing Communism into the bourgeois world?

There are two main reasons why the bourgeois world is interested in Moscow. There is, first, the question of trade with Russia. Industrial interests in Western Europe and America are urging their respective Governments in this direction, although the success of the Communist experiment would mean ruin for many of them, quite apart from the fact that the triumph of Bolshevism would mean the destruction of the non-Communist economic order. These states are giving economic support to a country whose dumping methods are already doing severe harm to various branches of industry. But it is an undeniable fact that there is not the slightest solidarity or foresight to be found in capitalist industry all over the world: everywhere momentary interests and temporary expediency alone are regarded. To overcome ephemeral difficulties the bourgeois world is ready to take steps which sooner or later must shatter its own position. Anyone who has spent any time in Moscow or Leningrad must know with what contempt the Bolsheviks and their press daily speak and write of the suicidal activities of capitalist economic circles.

It should be mentioned that in the present circumstances business relations with Russia mean one particular difficulty for certain states; and this is the unscrupulous way in which Moscow exploits all patents, models and special processes of the industries of these countries. Often enough business relations have been established with the sole purpose of obtaining this kind of information and utilizing it independently later. The losses caused to Germany by these methods during the years of business co-operation with Soviet Russia subsequent to the Treaty of Rapallo were very severe. Another factor of great importance is the guaranteeing by the State of industrial credits to finance business with Soviet Russia, which has taken the risk off the shoulders of the industries and businesses in question and transferred them to the State—in other words, to the taxpayer. This has resulted, strange as it may seem, in a direct community of interests between Bolshevism and Bolshevism's deadly enemies, the capitalists. In the interests of business these latter are now concerned in the granting of Government credits, and to this end their watchword has become: "All quiet in Russia." The last thing they want is to have business upset by anything directly or indirectly discrediting the business reputation of the Soviets; for this would endanger the placing of orders; and, after all, should anything go wrong, it is the State that will bear the loss.

A classic example of the part played by interested business circles in the conclusion of State agreements with Soviet Russia is furnished by recent events in the U.S.A., where the undertakings interested in Russian business exerted a decisive influence on the course of negotiations and on public opinion. If the desired result was not obtained, this must be attributed to quite different causes.

However, in Soviet Russia the decision rests with the Government, and consequently the benefits of Russian orders can only be enjoyed if it pleases Moscow to give such orders to the various concerns in the respective countries. We thus come to the inter-connection between business and politics in Russia's present-day foreign trade system, and with it we reach the core of the question: Moscow, by preference, places orders in accordance with political considerations. This explains why the Governments of all the states trying to do business with Soviet Russia act most vigorously to prevent such business from being hampered by public opinion.

The second reason why the competition for business relations with Soviet Russia has everywhere been so much intensified is to be found in the unhappy state of conflict which has existed among the European states since the Great War. This conflict has been a piece of luck for Moscow, since it has caused the various states to enter into the most degrading competition for Bolshevik favours. This fact was well illustrated by the events during and after the conclusion of the Treaty of Rapallo. The only valid reason which led the Germans to play off Soviet Russia against the victors of Versailles was the political duress in which Germany felt herself to be held at that time. All who lived through those hours of Easter 1920 in Genoa will confirm that for the Reich the real justification for that daring move—the sudden conclusion of a treaty with the Soviet Union—was the united front of the victorious Powers, which declined to accord equality of treatment to Germany. This tendency was undoubtedly promoted by the attitude of certain driving forces on the German side. At the moment when the influence of the neutrals and others had begun to bring about a certain solidarity between the victorious and the defeated European Powers during the first week of the general conference, the Moscow representatives, Chicherin, Litvinov and others, left no stone unturned to induce the German delegates to sign the Treaty of Rapallo forthwith and thus to force Germany out of the non-Communist front then in process of formation.[1] So if the Treaty was a triumph in Moscow, it is equally certain

[1] The remarkable diplomatic achievements of the Soviet representatives, whose first appearance it was on the international stage, especially Chicherin, must be emphasized. The Soviet diplomats employed every device; they succeeded in exploiting the personal relationships and ambitions of the other delegates; nor did they shrink from the dissemination of falsehood, with the one aim of reaching an immediate conclusion of the Treaty. This naturally prevented the formation of a united economic front of the non-Communist states of Europe, which, at the beginning of the Conference, had seemed within the bounds of possibility.

that it was only the differences between the Powers that made it possible.

There can be no doubt that the foundation for all future co-operation of the non-Communist states was thus removed for years to come. It will be remembered how the general race for business with Soviet Russia began immediately upon the conclusion of the Treaty of Rapallo—indeed, actually at Genoa. "The Conference smells of petrol," an important Paris paper wrote at the time.

It was at this time that the principle of "non-intervention," correct enough in itself, was adopted. The only question is whether there are any limits to this principle: should it not be suspended where purely humanitarian questions arise, like relief actions on behalf of innocent persons threatened by starvation?

I mentioned above that the non-Communist states were influenced by two considerations in dealing with Soviet Russia— economic questions, or, in other words, the question of business with the Soviets, and political interest in collaboration with Moscow. These two considerations are found dominating the attitude of the various states towards Soviet Russia. The influence of the respective factors vary, but in one way or another both are at work. I will now deal with the standpoint of the various Great Powers, and, later, with that of the neighbouring states.

Germany occupies a special position in relation to Russia, seeing that hundreds of thousands of German peasants have been settled in that country for more than two centuries. Apart from economic and political considerations tending in the direction of collaboration with Moscow, if only in defence against the victorious Powers, one might have thought that the fate of these German settlers would influence the attitude of the Reich towards the Soviets. Such at any rate should have been the case from the moment when the lives of these settlers began to be threatened. But it did not happen so. The *Temps*, the organ of the Quai d'Orsay, recently declared that German relief for Germans settled in Russia was hampered by the desire to maintain an entente with Moscow. (*Mais cette sollicitude pour cette population germanique était jusqu'ici genée par sa volonté d'entente avec Moscou.*) This single sentence from the *Temps* gives a correct description of Germany's policy with regard to her kinsmen in Russia. During all the years which have passed since Rapallo considerations of the fate of German settlers along the Volga, in the Ukraine and elsewhere, any readiness to render assistance to starving men, women and children in the forests of the north and in the famine districts of the south, have played second fiddle to the political factor which dictated co-operation with the Soviets. The result was that even when German influence at Moscow was greatest, the German populations in Soviet Russia had to perish miserably.

Neither official German policy nor a great part of the German public—excepting, of course, the relief organizations—ever took the slightest interest in the fate of the Germans in Russia, apart from the return of the 6,000 colonists who made their way to Moscow and thence to Germany. After Rapallo Germany sacrificed her own flesh and blood to her friendship with the Soviet State, and not a single energetic attempt was made to save the lives of these people. The fact is that Soviet–German relations during this period were determined solely by the two factors previously mentioned—the economic and the political; and that apart from certain charitable endeavours no attention was paid to the weal and woe of the Germans in Russia.

Then the new regime came into power in Germany. The National Socialist campaign had made the destruction of Communism in Germany its primary endeavour. To what change in Soviet–German relations did the revolution lead? The *Temps* of July 21, 1933, answered this question as follows: "To-day the German Government no longer considers itself bound by such considerations [i.e. friendship between Russia and Germany] and is openly starting a campaign on behalf of the German victims of the Russian famine."

It is true that during the summer the "Brethren in Distress" and the "National Union for the Support of Germanism Abroad" initiated collections on behalf of the victims of the famine. But the idea remained that Soviet–German relations must continue to be guided by the principle of non-interference in the internal affairs of another State, even in such a matter as the assistance of men of German blood in the Soviet Union. The old view was even maintained that a restoration of the former Soviet–German relations would amount to "a make-weight against the pressure of the authors of Versailles," as a Berlin paper put it.[1]

In the summer of 1933 the organ of the Central Union of Germans in Russia[2] contained the following passage: "We have for months been publishing, both in this periodical and wherever possible in other journals, extracts from letters written by Germans in Russia, in the hope that their appeals might be heard. A million Germans are threatened with destruction; but we look in vain in the German press for any cries of vengeance against Soviet barbarism. Here and there a solitary note is to be found, and that is all." Subsequently much more interest was taken by the German public and press; yet the prevailing opinion still is that, as things are, nothing further can be done by Germany in this respect.

At a later stage, however, it was seen that Moscow regarded the National Socialist regime as the chief and most fundamental enemy of Bolshevism, and hence of the Soviet State. Anyone who doubts this has only to look at the Soviet press for a few days, and read the flood of mockery and contempt which is daily poured upon the German endeavours. Acting upon this view, Moscow has made relief work for the benefit of the dis-

[1] In this connection reference should be made to a book by General von Seeckt, the former commander of the Reichswehr, which was circulated just at that time in Germany and abroad.

[2] *Deutsches Leben in Russland*, Nos. 1–5.

tressed Germans in various parts of Russia impossible by systematically persecuting the recipients. To-day, when even these slender possibilities of rendering help have ceased to exist, the German people is faced by the weighty question: What is to be done in future for the German famine victims in Russia?

It must be pointed out here that for a number of years the German attitude afforded the Soviet Union not only political and economic advantages, but also direct or indirect moral support. Numbers of German scientists and journalists endeavoured to make the public of Europe appreciate the "interesting" and even "extraordinary" experiments of the Soviets. From the time when the first German journalists settled in Moscow dates the method of describing this or that aspect of Soviet Russian life, such as industrial experiments, technical developments, social service, etc., without making any adequate attempt to describe the other side of the picture in Soviet Russia—above all, the actual conditions under which the majority of the population live. Only here and there, and to some extent only superficially, has anything been said about this side of Soviet Russian life.

It should be noted, however, that there were also German correspondents in Moscow, even in the period just following the Treaty of Rapallo, who paid some attention to the negative aspects of the regime.

The second State which provides a good illustration of the attitude of the European Powers towards the Soviet Union and the question of rendering relief to the victims of famine is France.

It was also the feeling of insecurity which induced France to seek close political, military and economic co-operation with the Soviet Union. This development was accelerated by the growing fear of the present Germany and of its alleged aggressiveness. The change at the Quai d'Orsay is the more remarkable because until recently the Moscow propagandists used to represent France as the type of the contemptible bourgeois state and subjected all her economic and social institutions to daily ridicule. The new relationship was promoted, if not made possible, by the intervention of M. Herriot. It was M. Herriot, and the effect of his journey to Russia, described in the preceding chapter, that drove France into the wake of the Soviet, despite many protests from various quarters. M. Herriot himself has openly declared that it was his ambition to counter the "dangerous intentions of Hitlerism" by an alliance with the "now pacific Soviet Union." At the same time the Soviet press, which quite recently had been describing France as the essence of capitalism and imperialism, hailed her as a friend of peace and of the Soviet Union.

When M. Herriot's journey for "private study" was followed by an official visit from M. Pierre Cot, then French Air Minister, the future attitude of France towards the Soviet Union, with all its consequences, was finally decided. The same thing happened ten years previously in Germany. The press, in so far as it was under official influence (and in foreign politics this is true of very many French papers) had to observe silence about everything that might hurt the susceptibilities of France's new friends in Moscow. The change of attitude of the *Temps*, the most influential paper in the field of foreign affairs, was particularly instructive. With M. Herriot's arrival in Russia all reports of famine and death in that country ceased to appear in its columns.

Naturally enough the *Temps* and official circles generally did not execute this *volte-face* in their treatment of Bolshevism and of Soviet conditions with perfect ease. It was felt that some explanation of the sudden change was due to the paper's readers. Accordingly, the *Temps* of September 30, 1933, published an article on *Diplomatie Sovietique*, by Etienne Fournol, which contained the following significant remarks on the new relationship between France and Soviet Russia. "There is a conflict between our moral and our political judgment. This is embarrassing to us. Both are justified, but they are of very different value. Our task now is to harmonize the two." The article goes on to declare expressly that all the moral principles are suppressed in the land of the Soviets. "The nation, patriotism, religion, property and even the family are treated as artificial inventions of the capitalist world. For fifteen years this view has been inculcated in all young Russians." But regard for moral principles must now conform to the demands of "political reason": this is the inevitable conclusion from the *Temps*'s arguments. What is meant by "political reason" is clearly stated—"a guarantee of the territorial *status quo*." A letter from Pierre Berland in Moscow published in the same issue of the *Temps* expresses this as follows: "The evolution which has taken place makes it possible to class the Soviet Union among the states which are interested in the maintenance of the present territorial status."

In other words, the Soviet Union has now, by the irony of fate, become for France a bulwark for the preservation of the Versailles Treaty: while Germany had hoped for ten years to make use of the Soviet Union for the modification, indeed the abolition, of this same Treaty. It ought to be quite clear that the Soviet Government does not care about the maintenance or the abolition of the Versailles Treaty, but seeks solely to exploit for its own purposes the conflict between the European Great Powers. Just imagine it! the Soviet Union is needed to remove the danger to the peace of Europe. Thus Pierre Berland writes in the *Temps* (September 21, 1933): "We need the alliance with Russia in view of the danger to European peace implicit in the Hitler regime, and it can be understood that the advances of the Kremlin meet with a favourable response in France and Poland." The present French view can be summed up thus: France and the peace-loving Communists will jointly preserve the Versailles system, and with it the bourgeois order (democracy) in Europe, against all attacks of the dictators and autocrats.

The reasons which induced Soviet Russia to conclude the

Treaty of Rapallo with Germany are correctly described by Berland: "The entente with the Reich meant for the Soviet Union a strong guarantee against the formation of a coalition between the so-called Capitalist Powers, the nightmare of Soviet diplomacy." Berland forgets to add that the same cause which underlay Soviet–German collaboration is the chief reason for the change in the Soviet attitude to the once so-hated bourgeois French Republic. The thought of a Franco-German understanding and, through it, a union of the non-Communist states absolutely terrifies the Moscow rulers. For Moscow there can be only one line of action—a fight against the non-Communist states, with or without capitalist support, until a victorious conclusion is reached. For eighteen years the Kremlin's one hope has been that the population of the non-Communist states—thanks to the quarrels and strife between them—may become ripe for the Communist revolution.

Anyone who has observed the inexorable persistency of Communist policy in dealing with the bourgeois world, and its contempt for the bourgeois regime and its institutions in Germany, France, Italy, England and elsewhere, can imagine the triumph felt by Moscow at this change in France's Russian policy. The struggle between the great peoples of Western and Central Europe will become, Moscow hopes, a permanent state of things. It is true that even now there exist in France circles and parties which see in a collaboration with Moscow a great danger. The more influential factors in the country, however—those who finally decide the policy—take up a different position.

Thus it comes that in the French press at the present time almost nothing is written about the negative side of life in the Soviet Union and of the conditions under which the unprivileged categories of the population live. "The moral judgment," as the *Temps* so lucidly explained, "has to give way to the political necessity." In view of this attitude, what is the use of a few French papers, such as the *Matin*, treating objectively the question of the Russian famine and the necessity of rendering assistance?

After the first spontaneous exchange of declarations of friendship between Moscow and Paris, a most significant event occurred in France—the discovery of a vast Bolshevik propaganda and espionage organization in Paris, accompanied by the simultaneous discovery of similar organizations in Finland, Bulgaria and elsewhere.

Etienne Fournol explained recently in the *Temps* how the French Revolution had been able to hold its own in the contemporary world, and added that the day might come when historians would discover "how it was that the Soviet diplomacy could prevail in the midst of the bourgeois system which had threatened to destroy it." These words are worth remembering.

While the French attitude towards the Soviet and the Russian famine is thus primarily guided by political considerations, economic elements also play a part, as they did formerly in the case of Germany. Moscow skilfully foments the hope that the old Russian war debts may after all be satisfactorily regulated owing to the new friendship. Nevertheless, economic considerations are a factor of comparatively small importance, from the French standpoint, in the friendship with Soviet Russia. For the Soviets the case is different; they are compelled to obtain a maximum of credits and economic advantages from France in exchange for their support in upholding the territorial provisions of Versailles. The relationship thus is similar to that between Soviet Russia and Germany, when the latter did much to enable the Communist experiment to be continued by the economic and to a certain extent also the moral support which it gave to the Soviet Union in the years after Rapallo.

Great Britain's attitude to the Soviet Union was also guided by the two considerations mentioned above—economic and political. It will be remembered how the representatives and employees of Moscow settled in London after the first Anglo-Soviet treaty, where they proceeded to found big organizations, and how, as the activities of these bodies extended, a large part of the British public showed signs of deep resentment. The publication of the Zinoviev letter caused an explosion of national anger. Whether this letter, with its revelation of Bolshevik activities in England, was genuine or forged does not matter, if only because overwhelming evidence of the activity of Bolshevik organizations in the bourgeois states has since been adduced. A second period in Anglo-Soviet relations began. Economic considerations began to predominate and Anglo-Soviet trade to expand, the balance of this trade being considerably in favour of Soviet Russia. Its policy of dumping raw materials, especially timber, did considerable injury to the Dominions in the home market. Simultaneously the propaganda of the Third International made itself felt in the various British spheres of influence in the East.

Thus Britain's attitude to the Soviet Union was also considerably influenced by economic and political considerations. Yet in one respect this attitude differs from that of many other states; for the British attitude has been influenced very largely by the treatment of British nationals in Russia, and considerations of the national dignity and solidarity in general.

When two English engineers were condemned by a Soviet court, for reasons of domestic politics, on the charge of counter-revolutionary activities, a spontaneous wave of indignation went through the entire country. People did not ask whether the resulting conflict and the ultimatum demanding the liberation of the arrested Britons would prove injurious to British trade; British policy was dictated entirely by the demands of national solidarity and dignity. The attitude of the British and the insistence upon their claims were a lesson to the world on the manner in which national dignity, the foundation of Britain's prestige in the world, must be maintained.

Nor has this attitude of the English had any disagreeable consequences for them; they have, in thèir commercial transactions with Russia, throughout been able to secure the same conditions as, say, France or the United States.

That this is actually the case is confirmed by the various paragraphs of the recently concluded Anglo-Russian provisional trade agreement; above all, two innovations which were not included in the old treaty. One of these is a clause by which the Soviet Union is bound from year to year, to 1937 inclusive, either to buy more goods in Great Britain than hitherto, or at least gradually to adjust the sales of its goods in Great Britain to its purchases in the British market, till the trade balance, until now unfavourable to Britain, is more or less equalized.

The second innovation is a concession to the Ottawa agreements, by which, as is known, Great Britain undertook to restrict those foreign imports which were calculated to injure her trade with her Dominions. In the new Anglo-Russian treaty it is laid down that Britain has the right even to suspend the most-favoured-nation clause conceded to the Soviet Union in the case of those categories of goods in which the Soviet Union might employ dumping methods. These important concessions, and, further, the granting of the British demand to be allowed to supply British citizens living in Russia with food supplies and goods from abroad free of duty—a demand which met with especially prolonged resistance in Moscow—clearly prove the correctness of the view that Great Britain's energetic measures against the Soviet Government in the affair of the condemned British engineers has in no way injured, but, on the contrary, strengthened England's position in dealing with Moscow. This lesson should be taken to heart elsewhere to-day.

But in the case of England, too, it must be pointed out that a considerable section of public opinion and the press is occupied almost exclusively with Soviet achievements and not at all with the negative aspects of Soviet life. This is, among others, due also to the activities of the so-called "Friends of Soviet Russia," at whose head is Mr. Bernard Shaw.[1]

As far as the attitude of *Italy* towards the Soviet Union is concerned, it is partly dictated by considerations different from those of England, France and Germany. Italy and the Head of its Government see, naturally, in Russia an important factor, if not a competitor, in their desire to obtain economical, cultural and political influence in the East. Rome has not yet forgotten the powerful and frequently decisive part formerly played by Russia in that sphere. Italy's one desire, therefore, is to free its trade, shipping and politics from Russian interference. The best means to this end is thought to consist in friendly relations with Soviet Russia, so long as she is so preoccupied by internal troubles that she cannot be a rival to Italy in the Near East. The firmly established dictatorship makes a Communist danger almost impossible and extinguishes in the Bolsheviks any desire to carry on subterranean intrigues in Italy. Hence this unnatural friendship between Communism and Fascism which existed for a long time.

If the two Governments had been true to their philosophies, they would have been obliged to turn and rend each other. The fact is that the attitude of each country was inspired exclusively by political calculation. It should be pointed out that Italy can take up such an attitude more easily than other states on account of her distance from Russia, her isolated position, etc. For years Italian support has been one of the chief political and also moral pillars of Soviet policy, and this is confirmed by the attitude which was taken up by the greater part of the Italian press with regard to the famine.

In the United States the supposed interests of trade and

[1] Letters written by Englishmen, seeking to refute all unfavourable reports about the Soviet Union, and in particular about the famine, constantly appear in the English newspapers. Englishmen, who do not speak a word of Russian, are continually being escorted through the Soviet Union, and then report with astonishment on the extraordinary achievements of the Soviet State.

industry are the decisive factor—the "vast advantages" to be obtained from trade with Soviet Russia. This attitude is mainly dictated by the special interests of a group of American leaders of industry. For if they succeeded in their plan of obtaining permanent Government guarantees for exports to Russia, the interests of these branches of industry in the maintenance of trade with Russia would cease to depend on the actual economic relations between the United States and the Soviet Union.

Yet this economic factor alone would not suffice to explain the changed attitude of the United States, which had refrained longer than any other country, on grounds of principle, from recognizing the Soviet State *de jure*. As in the case of France, there was also an important political consideration; for just as the German change of regime drove France into the arms of the Bolsheviks, so Japanese aggressiveness in the Far East had a similar effect on the United States. The Soviet Union and the United States are equally interested in preventing Japanese expansion in the Far East. Consequently, what, amid enthusiastic applause, a few years ago would have seemed the wildest fancy has become a fact, and Litvinov was able to describe the principles and achievements of Soviet Russia to 2,000 American millionaires and bourgeois, as well as their wives.

To-day American capitalism and Moscow Communism work together hand in glove. On March 3, 1934, *Pravda* published on the same page an appeal for the support of Austrian Communists, an eloquent summons to the fight against the bourgeois world, and a triumphant telegram from Chicago reporting that the Bankers' Club had given a dinner in honour of the Soviet delegate, Troyanovsky, which over five hundred representatives of American trade and industry attended. With barely disguised irony the names of these "sharks" of capitalism, as *Pravda* usually calls them, are revealed to the paper's readers. And what had Troyanovsky to tell the representatives of American capital in his loudly applauded speech? Naturally

s

enough, what they wanted to hear. As the report states, he explained the vast possibilities of Russian-American trade, the realization of which depended on a correct attitude towards trade questions being adopted. There can be no doubt what he meant by a correct attitude—a readiness to grant Moscow extensive credits. For this purpose, or, as Troyanovsky called it, in order to stimulate trade, the formation of a Russian-American export and import bank was decided upon.[1]

Since the summer of 1934, however, there has been a significant change in the relations between the U.S.A. and Soviet Russia, and in the attitude taken up by the American press in dealing with the famine and famine relief. This change was brought about by, among other things, the fact that the promised Soviet purchases were not forthcoming.

As mentioned elsewhere, the *New York Times* published the report of the Innitzer Committee with comments of its own. The *Chicago Tribune*, and other important papers, reported in detail the argument between the Russian Ambassador[2] at Washington and the writer. Troyanovsky's denials of the existence of a famine and of the number of its victims proved unavailing, and the discussion of the actual situation in Russia continued. On January 5, 1935, William Randolph Hearst broadcast a speech based almost entirely on the account of the

---

[1] While Litvinov was on his way to New York, the Profintern (the trades union counterpart to the Communist International) issued a publication called *Roosevelt's Famine Programme*, which contained this passage: "The leadership of the [American] masses must pass into the hands of the Communist Party and the revolutionary organizations. The dissatisfaction among the workers must be exploited to organize a gigantic struggle of the American proletariat against Roosevelt's plan." Thus, while the captains of industry and their wives were enthusiastically applauding Litvinov's words, the Communist International had already prepared its material.

[2] *New York Times*, July 11, 1934. Significantly enough, Duranty coupled his admission that the hopes of Soviet trade had been disappointed with a reference to the alleged prospects of an exchange of goods between Great Britain and Soviet Russia. No doubt this was intended to create the impression that unless the United States were to grant credits, etc., to Soviet Russia at the last moment, it would be Great Britain that would bring off the big deal with that country.

Innitzer Committee in the *New York Times*. The entire Hearst press next proceeded to deal with the Russian famine. Early in summer the American-Russian negotiations had almost been completed; now they began to lag, and, indeed, could not be continued on the old lines. At this period even Walter Duranty had to admit that all the hopes of Soviet purchases had not been realized.

The plan formed by Moscow and her friends to make America pay for Soviet Russia's foreign trade and hence for the continuance of her economic experiment, may be regarded as a failure.[1]

Next in importance to the relations between Soviet Russia and the Great Powers stand those with neighbouring countries —and especially Poland. Here again Moscow has attempted to employ its tactics of profiting by the quarrels between the bourgeois states. When the friendship between Soviet Russia and Germany came to an end, and Moscow, from being an opponent of the peace treaties, suddenly became a champion of the *status quo*, the time was considered ripe for an attempt to woo Poland, like France, on this basis. Karl Radek was despatched to Warsaw as emissary of the Soviet Government—the same man who for years on end had described the "scandal of the Versailles frontiers" and quoted the Polish Corridor as an example of the necessity of altering them. As guest of the Polish press in Warsaw Radek declared the opposite of what he had been maintaining for years. But there was a special reason why his attempts to win over Polish public opinion were bound to fail. The Poles remembered the part played by Radek, who was born in Poland, while he was a journalist at Cracow and more especially in 1920 during the Bolshevik attempts to conquer Poland.[2]

[1] I describe elsewhere the growing interest displayed since the summer of 1934 by religious bodies in the famine victims in Russia and the question of their relief.

[2] In this connection the *Kurjer Bydgoski*, the organ of the Poles of Posen and Pomerellia, who are particularly interested in the Corridor question,

Naturally enough, the Poles are well informed about Soviet conditions, and no Polish statesman could have been deceived as M. Herriot was. Nor are there any illusions whatever as to the position in the Soviet Union. But neighbourly relations with Russia are among the main foundations of Poland's foreign policy, and even her interest in the fate of the Poles settled in Russia, whose position, like that of all the other nationalities, is extremely difficult, has to take a secondary place.

An important element in the situation is the new agreement between Germany and Poland, for it goes without saying that it would now be difficult for Moscow by means of its usual tactics to gain advantage from the quarrels between these two countries.

The position of Russia's four neighbours to the north of Poland—Finland, Estonia, Latvia and Lithuania—is similar to that of Poland. All these states have large groups of their nationals inhabiting Russian territory. In relation to the total number of Finns, Estonians, Latvians and Lithuanians, these minorities are fairly important; in some cases they form 10 per cent of the total nationals of the country in question. In the Pleskau region alone there are about 180,000 Estonians, and there are Estonian, Latvian and Finnish settlements in various districts as far as Siberia and especially along the Volga and in the Ukraine.

Each of these countries had formerly to suffer under Moscow's tactics of *divide et impera*, more especially in the economic

wrote as follows: "One cannot help making certain reservations with regard to this gentleman who is paying us the return visit [following a Polish visit to Moscow]. Could not someone else have been chosen for this mission? We in Poland recall the answer which a Zamoyski gave the King of Sweden under the walls of Zamosc, when the King of Sweden sent a Pole as negotiator. Zamoyski demanded that a Swede should be sent, for a Pole in Swedish service might have the dogs set on him. This Mr. Radek is in the same position. He comes from Tarnov and once worked for the Socialist *Naprzod* at Cracow, but he went over to the Bolsheviks and, in 1920, joined the traitor Marchlevski and others in attempting to seize Warsaw and instituting Communist rule."

sphere. They are, however, too small to form a counterweight to Soviet Russia, the largest military power in the world, and, being compelled to rely on their own strength alone, are weak both economically and politically. They rightly feel that they cannot do anything to offend their eastern neighbour, even when the existence of their kinsmen in Russia is at stake.

The position of Finland is unique in so far as the Soviet Union, by the Treaty of Dorpat, assumed obligations valid in international law, guaranteeing the rights of the Finns in Ingermanland, and of the population of Karelia. The subject was dealt with in an earlier chapter.

The position of Roumania, the southern neighbour of the Soviet Union, is rather different. Probably more is known in this country about the famine in Russia and the number of its victims—including Roumanians—than anywhere else. Nor is there any illusion as to the fact that the Soviet Government (the Komintern) has for years been making Roumania in particular the scene of its endeavours to bring about a Communist revolution. The discovery of widespread secret organizations has proved this. But Roumania's relations with her neighbour are decisively influenced by one question—that of Bessarabia. Now Soviet Russia has conceded Bessarabia to Roumania, and consequently the view is held at Bucharest that the Soviet Union must be treated with all possible consideration and must even be regarded as a potential ally.

Czechoslovakia, another member of the Little Entente, does not border on Russia, but many Czechs live in that country. Czechoslovakia's attitude to Russia is a good example of the way in which the public opinion of a country can be influenced by a political change of front. How quickly the Czech change of front took place can best be seen from the following dates. In July 1934 diplomatic relations between the two states were initiated and on March 25, 1935, the trade treaty was signed. A few weeks later Moscow achieved a success it had been seeking for many years in other states: it secured a loan of

250,000,000 Czech crowns to run for five years at 6 per cent. The Soviet plenipotentiary, Rosengoltz, rightly said of this credit that it was the first instance where the principle of bill debts had been broken. The threatening methods employed by Moscow in order to carry its economic negotiations to a successful conclusion are illustrated by the fact that previous to the signing of the treaty the Soviets had cut down imports of Czech goods from 34,000,000 roubles in 1931 to 2,000,000 roubles in 1934.

The collaboration between Czechoslovakia and Soviet Russia was, however, not confined to the economic field. Since M. Benes's journey to Moscow, concrete measures have been taken to promote a cultural interchange and strengthen the intellectual relations between the two countries. This is certainly a considerable advance for the Soviet Union in its relations with the non-Communist world; for, despite economic collaboration, the latter had refrained as far as possible from a cultural interchange with Moscow on account of the different nature of the fundamental views on cultural matters held by the Bolsheviks. A further sign of progress is Prague's endeavour to involve Moscow in the settlement of Central European problems —for example, to obtain its guarantee for the independence of Austria. From what has been said it will be readily understood that Soviet Russia, if involved in any Central European dispute, would follow her constant maxim of *divide et impera*.

There is, however, an important part of Czech public opinion which, under the leadership of Dr. Kramářsch, vigorously resists the policy of an alliance with Moscow. Others point out the dangers of confusing friendship with the Soviet regime and friendship with the Russian people or peoples. Dr. Kramářsch emphasized his attitude with particular vigour when it was found that Yugoslavia refused, despite the pressure of certain friendly states, to recognize the Soviet Union *de jure* or to adapt its policy in dealing with Moscow to that of Czechoslovakia or Roumania.

The attitude of another Slav Balkan state, Bulgaria, differs from that of Yugoslavia and rather resembles that of Czechoslovakia and Roumania. This also applies to Hungary, which, despite its objection to Bolshevik principles, proceeded to conclude a trade agreement with Soviet Russia even before the Little Entente. Hopes as to the result of such co-operation are entertained at Budapest no less than at Prague; in this respect there is not so much opposition as competition between Hungary and the two Little Entente states. Everywhere hopes of successful collaboration with Moscow are entertained.

I will touch briefly on the attitude of the so-called neutral states—Switzerland, Holland and the Scandinavian countries—with regard to Soviet Russia so far as the famine is concerned. With the exception of Switzerland and, to a certain extent, of Holland, these states hold the view that everything must be done to maintain friendly economic and political relations with Moscow and to avoid anything which might lead to complications. This applies especially to the question of the famine, a tender spot for Moscow; it is perhaps best illustrated by Dr. Mowinckel's change of attitude in this connection. It is hoped above all to improve business by trade with Russia. Switzerland is an exception in this respect. When its delegate, M. Giuseppe Motta, spoke on the question of admitting the Soviet Union to the League of Nations, he was practically the only man to insist upon the principles of the League. His speech met with universal applause. He ceased for the moment to be a Swiss delegate and became the mouthpiece of the world's conscience. This is the only explanation why the delegates, who next day had to vote for the admission of Soviet Russia, gave him a spontaneous ovation.

The position of the Vatican is entirely different from that of any other state. It is a power whose influence is not based on land, population or armed forces, but only on the moral authority which the Holy See enjoys in the world in general and more especially among hundreds of millions of faithful

Catholics throughout the various countries. Although the Vatican in principle rejects all Moscow's methods, the intentions held by Rome in regard to Moscow were uncertain, for it was maintained that there were old plans in existence by which the Vatican was to conclude a treaty with Russia to enable it to prepare its mission in the East in order to win over Russia to Rome. It is no secret that there were tentative soundings of the position by the Archbishop of Genoa and the Foreign Commissary Chicherin at the time of the Genoa Conference. At that time, however, the position was different; the persecution of all the Churches and of their dignitaries had not yet become the order of the day. At present the Vatican supports relief works on behalf of people suffering from famine in every way.

It is important to note here that a few Polish and Lithuanian Catholic priests, who had been kept for many years in Soviet prisons and who had been after long negotiations allowed to leave that country, proceeded to the Vatican and reported there personally the condition of the starving people in the Soviet Union.

Now, when the attitude of the states is determined almost entirely by political and economic considerations, it should be the mission of the Vatican and other Churches to act in accordance with their principles and regardless of all other factors. It should be their task to put themselves even more than before at the head of all efforts to bring an ample measure of relief to the Russian population. If this were done, there would be a possibility that despite the political and economic obstacles prevalent in the individual states and despite the principle of non-intervention, the view might after all prevail that some action is necessary in consideration of the purely humanitarian nature of the work.

CHAPTER VIII

THE PROBLEM OF RENDERING ASSISTANCE

PRECEDING chapters have shown why the various states and also the public opinion of the world have hardly concerned themselves with the Russian catastrophe. They have shown, too, that Soviet wishes and the interests of the states have been at one on this question. Only so could it happen that, while the famine was taking so heavy a toll of human life, the agricultural districts abroad were positively "suffering" from a surplus of grain (in certain regions, e.g. in Kansas, industry used corn and maize for fuel) and numbers of vessels which might have brought the surplus grain in a few weeks to Odessa, Nikolaiev, Rostov, etc., were laid up unoccupied. Despite the attitude of Moscow, however, and the indifference, indeed opposition, of most of the states, or rather of their Governments, to the question of the Russian famine being taken up, there were forces available which urged a general relief undertaking—a work of pure charity—on behalf of the people perishing in the Soviet Union. That their efforts have hitherto been unsuccessful is doubtless a sign of the times in which we live.

Before discussing these efforts to bring assistance to the starving populations in the Soviet Union during the last few years, I must explain that there is a fundamental difference between the two classes of victims of the events in Russia. First, there are those who, rightly or wrongly, are treated as enemies and offenders against the State and are openly opposed, persecuted, even executed, as such. Their numbers are appallingly large. Any assistance for members of this class was naturally restricted within narrow limits. Nevertheless, a good deal was done for them during the earlier period of the Soviet regime. In this connection a courageous woman must not be forgotten whose name is held in great esteem and mentioned with gratitude by numbers of political prisoners in Russia: Maxim Gorki's first wife, Madame Peshkova. As president of the Political Red Cross, which specialized in assisting this category of prisoners, Madame Peshkova did wonders. She visited all the important prisons of Moscow almost daily, maintaining direct contact with the prisoners. But the assistance that could be given in this way was, as will be understood, very limited; the numbers saved were insignificant compared with those of political opponents or simply of non-Communist elements exterminated throughout Russia during this period.

The victims of this category were particularly numerous in the years between the Revolution and the beginnings of N E P in 1921. There followed a period of improvement, until a new climax was reached during Stalin's first five-year plan. The chief victims now were the so-called *kulaks*, i.e. not persons politically suspect, but all peasants who had any property, who were attached to the soil, their family and their religion and who were consequently reluctant to accept collectivization. Thousands of these were condemned to forced labour in the forests of the north, in Siberia and elsewhere. The only difference was that during the first, or "pre-Nep" period, most of these "enemies of the State" perished in prison, whereas the victims of the second period, that of Stalin's five-year plan, were not put in prison, but became "invisible" in the forests of the north and Siberia. Moscow's policy in dealing with its enemies at home has thus undergone a complete change: the prisoners are not allowed to die unproductively in prison, but are deported to the forests of the north and east, where a maximum of labour on a minimum of food, for the purposes of the dumping policy, is wrung from them before they die. In the case of victims belonging to nationalities whose main branches are outside Russia, the countries in question have felt unable to intervene effectively on their behalf: any representations made were met by the reply that the persons in question were "enemies of the

State undergoing proper punishment." This also explains why even a purely charitable relief action for their benefit met with the greatest difficulties.

The victims of the present period are a very different body of persons. These are simply the victims of a catastrophe, and even the Soviet Government does not attempt to describe them as saboteurs, *kulaks* or enemies of the State. Here we are faced with the fact that the daring experiment of agricultural communization has involved the death of an appallingly large number of people who were innocent even in the eyes of Moscow. This is, in my opinion, the most striking feature of the most recent events in the Soviet Union. The usual explanation that the interests of the State demanded, and therefore excused, these sacrifices, is not valid in this case; there is an obligation to render help in need, and from this standpoint a situation has now arisen which cannot possibly be confused with the question of political offenders against the Soviet State.

Human charity has always been ready to help when the lives of innocent people have been imperilled from inability to overcome economic forces, or from other causes. But now it seems that this rule did not exist, and that people in the Soviet Union, even when not regarded as politically or criminally "guilty," are to be sacrificed in masses to the Communist experiment while the world looks on and does nothing. It is not sufficient to explain this by saying that the groans of these unfortunates are not audible, because their voices are too feeble to cry for help, or because the foreigners visiting Russia see or hear nothing of their misery—since they themselves are the victims of Russian propaganda. No, it is also because they only too often avoid the sufferers as being a painful spectacle to them.

There is no doubt that this factor has contributed largely to the "conspiracy of silence," for it is in fact unpleasant to associate with persons who are mentally and physically at the very end of their resources. Not for nothing did Mr. and Mrs. Lang, whose studies were concentrated on the distress among members of the non-privileged categories, find themselves compelled to break off their visit after four weeks, although they had originally intended to stay for six, the sole reason being the torment which the witnessing of these human tragedies had caused them. The Langs returned from Russia profoundly shocked, and live now with but one aim—to serve the cause of relief for these unfortunates.

When Stalin began the radical communization of industry and agriculture, and the number of innocent victims of economic distress reached its maximum, those peoples outside which still had kinsmen settled in the Soviet Union began to react more and more strongly to the appeals for help which reached them. These came from the Jews in the Ukraine and White Russia, from German colonists, Catholic priests and Lutheran pastors—in short, from all who could hope for assistance from abroad.

These appeals naturally fell upon ready ears, and attempts were made to regulate and extend the remittances of money and food to individual persons in the Soviet Union which were already being sent. This was done in particular by the Jews, who have their own organizations in Vienna, London, New York, etc.; by the Germans, whose relief work is organized through the "Brethren in Distress"; by the European Central Office for Inter-Church Aid at Geneva, whose Russian relief is conducted by Professor Keller; by the "Baltic Work for Russia," directed by Oberpastor O. Schabert of Riga; and by various other organizations which need not be enumerated in detail. It should be mentioned, however, that Russians and Ukrainians living abroad possess organizations of their own to assist their friends in Russia.

Hitherto relief has been organized partly on national and partly on religious lines; it being noteworthy that different Churches have successfully collaborated, e.g. in the European

Central Office for Inter-Church Aid at Geneva.[1] Yet up to now measures have not been taken to bring about an international and interconfessional relief action of a purely charitable nature. So far assistance has been rendered exclusively on an individual basis, especially as regards the so-called Torgsin operations. Moscow's attitude towards this individual relief is certainly of the greatest interest. At first suspicion was displayed, and various difficulties were made for the recipients of food or money. Soon, however, it was grasped that this relief to individuals could be admirably exploited to obtain foreign currency and thus to improve the Soviet balance of payments. New tactics were adopted. Instead of being merely food parcels (which had not the slightest interest for Moscow, for, as has been shown elsewhere, Moscow is not interested in the preservation of individual lives), the Torgsin presents became a financial operation which was regularly to provide the State with

[1] Concerning this great organization which has its headquarters at Geneva, its proceedings up to the present day have been so noteworthy that we must here, if only in few words, draw attention to it.

In 1930, when many reports, all agreeing about the distress prevailing in Soviet Russia, had been received in Geneva, the European Central Office for Inter-Church Aid summoned its first international and interconfessional conference at Basle, at which there were representatives of more than twenty societies already giving practical help—and not only representatives of Lutheran, Reformed, Methodist and Baptist, but also of Anglican and Orthodox organizations.

The conference sought to co-ordinate the work of already existing relief societies. The European Central Office for Inter-Church Aid was entrusted with this task, and an International Russian Executive was formed, on which the European Central Office, the Relief Committee of the Archbishop of Canterbury, and continental organizations were represented. The Bishop of Zagreb and Professor Bulgakoff were also members of it. How successful was the work of the European Central Office may be seen from the fact that it collected several hundred thousand Swiss francs, which were sent through Torgsin to individuals in the Soviet Union. On the initiative of the European Central Office another specially representative Commission was formed later which included representatives of the World Alliance for International Friendship through the Churches, the Universal Christian Council for Life and Work, and the European Central Office.

The achievements of the European Central Office for Inter-Church Aid, and above all its widespread influence in Anglo-Saxon countries, are ultimately due to the great international reputation and the untiring zeal of Dr. Keller, for many years its leader.

millions of pounds sterling, dollars, Swiss francs, reichsmarks, etc. As the philanthropic activity of persons abroad for the benefit of starving individuals in Russia now serves the economic interests of the Soviet State, no objection is made to it—though a number of quite definite conditions have to be observed. Moscow has recognized that the judicious exploitation of human generosity contains immense possibilities. If any further proof were required to show how the Soviet regime uses any and every means for the realization of its economic ideal (the fulfilment of the Five-Year Plans), the so admirably organized Torgsin system affords a perfect example.

The theory of the system is as follows. The Soviet regime, from the politico-financial point of view, has not the slightest interest in the sending of food parcels, or even at the setting on foot of a general relief action by the importation of grain or any other method. For, as I pointed out in an earlier chapter, Moscow believes that it still disposes of sufficient reserves of man-power, so that the loss of a few million peasants can have no economic significance. This explains, too, the methodical exportation of food supplies. Now in the event of a general relief action being set on foot (Moscow thinks) the first condition of foreign participation would be an entire cessation of grain exports. This is one of the reasons why Moscow would think of allowing a general relief action only *in extremis*.

But it is quite another matter when foreign help takes the form of a transfer of pounds, dollars, reichsmarks and so on, foreign currency which the Soviet Government can use for its own purposes. By the ruthless extraction of grain and food supplies from the producers, and an unduly low allowance of rations to the consumers, these, or at least a whole series of categories, are reduced to a permanent state of want, while the Government obtains possession of adequate supplies. Thus the nationalities, and the former Russian bourgeoisie, are compelled to address continual appeals for help to their

ago as the autumn of 1933 there were reports of political accusations having been made by the Soviet authorities against people who received Torgsin parcels. It must be realized that while Moscow allows the Torgsin deliveries solely for the sake of the financial advantages they bring, and, indeed, sees that they reach those for whom they are intended, it none the less regards with suspicion, and even with open hostility, all those Soviet citizens whose relations with people abroad are thus revealed. This is especially true of the local Soviet officials. It only too often happens that vengeance is taken on the recipients of supplies on some other ground which has no direct connection with the Torgsin. Harry Lang and many others have testified to this.

Experience has shown that when the political relations between the Soviet State and any country deteriorate—and this seems to the Soviet rulers to outweigh the economic importance of the Torgsin remittances—they decide to take ruthless action against all those who have received supplies from the country in question.

The persecutions to which the German colonists in the Ukraine and in the Volga region have been exposed—for receiving or seeking help from the "Brethren in Need" Committee—since the relations between the Soviet Union and the Reich grew worse, is an example of this. In the autumn of 1934 the relief work of the "Brethren in Need" Committee, which from the beginning had been composed of the representatives of the different religious communities, was completely prohibited in the Soviet Union. All who had received help from the Committee were persecuted, and even more the clergy who acted as intermediaries.

Many death sentences have lately been pronounced, doubtless with the object of impressing foreign opinion, and even of creating the impression that the German colonists—alleged to be agents of "Fascism" in Berlin—are a menace to the Soviet State. The nature of the "crimes" committed is

co-religionists, people of the same race, or relatives abroad. The latter are afforded an opportunity of giving help by the following well-calculated method. The Moscow Government invites them to place at the disposal of one of its missions abroad, or to official quarters co-operating with its missions, a sum in foreign currency, on which the Government will hand over to any person indicated, from its stores in the Soviet Union, a corresponding amount of flour, oats, sugar and so on. In other words, a German peasant (for example) in the neighbourhood of Odessa, whose harvest has been taken away from him almost in its entirety, will have a part of this minimum necessary for existence restored to him if people abroad will pay over to the Soviet Government a sum in foreign currency. The net result of the Torgsin system is that a few lucky people are moved up into the privileged category, and receive help at the cost of the suffering masses.

What are the advantages of this system to Moscow? In contrast to the export of grain, which is very costly, this system, involving no expenditure abroad, is probably the most profitable method of exploiting the distress of particular human categories for the benefit of the national budget. At present much better terms can be obtained by the Soviet from people abroad for the food they buy in Soviet Russia for their friends and relatives than by exporting it in the usual way. For years Moscow has taken inordinately high payment for its toleration of individual help.

On the other hand, Moscow thus publicly admitted once and for all the existence of a state of distress in the country, and the fact that hundreds of thousands could only support life with help from abroad, as well as the moral justification of such relief. This disadvantage was accepted, because it was counterbalanced by the extraordinary advantage of receiving foreign currency in place of food parcels.

The slogan applied to these proceedings was characteristically not "help for the suffering," but "presents for the Soviet

Union." The Torgsin system enables the Soviet Government to turn even their greatest enemies, the Russian emigrants living abroad, to its own financial advantage. Anyone who has the opportunity of inspecting the archives of the great relief organizations, and looks through the countless letters from people in want, will realize clearly that the Torgsin transactions are meant simply and solely to help those in want and even starvation, and that there is no question of "presents" in the ordinary sense of the word, as the slogan suggests. The fact that the Torgsin system could reach such enormous dimensions —it extends all over the world—is a further and irrefragable proof that great numbers of people in the Soviet Union are living in misery and starvation.

The development of the Torgsin system has necessitated the creation of an organization which now extends over many countries. All over the world there now exist organizations, committees and private firms of a purely business character, which co-operate very closely with the Soviet trade delegations. If an American, Englishman, Dutchman or Jew wishes to send a present to any relative or friend in Russia, and has paid in the prescribed sum in foreign currency at one of the places fixed for the purpose, the instructions are forwarded to Russia and immediately carried out by the officials of one of the food stores which exist in all parts of the Union. It is greatly in Moscow's interest that the Torgsin machinery should work swiftly and without friction, because there are agreements between most of the relief organizations abroad and the Soviet missions, according to which remittances are considered as having been effective only when an acknowledgment is to hand from the recipient of the supplies.

In so far as it helps individuals, even the Torgsin system is to be approved. But as for its effect on the lot of the bulk of those in want and starvation, it must be emphasized that this help which reaches a few elect does nothing to mitigate the sufferings of all the rest—indeed, it sometimes aggravates them.

It would be otherwise if the certainty existed t Government, in view of its larger receipts of fo would at least diminish correspondingly its expo use its surplus to relieve the rest of the famir this is not done; the export of grain goes on method may be the only way of giving individu saving a limited number of victims; but still that the Torgsin system as such is harmful, in above all, because it involves a differentiati victims.

Moscow has at the same time gained anothe advantage through the Torgsin system. It h to some extent a guarantee against too se conditions in the Soviet Union from those w indirectly interested in the Torgsin operatio must be glad that Moscow permits the relief t sin machinery, and their one anxiety must disposition to allow the Torgsin operations suddenly come to an end. It is, therefore, t urge that Moscow shall not be irritated and criticism of existing conditions.

In yet another way does Moscow exploit to obtain foreign currency. There are plen ready to pay large sums to get this or tha out of the country. So in exchange for a su often depends on the negotiations which h with the "Intourist" (it is usually several l persons designated are handed over, ass considered harmless on account of advan reasons. As some of the people who hav their friends and relations abroad have Soviets by the information they have transactions are now comparatively seldo

The effect, direct or indirect, of th parcels on the recipients is a question of

shown clearly by the report of the case of the peasant Derksen in the German Communist paper *Das neue Dorf*.[1] This agent of Fascism," the paper wrote, "had in his possession the addresses of Fascist organizations and wrote to them slanderous counter-revolutionary letters about 'hunger and distress' in the Soviet Union. . . . For these counter-revolutionary provocatory letters he received from the Fascists eight remittances of money and two parcels. It was shown at the trial that the collective farm peasants, on whose behalf Derksen wrote, were fully supplied with produce by the collective farm. . . . The proletarian court sentenced Derksen to be shot as an agent of German Fascism."

A similar procedure and similar arguments are used against the clergy. The measures taken against the German Lutheran and Catholic clergy since the spring of 1935 amount to nothing less than their methodical extermination.

I quoted in an earlier chapter the "spontaneous" retorts of peasants in various districts to offers of help from abroad—"We are not your suffering brethren. . . . We do not need one Fascist penny," and so on, including a resolution (from the Minsk region) "to work on a holiday and send the proceeds to the unemployed in the Capitalist countries." They suffice to show what difficulties are placed in the way of the Torgsin remittances and how vulnerable it is to the tyranny of the Soviet regime. Whenever the interests of Moscow demand it, all relief from abroad is treated as suspect, jeered at and obstructed as a "Capitalist" or "Fascist" intrigue.

In the autumn of 1935 the sensational news suddenly appeared in the world press that Moscow had decided to liquidate and close down Torgsin. It was debated whether now indeed the whole system by which help was sent to starving people in Russia was to come to an end. Newspapers under Moscow influence hailed this decree as a new proof of progress in the Soviet Union. However, it soon became clear that the

[1] February 26, 1935.

liquidation of Torgsin had not altered in the slightest the system of exchange operating in the case of remittances sent to the distressed in Russia. Here we had before us again one of those clever, psychologically well-thought-out moves of Moscow, whose aim it is, by the change or complete abolition of the name of a department greatly discredited abroad, to give the impression that the department itself has ceased to exist. (One has only to recall the various designations of the Soviet secret police—Cheka, Ogpu, Narkomvnudel, etc.—which, in spite of the change of name, remains ever the same.) Simultaneously with the announcement of the liquidation of Torgsin there appeared in the press of various countries, even in the Russian émigré press of Paris (*Vozrejdenie* of December 14, 1935) the advertisement of different banks which undertake the trans-mission of remittances from the public to relatives and friends in Russia. So that the system remains fundamentally the same, except that the Soviet representative abroad, contrary to his former practice, from now on will demand that his clients send their remittances in Soviet instead of in foreign currency. This means that anyone who hitherto has sent remittances in dollars, pounds, francs, etc., now carries through this transaction in Soviet roubles *at the rate arbitrarily fixed by Moscow*. It is obvious from this that the most important result of the liquida-tion of Torgsin is a substantial increase in the cost of the operation to senders of help, and a correspondingly increased profit to Moscow.

As a result of these developments, culminating in a direct threat to all colonists who received Torgsin supplies or any other kind of help from Germany, the German Government, on March 15, 1935, took a drastic step to check the sending of help from Germany to the Soviet Union. The Reichsbank issued a notice referring to the persecution, imprisonment and banishment of the recipients of supplies through the Torgsin, and announcing that it would no longer give the senders of these remittances the usual authorizations to send German currency, but only a permit to send fifty marks for the purchase of food.

Thus all help from the Reich to the Germans in the Soviet Union was completely stopped. Nothing more can be done now to help the starving colonists in the Ukraine and the Volga region. The European Central Office for Inter-Church Aid at Geneva has also, since the autumn of 1934, had to work under similar difficulties; the recipients of its remittances have also been persecuted. It must therefore be admitted that the whole system of individual help by means of Torgsin remittances was faced with a crisis, and that no one could guarantee that assistance sent through this channel would not be highly dangerous to the recipients in the Soviet Union. The prediction that individual relief would be no solution of the Russian relief problem has thus been shown to be correct—as regards the safety of the recipients, not to mention other considerations.[1]

Even in 1933, when men began to die like flies in various Russian famine areas, it was clear that individual help with Torgsin parcels was like filling the ocean with a bucket. It was like the rescue of just a few of the many occupants of a huge burning house. This led the author, who, as Secretary-General of the European Congress of Nationalities, had obtained from the peoples and nationalities represented on that organization authentic news of the effects of the Soviet Russian famine, to publish his memorandum calling for a general relief action, based on definite proposals. In my view the stores of grain in the American ports and other surplus areas, which were, to some extent, unsaleable, should have been shipped at once to Odessa, Nikolaiev, Kherson and Rostov, the great Black Sea ports in the immediate neighbourhood of the famine area.

The principles and ideas on which this plan of relief action

[1] The author in a memorandum of August 1933 set out in detail the general objections to relief through the Torgsin system.

was based for the most part hold good to-day. They were published at the time in various newspapers and periodicals in many European states.[1]

Thus the question of the actual situation of millions of starving people in the Soviet Russian agricultural regions, and with it the question of a general relief action, has been under discussion since the summer of 1933. There followed soon afterwards various manifestations in favour of a general relief action on humanitarian lines. Above all should be mentioned an appeal issued from Lvov (Lemberg) by the Prince Metropolitan of the Ukrainian Unified Church, the aged Count Andreas Szeptyczkyj. Then, on August 20th, came an important event. The Archbishop of Vienna, Cardinal Theodor Innitzer, addressed to the world public an appeal to join in a relief action for those starving in the Soviet Union, and announced at the same time that an interconfessional and international committee, to embrace the representatives of all the creeds and national groups in Vienna, would be formed by him in the immediate future.

This manifestation in Vienna in favour of comprehensive action to bring help to the people in the Soviet Union then

---

[1] They were set out as follows in the Vienna *Reichspost* of July 15, 1933:
1. The work must be of a purely humanitarian character.
2. It must on principle exclude all political factors and considerations.
3. It must be instigated by the humanitarian organizations.
4. An international relief committee should be formed on its initiative.
5. The whole of the work in Russia—importation, transport and distribution of the supplies of corn, etc.—must be done under the supervision of the relief committee. It must be carried out by the representatives of the relief organization in co-operation with the officials of the Soviet Government.
6. The work must be international and interconfessional.
7. Public opinion must be in a position to exercise complete control of the relief work.
8. The relief work must in all events be facilitated and promoted by consideration of the economic factors; above all, advantage should be taken of the circumstance that the grain-producing areas overseas have long been suffering from an economic crisis owing to overproduction and are themselves interested in getting their surplus grain taken off their hands and utilized by the relief action. International shipping has an equal interest in the setting on foot of the relief work.

found a strong echo in the various states of the world. A few days after Cardinal Innitzer's declaration there were others of the same kind from the peoples and nationalities in other European countries which were concerned for the fate of their kinsmen. There were also protests by the great international associations, especially those of a religious nature. They all demanded that humanitarian principles should be placed before current political considerations. One of these associations, the European Centre for Church Assistance at Geneva, at whose head was Professor Keller, addressed a fresh and emphatic appeal to the evangelical Churches of the world to set on foot without delay relief action "on a broad basis."

Then the ninth European Nationalities Congress at Berne took up the question shortly before the meeting of the League of Nations Assembly at Geneva. Here, it must be emphasized, traditional enemies like the Russian and Ukrainian nationalities for the first time expressed full agreement with each other's views and demands. One after another the representatives of all the Russian and all the Ukrainian national groups in Europe—not those of the *émigrés* living in the various states—solemnly demanded that the relief plans should be immediately put into action.

The Congress passed a special resolution welcoming the secretary-general's memorandum and the concrete proposals contained in it. It also declared that the circles it represented would do everything in their power to support the relief action.

From Berne, on the conclusion of the Congress, the members of its presidential body proceeded to Geneva to convey its resolution to the then president of the League Council, the Norwegian Premier, Dr. Mowinckel, and to beg him to use his influence to take up the question of a relief action for the starving in Russia. The representatives of all sections of the Ukrainian people outside the Soviet Union also went to

Geneva to appeal to the League Council and its president. The Russians did likewise.

The question now was whether among the statesmen at Geneva one would be found who, ignoring all the narrower political considerations, would be ready to call the attention of the League of Nations to the fact that millions of innocent people were starving in the middle of the continent of Europe, while at the same time large supplies of food were available or had even been destroyed in the regions possessing surpluses. Would there be a statesman with the courage to put before the League the question of organizing relief in the Soviet Union, a man round whom the others could group themselves in the fight for the most elementary human solidarity and against the domination of selfish interests?

Such a man there was in the person of Dr. Mowinckel. The successor of Fritjof Nansen as Norwegian representative in the League Assembly, Dr. Mowinckel was fully conscious of the great tradition his people had to maintain. The authentic documents submitted to him left him in no doubt as to the terrible situation of the people in the Soviet Union; and this decided him. It may be presumed that he was also influenced by the fact that the people especially affected by the fearful calamity was one which was not represented at Geneva and had there no defender of its rights and interests. Dr. Mowinckel entered the lists courageously and unselfishly against short-sighted state interests and misconceived political considerations.

All the initiated followed this move of Dr. Mowinckel, his championship of the relief action which the most elementary humanity dictated, with the keenest expectation. But what followed will stand on record as characteristic of the difficulties which hamper the League of Nations, and above all as proof that current political interests are predominant there. It would take us too far to describe in detail how, when the president of the League Council proposed that this body should take up the question of relief for the starving in Russia, all kinds of formal difficulties were placed in his way.[1] This was done, of course, mainly for political reasons, out of consideration for the Soviet Union and the friendly relations which were being established between it and many of the states represented at Geneva. It was thus possible to prevent the question from coming up for discussion at an official session of the League Council. Thus the issue was already decided against Dr. Mowinckel. It is impossible to give any details of what took place at the private session of the Council called by Dr. Mowinckel; it was a stormy meeting which lasted two hours, and Dr. Mowinckel spoke several times in defence of his standpoint. We only know that there was a sharp conflict between the two views—that which emphasized the moral duty of the community of peoples towards the victims of a fearful disaster, and that which placed first considerations of political factors and interest. Dr. Mowinckel, though supported by some of the delegates, had at last to own himself beaten. It was pointed out to him that, in spite of its statutes, which allow of any question being brought up which is of importance to the comity and peace of the nations, the League of Nations must in practice not lose sight of political factors—for example, the fact that the Soviet Union was not at that time a member of the League.

The Council finally decided that Dr. Mowinckel's motion should not be placed upon the order of the day of the League of Nations, but asked him, as President of the Council, to approach the International Red Cross. It was obvious from the first that this could not be successful, in view of the dependence of the Red Cross Societies, and therefore their international committee at Geneva, on the various states and their interests.

Now the view may be taken that the League of Nations,

---

[1] According to the Statutes of the League of Nations the president of the Council has the right to bring any question whatever before it at his own discretion.

if it were to act strictly in accordance with the political factors, should on principle not exceed the scope of the special interests of the member states. But what is the actual position? For more than sixteen years, in declarations, resolutions, manifestos of all kinds, it has always been insisted that the actions of the League were guided above all by the great principles of law and humanity. For sixteen years Geneva delegates, great and small, have paid tribute to these principles (the author has been present at every single Assembly of the League). This was the one *leitmotif* of all the speeches of Aristide Briand and many other brilliant orators. But it was only too soon to become clear that in the proceedings of the League of Nations there was an extraordinary, ever-growing discrepancy between words and deeds, between theory and practice. Geneva had become the playground of the most gifted orators from all the world's states. Every one of their ringing declarations was welcomed, but when it came to action, no one would deviate a hair's breadth from a misconceived political egotism. Very often —just as an example—"the sacred rights of the nationalities" were spoken of. But when one or another of the national groups addressed a petition to the League, as provided in the treaties for the protection of minorities, it happened only too often that it led to no positive results, not even on the most modest scale.

Another example! A few years ago the delegates congratulated each other with especial joy on the acceptance of a resolution in favour of the beginning of a reduction of the existing Customs barriers. Many were inclined to see in this event a significant turning point in the economic development of Europe. But what happened? A year later, when another meeting of the League was to continue the attack on economic barriers of a political nature, the president was obliged to declare that in the meantime, despite the important decision taken a year before, Customs tariffs had been raised still higher in almost every state instead of being lowered.

Under the same heading may be classified Aristide Briand's famous "European luncheon," followed by the foundation of the League's European Committee. This event, too, was hailed as the "beginning of a new era." But scarcely one of the Foreign Ministers of European states then present at Geneva, who, as usual, rhetorically congratulated Aristide Briand and themselves on this new achievement, thought seriously of utilizing this turn of events in their own policy. Of the plans of M. Briand's European Committee—apart from an excellent photograph of those present at the luncheon—nothing exists to-day.

And then there was an affair which is directly connected with the question of help for those starving in Russia. For years the League of Nations had in hand an Italian scheme for the rendering of immediate help in cases where the population of some region was vitally threatened by a natural catastrophe. It debated fully what should be done in order to bring help without the slightest loss of time, to spread the news of the catastrophe through the quickest and most reliable channels, in order that some radical step might be taken at once to alleviate the distress. This proposal, too, was recommended for acceptance in the name of international solidarity, the united opinion of the civilized world, the human instinct to help others in distress, and so on.

But the reality! The terrible disaster in the south of the Soviet Union compelled the president of the League Council to bring the question before that body. But, as always at Geneva, he came into collision with political interests. Indeed, in those days—and nothing could better characterize the situation— the Norwegian Premier was openly pitied by the statesmen and newspaper correspondents at Geneva. They spoke with compassion of the man who was attempting to resist political tendencies. It was not that there was the smallest difference of opinion between these men on the fact that millions of people were dying in the Russian famine areas. On the contrary, what they simply could not and would not understand was that the Norwegian Premier in particular should suddenly attempt to override considerations of rationalistic politics. Why could not Dr. Mowinckel see, like the rest, that many of the states, including some Great Powers, saw in the Soviet Union a business colleague, even a future ally, for which reason they themselves, even in a humanitarian question like this, must treat with consideration the co-signatory of a future treaty.[1]

It was shown once more that this predominance of political interests in Europe means a death sentence for every attempt to bring developments at Geneva on to a higher plane. The fiasco of the disarmament conference is a further proof of this. Is it surprising that the League of Nations is to-day passing through a severe moral crisis, that its prestige as the representative of the ideal of supernational co-operation for the realization of loftier and better principles is sinking lower and lower?

If Dr. Mowinckel had succeeded in persuading the Geneva Assembly to inform the Soviet Government in suitable language that the question of the famine or of relief must be cleared up without further delay, and that if the existence of the famine was denied, the matter must be investigated—for example, by sending a committee of experts to Russia, the League of Nations would have done a striking service not only to the good cause, but to its own prestige. Even if it had taken some time to break down any resistance offered by the Bolsheviks, Moscow must in the long run have given way under the moral pressure of the world's public opinion.

In view of the attitude of the majority of the League Council the Norwegian Premier had no choice but to approach the

---

[1] A well-known Geneva correspondent observed to the writer: "What is the use of all this talk about the people who are dying in Russia? You are pushing at an open door. No one but Herriot thinks of denying that there is a famine in South Russia. But, for the well-known political reasons, there is no possibility now of a discussion of the famine, an awkward question for Moscow and so for its friends too—let alone any talk of relief."

International Red Cross at Geneva, as he had been requested to do. This sealed the fate of his endeavours. The Soviet Russian Red Cross has long been one of the members of the International Committee. This means that the International Committee cannot act in any question concerning Russia without first asking the Soviet Russian Red Cross in Moscow for its opinion. So, with reference to Dr. Mowinckel's proposal, the International Committee sent a letter to the Soviet Russian Red Cross. That body—as was only to be expected—returned a purely negative answer in the usual tone, expressing surprise that such statements and suggestions could come from the Geneva Committee.

Even in face of the irrefutable evidence, since forthcoming, of the vast number of deaths in South Russia, Moscow still flatly denies that there has been any famine or any victims. This confirms what has often been said, that any discussion with Moscow about relief action can only be successful if the negotiators have the support of world opinion. Negotiations set on foot without any such support from world opinion cannot possibly end in anything but failure, for otherwise Moscow has not the slightest interest in abandoning its point of view. Only considerations of world opinion—or, more correctly, of its reactions on its economic and political interests, can cause Moscow to modify its attitude. For as things are to-day, the Soviet State, politically and economically, is still largely dependent on the shaping of its relations with the Great Powers and many other states.

There could, then, be no doubt that a modest inquiry in Soviet quarters regarding the possibility of relief action, if this went beyond the scope of the Torgsin operations tolerated by the powers that be, was doomed to failure in advance. But the boldness with which the Soviet Government flatly denies the existence of the famine is doubtless explained by another circumstance, and one which perhaps shows as clearly as any the dependence of European statesmen on the immediate interests of their states. When Dr. Mowinckel took up the question at Geneva he could reckon not only on Norway resigning from the League Council—in which case she would have had to pay less consideration to the other states on the Council—but also on his not remaining at the head of the Government on account of the expected change in the strength of the respective parties in Norway. He had good grounds for supposing that after the assembly of the newly elected Parliament another Norwegian party leader would take over the reins of government. But now fate willed it that the relative strength of parties after the elections compelled Dr. Mowinckel —although his political opponents were stronger than before— to take upon himself the burden of the Premiership for a further period. But that meant that in all questions affecting Russo-Norwegian relations he had to confront the Soviet Government as chief representative of Norway and all her economic and political interests. Moscow, as usual, had exploited this situation for its own ends in masterly fashion. Before it replied to the letter from the International Red Cross, it asked in Oslo for a statement to the effect that Dr. Mowinckel's idea of the state of things in the Soviet Union had been based on information placed at his disposal by "the other side," and not on his own personal observations on the spot. It is said that Dr. Mowinckel's statement—which it could not be difficult to extract from him as Norwegian Foreign Minister and negotiator in all dealings between his country and the Soviet Union—figured in Moscow's reply to the International Red Cross as one of the main planks in its denial of the existence of a famine and rejection of any offer of help.

These events need no further commentary. But they show that the strength of men like Fritjof Nansen lay in the fact that they were never obliged to champion the immediate political interests of their states.

The failure of Dr. Mowinckel's attempt to get the League of Nations to act, and the deplorable effects of M. Herriot's attitude, did not, however, bring the endeavours to set on foot a relief action to a complete standstill. The nationalities interested in the fate of their kinsmen in Soviet Russia, and the international organizations, continued their efforts with the greatest determination. The Interconfessional and International Relief Committee was founded in Vienna in October 1933 at the instance of the Cardinal Archbishop Dr. Innitzer; and on December 16 and 17 a European conference of all organizations interested in relief work in Russia sat in the Archbishop's Palace in Vienna. The writer was appointed honorary secretary of this conference.

In the words of thanks which they addressed to Cardinal Innitzer at the close of the conference the leaders of various groups[1] emphasized the fact that this was a joint movement dictated by the purest humanity, which had nothing to do with politics. The short and pregnant resolution of the conference has real significance even to-day.[2]

[1] Colonel Sauter, of the European Centre for Church Assistance at Geneva, in the name of the Protestants; the Bishop of Lemberg, Dr. Budka, on behalf of the Ukrainian-Unified organization; Professor Kurtschinsky, of Tartu (Dorpat), the leader of the Russian minorities, in the name of the Russian organizations; and the Chief Rabbi of Vienna, Dr. Feuchtwang, for the Jewish relief organizations.

[2] The text of the resolution was as follows: "The supernational, interconfessional conference of representatives of all organizations participating in the relief action on behalf of the starving in Russia sat in Vienna on December 16th and 17th, 1933, and came unanimously to the following conclusions on the basis of authentic reports and documents, including a large quantity of photographs:

" 'Despite all attempts to deny the existence of the terrible famine which raged in the Soviet Union down to the last harvest, there is proof positive that in the course of this year millions of innocent people have perished of starvation even in the most fertile regions of the Union, such as the Ukraine and the Northern Caucasus. It is equally certain that the most horrible attendant phenomena of every famine, even cannibalism, have accompanied this famine. These sacrifices could have been avoided! While this tragedy was being enacted in the Soviet Republic, the grain-growing areas overseas were suffering from over-production. World conferences have taken up the problem of reducing wheat production. Vast quantities of excess supplies of food have been destroyed, a thing which is in conflict with the most elementary principles of reason and humanity. These surpluses could very quickly have been shipped to the ports of the famine areas—Odessa, Rostov,

The writer, as emissary of the Vienna relief committee, had, in the spring and summer of 1934, the opportunity of explaining its standpoint in England, Scotland, the United States and Canada, and noted with satisfaction the great interest taken in the relief question by the various Churches and creeds in those countries. At the end of July 1934 the Archbishop of Canterbury made his great speech on the question in the House of Lords. Speaking as head of the Church of England, he most strongly emphasized the point that helping the victims in Russia was a work of purely humanitarian character, in which the whole of Christendom must take part. The entry into the lists of the Primate of Great Britain was certainly an important event, and all the more so that other prominent members of the Upper House supported him. Of these speeches I would mention that of Lord Charnwood. He quoted the relevant clauses of the League Covenant and showed that the conditions in which large numbers of the population of Soviet Russia lived (especially those doing forced labour in the concentration camps of the north) were far from fulfilling the demands made by the Covenant on all states belonging to the League. Lord Charnwood demanded that the Soviet Union should be admitted to the League of Nations only if it fulfilled these conditions—and the Archbishop of Canterbury expressed the same view at the end of his speech, if in a different form.

Since then almost all the English Churches and religious bodies—in so far as they had not done so already—have set up

etc.—by using the available means of transport (the laid-up ocean steamers). The comparatively good harvest of 1933 could bring only temporary alleviation.

"'It is not enough to save a few lives by individual help, as has been done hitherto; measures must be taken without delay to prevent severe loss of life in the future by relief action on a large scale and as swiftly executed as possible. Should any attempt be made to cast doubt upon the evidence of the devastating effects of the famine, the Conference believes that the world public, through its proper representatives, can find ways of ascertaining the real conditions.' "

special Russian relief committees. Further, since the spring of
1934 joint sessions of representatives of all these relief committees have been held under the presidency of Dr. Rushbrooke,
formerly head of the Free Churches; and at these meetings the
unanimity of all these organizations on the necessity of bringing
help to the distressed in Russia has been clearly expressed.
Alongside these efforts in England I should mention the
exemplary work of the Scottish Church, which has long possessed a special bureau to deal with the Russian relief question.

Among the various Churches and creeds in the United
States and Canada, which I visited soon afterwards, I found
just as keen an interest. Discussions between delegates of
different creeds on the Russian relief question took place in
New York with Dr. Atkinson, of the Church Peace Union, as
chairman. Representatives of the Philadelphia Quakers also
took part in these conversations; like the English Quakers, they
are particularly interested in the question.

The same happened in Canada. At Winnipeg, the centre of
the Canadian grain area, in whose neighbourhood are settled
many emigrants from Russia belonging to the most diverse
creeds (Ukrainians, Russians, Germans and Jews), all the local
forces (Mennonites, Catholics, Lutherans, Orthodox Church,
etc.) were united under the presidency of Dr. Mackay of the
United Churches. The representatives of all the Churches and
religious sects in Winnipeg addressed a joint manifesto to the
Canadian Prime Minister, Mr. Bennett, begging that Canada
should give her consent to the admission of Soviet Russia into
the League of Nations only on condition that measures were
taken to save the victims in Russia. This manifesto proposed
that Canada and the other states should request the Soviet
Union to allow an international commission of inquiry to go
to the famine areas, and offer to co-operate with the Soviet in
relieving the distress. The Canadian delegate at Geneva did,
in fact, declare that his country voted for the admission of Soviet
Russia into the League in the expectation that it would in

U

future be made possible for its citizens to assist their kinsmen and co-believers in the Soviet Union.

All this happened in the summer and autumn of 1934, shortly before the opening at Geneva of that League Assembly which was to decide whether and on what terms Soviet Russia was to be received into the community of states. Then, in September 1934, when the Soviet Union had resolved to join the League, the moment had come to make its admission dependent on certain conditions being fulfilled—a unique opportunity which could have been exploited in the interest of the victims in Russia. But the efforts to induce the delegates of the states assembled at Geneva to take care that the most essential provisions of the Covenant were observed by Soviet Russia— which would have been in accordance with the Covenant itself and the usage hitherto employed in the case of almost all states newly admitted to the League—were from the first doomed to failure. This was because the admission of Soviet Russia into the League was really nothing but part of a whole system of political alliances, which necessarily involved concessions to and obligations towards the Soviet State. The countries directly or indirectly interested in Moscow's admission were, therefore, bound to oppose the making of any stipulations.

Indeed, the first impression was that the Soviet Union had even been promised a kind of triumphal entry into Geneva— the claims which Moscow's representatives addressed to the Powers on the Council showed that this was the case. It was proposed that the states at Geneva as a body should hand a written request to the Soviet Union to enter the League. That this was not done was due mainly to the determined attitude of a number of delegations, in particular those of the British Dominions. But, as things were at Geneva, there could be no question of any conditions being imposed upon Moscow. The Soviet's admission was to be decided upon in silence, without any discussion either in committee or in full session of the

Assembly. It was thanks only to the representative of Switzerland, M. Motta, and a few other delegates, that all the questions in which the Soviet State's performance fell short of the requirements of the League's Covenant were openly discussed at the now historic sitting of the committee. M. Motta in his great speech dealt not only with Moscow's endeavour to bring about revolution in other countries, but also with the persecution of religion, the suppression of the nationalities, and the state of misery in the famine areas. The representative of a small country, he had the courage to insist on the real facts of the case. The result was—and this will be on record as especially characteristic of conditions at Geneva, or, rather, in all Europe to-day —that M. Motta's speech, giving the reasons for Switzerland's "no," was received with enthusiastic applause from those very delegates who were obliged to vote for Moscow's admission. That applause without doubt pronounced moral judgment on Moscow's qualification to be received into the League.

Besides the efforts to set on foot a general relief action for those in want in Soviet Russia, there is the special question of relief for national groups whose main bodies are situated outside the Soviet frontiers—of help from their mother-countries for the Finns, Germans, Poles, Latvians, Estonians, etc., living in the Soviet Union.

I have already pointed out that in the Treaty of Dorpat in 1920 Moscow gave Finland assurances regarding the treatment and rights of the Finns both in Karelia and in Ingermanland —Soviet citizens who had always lived in Russia, never within the boundaries of Finland. This is of fundamental importance, for here the right of a nation to interest itself in and feel anxiety for its kinsmen living abroad was clearly recognized.

It was a positively tragic setback when, in concluding the Treaty of Rapallo, the German Government—despite its favourable position *vis-à-vis* Moscow—failed to obtain similar assurances, legally binding, for the lives and the most elementary national rights of its kinsmen and co-religionists in the Soviet

State. This made it possible for Moscow thenceforward to uphold with the greatest persistence the theory of "non-intervention in the internal affairs of a foreign state." Thenceforward, to take only one example, the representatives of the Reich in Moscow and the provinces had to look on quietly while Germans were being banished and executed close by on trumpery pretexts. If any attempt at protest was made, the Russians pointed out that such protest was inconsistent with the theory of non-intervention which had been recognized by the Reich Government itself.

As an example of the outrages practised on Germans in Russia, take the execution of Dr. Ernst Schiele, the last president of the German Academy in Petrograd, who was shot with his wife, on the usual charge of being a counter-revolutionary, a few miles from the German Consulate-General in Petrograd. Dr. Schiele was a German Balt from what is now Estonia, and could, had he chosen, have returned to Estonia and secured a good medical practice there. But when I visited him in Petrograd in 1921 he declared that "the captain must be the last to leave a sinking ship." Thousands of Germans have perished as he did, some dragged away to forced labour in the north and in Siberia, others starved to death in the very towns.

Only Finland, as mentioned above, is in a special position. The result of this was that when the persecution and extermination of Finns in Karelia and Ingermanland became particularly severe in 1926, Finland brought the question before the League of Nations, i.e. the Court of Arbitration at The Hague, pleading the assurance given by Moscow in 1920. The only result, it is true, was that the Soviet Government ignored Finland's move, pointing out that it (the Soviet) had nothing to do with the League of Nations.

Now, when the Soviet Union is a member of the League, of course the situation has quite changed. Profound indignation is felt in Finland at the latest measures taken by Moscow to annihilate the Finns in Russia. It is said that Moscow has informed Finland that it feels itself under no legal obligation to recognize the Finnish claim to interest itself in the situation of the Finns in Karelia and Ingermanland; so that this question has become more than anything a purely legal dispute. Are the assurances of 1920 still legally existent? The decision on this point, now that both states are members of the League, lies— assuming Finland takes the initiative—solely in the hands of the League of Nations.

I am anxious to emphasize once more that the raising of the question of help for the Finns who are perishing in the Soviet Union cannot, in view of the Dorpat assurances given in the Dorpat Treaty, or, indeed, on general grounds, be regarded as an act of political unfriendliness against the Soviet Union. No one can prevent the Finnish people, hardened by long struggles for freedom, from publicly taking up the cause of its perishing kinsmen in Ingermanland and Karelia—the cradle of the mythical Finnish heroes—through relief action of a purely humanitarian nature approved by the League of Nations.[1]

The only exception to the general rule has been Sweden, which, in a manner that might serve as a model for other states, has succeeded in rescuing its kinsmen living in the Soviet Union. Through negotiations with Moscow, Sweden was able to secure permission to return to Sweden, or to emigrate elsewhere, for the whole population of the Swedish settlement in South Russia, conducted by its evangelical pastors. And even if some of the repatriated persons, as a result of Communist impressions received in Russia, later caused their motherland some difficulties, the Swedish people has the satisfaction of feeling that its kinsmen in Russia were rescued

---

[1] It may be recalled that the Association of German National Groups in Europe urged, as long as two years ago, that it was both the right and the duty of the German Reich to urge that Germans in Russia should be allowed to leave the country on the strength of the assurances given them many years before (e.g. to the Volga Germans in the decree of the Empress Catherine II in 1776).

in time—before the famine set in which was the result of Stalin's collectivization of agriculture.

The other nations interested in the fate of their brethren in the Soviet Union have been able to exchange Communists arrested in their countries for clergymen, or for other banished or arrested members of the national group. They could apparently do no more in view of the political and economic relations of their states with Soviet Russia.

I explained above why M. Motta's speech at the historic committee session at Geneva on the admission of the Soviet Union to the League of Nations is of such great importance. But it is of peculiar significance from yet another point of view. It laid down—and the president of the League Assembly confirmed this later in language that left no room for doubt— that Moscow by entering the League bound itself to observe in future all the stipulations of the Covenant.

Thus the entry of Moscow into the League has altogether changed the situation. All the more so that no other speaker contradicted M. Motta on grounds of principle. Quite the contrary; even the French Foreign Minister, the late M. Barthou, confined himself to arguing that conditions would improve in the Soviet State once it had entered the League. The fact that this view was taken of the Soviet Union's admission cannot, therefore, be disputed. What conclusions can be drawn from this?

In a long discussion in *The Times* on the subject if the proceedings at Geneva—carried on in letters to the editor of the paper from a number of well-known people—Lord Cecil expressed the opinion that it would be much easier to deal with a Soviet Russia that was a member of the League than with a Soviet Russia outside that body. This view was opposed to that of most of the writers, who held that the unconditional admission of Soviet Russia to the League must have a harmful if not positively disastrous effect; besides which it was quite contrary to the principles of right on which the

League was based. How are Lord Cecil's words to be inter-
preted? In my opinion only thus: either M. Barthou's view
that conditions in Soviet Russia will improve is right, or
the community of League States will be compelled to raise
the question of the non-observance by the Soviet Union of the
principles of the Covenant—and more, to see that they are
observed.

The preceding chapters of this book show beyond all doubt
that the behaviour of the Soviet Union as regards the
persecution of religion, forced labour in the areas to which
people are banished, the ill-treatment of the nationalities,
and, above all, its attitude towards a relief action for those
in hunger and want within its borders, has certainly not yet
improved, but grown worse. What is to be done now?

Article 23 of the Covenant speaks very plainly. All members
of the League, it says, are bound "to secure and maintain fair
and humane conditions of labour for men, women and children, both in their own countries and in all countries to which
their commercial industrial relations extend, and for that
purpose will establish and maintain the necessary international
organizations."

Will the Great Powers and civilized peoples who take their
stand on the principles of the League of Nations, and who
to-day loudly demand that the Covenant of the League shall
be observed, be able to overlook this clearly formulated obligation? Or will they exert themselves to make the Soviet Government respect the principles which it adopted when it joined
the League of Nations—by allowing, for example, a commission
to visit Russia and investigate the real state of affairs in the
agrarian districts and in all those places where exiled persons
and prisoners are employed in forced labour for the State?

The answer to this question is, in my opinion, of quite
decisive importance; on it may well hang the fate not only of
the people in the Soviet State, but of our Western civilization.

EPILOGUE

I HAVE dealt fully in this book with the reasons why, despite the fact that we live in the age of radio, air mails and other swift means of communication, so little is known of such extraordinary events as millions of deaths from starvation in a neighbouring country. Extraordinary also is the lack of interest roused even when the facts come to be known. At the time that I was putting the finishing touches to this book, I happened to be present at two international gatherings, the proceedings of which throw light on this state of affairs.

At Geneva, in September 1935, the great banquet of the association of journalists attached to the League of Nations was being held at the Hôtel Les Bergues, as it is every year at the conclusion of the League Assembly. At the top table were the vice-president of the Council, Dr. Eduard Benes, M. Paul-Boncour, M. Titulescu, and many other statesmen of different nations. The informal speeches of the League "stars" are without doubt the "high spot" of this annual banquet. This year too a number of them spoke—last of all M. Edouard Herriot. His toast was warmly applauded—loudest of all by the Foreign Commissary of the Soviet Union, M. Litvinov. Was this enthusiasm due solely to the fact that M. Herriot, at the very beginning of his speech, had addressed M. Litvinov as *mon cher ami*? No. There was a further reason. M. Herriot's speech was devoted to the war they were waging in common for liberty, peace, humanity and the rights of man.

A few weeks later. Once more hundreds of statesmen were assembled at a banquet, held this time in Paris, at the close of the Congress of the largest French party, the "Radicals." One of the last speakers was the former Prime Minister, M. Daladier. His speech too was a glorification of a common fight for peace, freedom and right. But he did not refer, as M. Herriot had done, to co-operation in the international field, but to the alliance of Socialists, Communists, and bourgeois Left in France. When M. Daladier finished his speech, his supporters raised their clenched fists in the Communist salute, the salute of the *Front Populaire* to-day.

These two pictures illustrate better than anything else, perhaps, the remarkable success of Moscow's policy in the course of the last few months. What I would particularly emphasize is not the mere fact of co-operation of the non-Communist states with Moscow, but—far more important—the fact that those who promote and laud this co-operation do so with references to peace, liberty and the rights of man. The hatred and passions which divide the peoples of the Continent to-day have enabled Moscow to win at Geneva a quite unique position; a position often almost equivalent to that of an arbitrator. Indeed, the representative of the Soviet State on the Council is at liberty again and again to contrast mass terrorist methods, the exploitation of the coloured peoples by the Europeans, and so on, with the truly model principles of Soviet Russian policy.

Is it astonishing that Moscow, having won these unique successes, is ceasing to show the same consideration for the bourgeois world as hitherto? This is the only explanation of the manner in which it dropped the veil at the Congress of the Communist International held in the autumn of 1935. The resolutions of this Congress have shown as clearly as possible that the Soviet Government refuses on principle to dissociate itself in the future from the activities of the Komintern, whose object is to bring about revolution in the bourgeois states. On the contrary, Moscow is now openly and most thoroughly co-ordinating the activity of the Soviet Government with that of the Komintern. No wonder that some countries, notably the United States, felt obliged to take exception to the attitude of the Soviet Government on the question of the Komintern.

But since the new president of the Komintern, Dimitrov, has declared his guiding principle of "Trojan horse" tactics, which the Communists must employ in future in their revolutionary work in the different states, it has been clear that these tactics are already being vigorously pursued in various countries.

In some countries—above all in France—a second principle proclaimed by Dimitrov, the formation of a Left or concentration *bloc* with the Socialists and the bourgeois parties of the Left, has been successfully realized. This development has materially extended Moscow's opportunity for propaganda. Hundreds of non-Communist papers in France and elsewhere are now busy praising and glorifying the achievements of Moscow, entirely out of consideration for their Communist ally.

I am obliged to dwell upon this point, because it has made the endeavours to ascertain the real position of the victims of want in the Soviet State vastly more difficult than before. Quite independently of any fight "for peace" or "against Fascism," numerous papers in the bourgeois countries which in themselves have nothing to do with Communism (these should be distinguished from the camouflaged Communist papers) now propagate the familiar Soviet Russian catchwords. For example, those which declare the abolition of all ration cards to be the proof of a great economic improvement, and which represent the Soviet Union as the only state which has solved the nationalities question in an ideal manner.

And how have things been going lately in the Soviet State? Perhaps I have been wrong, and the forecast of the *New York Times* correspondents in the autumn of 1934 that in the following year, thanks to the surplus of corn, famine would be avoided, has been right? To-day I am able to say that the *New York Times* correspondents now themselves admit the terrible distress of the peasants in the Russian agricultural regions—and not only in 1933 and 1934, but also quite lately, at the end of the summer of 1935. In a telegram dated July 7, 1935, Mr. Denny reported that according to reliable reports which had reached Moscow the demands of the State grain collectors had left the peasants too little corn after the harvest; the peasants, therefore, when their supplies were exhausted, had to buy back corn from the State at one rouble per kilo, while they had previously received only eight kopecks per kilo for the sale of the corn which the State took from them.

Mr. Denny, characteristically, telegraphed this report to his paper along with statements on the favourable supply position in the Soviet Union. It was doubtless this fact which led the editor of the paper—who, in contrast to the "optimism" of its Moscow correspondents has endeavoured to get the real position in the Soviet State cleared up—to publish the message under headlines to this effect: "The country as a whole has food enough, but the peasants buy back corn at twelve times its sale price." What does this statement mean? It means that the peasants, who have been deprived by the grain-collecting policy of the Soviet Government of the minimum requirements for bare existence, have to die of starvation if they are unable to buy back their own corn at an exhorbitant price.

And what about the statement that the abolition of bread and ration cards are ample proof of the abundance that now prevails in the Soviet State? Can the state of things I have described have changed so much of late that the situation at least of the non-privileged classes has improved? Since the autumn of 1935 miserably clad figures have often been visible in the neighbourhood of the Bulgarian Legation in Vienna. These are Bulgarians who have lived for many years in the south of Russia as fruit growers and so on, but remained Bulgarian subjects and have now been enabled by the mediation of their mother-country to leave Russia. If one asks why they have left, one always gets the same answer: they have been compelled to leave by starvation and want. One kilo of black bread—a Bulgarian from the Armavir district in the Northern Caucasus told me—has cost 90 kopecks since the bread cards were abolished, and a kilo of white bread one and a half roubles.

But the earnings of an average workman in this region are from 80 to 100 roubles. How can a man live on that if he has no claim to privileged treatment as a member of the party or the privileged classes? Foreign specialists who have lived in Russia for years have proved by documents and figures that in consequence of the abolition of ration cards—i.e. in consequence of the raising of the price of bread, etc.—the actual wages of a workman in the Soviet Union have fallen by about a quarter from the beginning of the first five-year plan down to the autumn of 1935. Despite, or just because of, the abolition of ration cards the difference between the position of the privileged and non-privileged classes in the Soviet Union has become greater as compared with the end of 1933. This is why foreign visitors to Moscow and other centres, seeing the luxury and dissipation of the privileged classes, report the development of a bourgeoisie in the classless state.

In his telegram mentioned above Mr. Harold Denny spoke of the (in his belief) excellent harvest and announced that the Soviet Union was likely to increase its exports by about 5,000,000 tons to the level of 1930; indeed, he even mentioned the pre-war export figure of 100,000,000 tons. When journalists friendly to Moscow make announcements of this kind, it usually means that the Soviet Government is preparing the world public for what it intends to do. Thus the proceedings described elsewhere are repeated. The grain taken from the peasants is exported so far as it is not required for the needs of the State and the privileged classes. Indeed, it looks as if the exportation of this "famine corn" would assume ever larger proportions in the near future. Correspondingly large numbers of the producers and of the "non-privileged" categories in the towns, thus deprived of the minimum necessary to existence, will be abandoned to privation and famine. Is this spectacle to continue for ever? Is human life no longer to have any value or significance just because the humans are in the Soviet State?

If the bourgeois states, indeed the whole non-Communist

world, to-day regard with interest, if not actually with benevolent sympathy, the Communist experiment that has already cost the lives of millions, it is no business of mine to protest. But to avoid misunderstandings, I should like to emphasize that I have no intention of proclaiming the advantages and the achievements of the capitalist system. I do not hesitate to affirm that it is going through a crisis of its own making; indeed, that the Soviet Russian criticisms of the negative aspect of the present-day capitalist system are largely justified. (The fact that the remedy which Moscow proposes to apply is far more harmful still is quite another question.) I should like, moreover, to declare with equal emphasis that what is really demoralizing in Bolshevist policy is not so much its insistence on the new economic system as its fundamental disregard of the Western principles of attachment to nationality, religion and family. In branding everyone who protests against the oppression of the nationalities, religion and family life in Soviet Russia as a defender of the present harmful regime in the non-Communist states, Moscow is certainly employing maybe the cleverest tactics in its whole propaganda system.

It is not my task in this book to controvert the views of Joseph Stalin. It is useless to enter into controversy with people who openly and on principle avow that the annihilation of whole masses of humanity is justified to secure the realization of the Communist ideal. My protest is addressed solely and exclusively to all those in the non-Communist world who still confess to the principle of human, in particular Christian solidarity in the face of catastrophes, indeed of unmerited disaster overtaking others—but who are blind and dumb where the fate of the luckless population of the Soviet State is concerned. I remarked above that a protest against the benevolent attitude of these people towards Moscow and its experiment is not justified. But this attitude—on this I must insist with all possible emphasis—in no way relieves them of the duty of defending the innocent victims of this experiment. On the contrary, their attitude greatly increases their responsibility towards the victims. Human life in the Soviet State has in my opinion the same claim to protection and help as in any other country in the world.

I do not claim that what I say in this book shall be believed without confirmation. But I think I am entitled to claim, on the strength of the data collected not only by myself but by others of greater authority, that the question of confirmation—the elucidation of the true position of the distressed in Soviet Russia—shall be taken in hand without further loss of time. The possibility of doing this has increased now that the Soviet Union has been admitted to the League of Nations.